WINGED BUILDERS

WINGED BUILDERS

*a book of bird lore, chiefly concerned with
the nesting, building, and family
habits of British birds*

by

NANCY PRICE, C.B.E.

GEORGE RONALD
LONDON

SET IN PLANTIN AND
PRINTED BY THE BROADWATER PRESS LIMITED
WELWYN GARDEN CITY, HERTFORDSHIRE

PREFACE

MISS Nancy Price has called this delightful book *Winged Builders* but I would sum it up as *The Joy of Birds*, for every page is full of the joy and wonder of bird life and that whether she is writing of a hedge-sparrow in the home garden or a tystie—black guillemot—on an Orkney island.

As she says on her first page, every day finds more and more people turning to the quiet delights of bird-watching and the joy, solace, and refreshment of bird study, from the severely scientific ornithologists to those who love birds just as birds. Never have there been so many bird societies, never such a mass of bird literature, both scientific and popular, in short, never has there been such a widespread interest in wild life, in particular bird life.

There is always room for another book on this subject particularly when it comes from the pen of one who loves birds so keenly and to whom they mean so much. It is obvious that in the course of her varied, interesting, and exciting life, Miss Nancy Price has found ever-increasing joy in the creatures of tree and bush, meadow and hill, and of the waters salt and fresh. Birds have obviously meant much to her; this can be felt when reading these pages. You sense the solace and refreshment, the wonder and joy that she has derived from watching birds and studying their ways. I feel sure that countless readers will find delight in joining her in her studies of the wondrous army of *Winged Builders*.

FRANCES PITT

CONTENTS

LIST OF ILLUSTRATIONS

WINGED BUILDERS

1

BUILDING THE HOME

'I come in the little things, saith the Lord, the glowing wings of eager birds. I stand confest on every nest where feathered Patience is content to brood—and leaves her pleasure for the high emprize of motherhood. There doth my Godhead rest.'—Evelyn Underhill

THERE is no question that every year more people are becoming attracted to the observation of wild life, regarding it not merely as a source of food, clothing, or sport, but finding in it an enrichment of life. I have certainly found that watching and listening to birds has given me more pleasure than I can well express.

In this book I have concerned myself chiefly with the variety of nests and have tried to arrange the birds under characteristic headings that have been suggested by the manner of their building and choice of site, though every bird has individuality, which it exhibits in various ways. The chief interest to me has been not so much in the discovery of a nest, but in finding out how and why birds build in particular ways or places. I have found this is most successfully achieved by disturbing them as little as possible.

The best way to observe birds is to appear uninterested for, like us, they resent a prying eye. But when they realize there is nothing to fear from the watcher they will carry on with their occupation. It is essential to convey, in every way possible, that the watcher's presence bodes no ill. This requires, among other things, concentration and control of movement.

Birds are very timid; they have countless enemies, and if a nest is touched or the surroundings interfered with they usually desert. Although I am filled with delight that birds favour my garden for building, I never search for their nests, preferring to rest satisfied in the knowledge that they can build and brood in peace.

A hen during her first brooding is more nervous than later on when she has learnt to distinguish friends from enemies and is aware that certain familiar objects may not necessarily be dangerous. It is noticeable that birds who build two or three nests in a year will build the second and third much more quickly than the first.

A nest represents an unceasing labour of weeks and is a miracle of ingenuity, persistence, and patience. Whenever I see one I think of a verse by the poet Hurdis:

> It wins my admiration
> To view the structure of this work—
> A bird's nest. Mark it well, within, without;
> No tool had he that wrought; no knife to cut,
> No nail to fix, no bodkin to insert,
> No glue to join; his little beak was all;
> And yet how neatly finished: what nice hand,
> And every implement and means of art,
> And twenty years' apprenticeship to boot,
> Could make me such another?

Soon after I began seriously to watch birds, I understood the truth of my father's words when he said that the man, woman, or child who interfered with a nest must lack imagination, while anyone who would disturb a brooding bird was actively cruel. Whether a bird's nest is stoned or a town destroyed, the impulse differs only in degree. In an old Irish lament called *The Deserted House*, written in the eleventh century, there are two lines that always remain in my mind as a vivid picture of the desolation created by a nest robbed and destroyed:

> No bird now comes from out their house,
> Across its edge the nettle grows.

The site for these 'winged buildings' often induces a more intimate enjoyment of the beauty of branches, leaves, and buds. The lark's nest recalls the near smell of clover or the sight of a bumble-bee in his plush coat, carrying his honeyed load. The garden warbler, yellowhammer, and linnet bring the close companionship of the gorse. Here are lulling sounds, comfortable and consoling, arising from the favoured haunt of velvet-winged butterflies. When we listen to a bird singing his love-song or voicing encouragement to his brooding mate, the sound is accompanied by innumerable fragrant scents and sweet sounds. The spirit is lifted for a time out of a morass of perplexities to another world, equally active but almost unknown, where the earth-bound mortal glimpses the wonderful country of the winged creatures.

Some birds seem to spend not only an infinity of care but also of artistry in the making of their marvellous nests; others appear to trouble less, but all build according to their particular need. This has been ascribed to inheritance, but is that the whole explanation? So many birds' ways remain a mystery, and I personally am satisfied that it should be so.

I have always been puzzled as to how birds keep the first twig or blade of grass in place. It is one of the many things that constantly confounds the watcher: not only the consummate art of the whole construction, the foreknowledge of requirements, but how the actual foundation is effected, the first twig entwined, the first stick laid in its place, the first beakful of mud fixed. In spite of careful watching I have only once been fortunate enough to see the initial brick laid, if one may so express it.

At a hospital where I was daily visiting a patient in the top storey, the ground below sloped away so steeply that I found myself almost level with the tops of near-by trees in which rooks were building. With the pair that I was able to observe, the first twig was brought by the male and presented to the female, who held it carefully in place with her claw. The male then flew down to some sweet-chestnut trees immediately below the window and peeled off some fine strips of bark, several inches long, which he carried back to his mate. With these the pair proceeded to fasten the twig firmly in position. The process was repeated until two or three twigs had been safely fixed. I do not imagine this would be a universal practice among birds but it is the only time I have seen the initial foundation laid.

All nests are completed with a mixture of energy and ecstasy; the male may choose the site, but the female decides exactly where in that territory the nest shall be and she is usually the architect. I have noticed that birds building in bushes and trees which are more liable to draught always have a good lining to their nests; not so much is found in the cosy cradles of the warblers. Mud is often used by those birds who start breeding early and this is carefully laid between the inner and outer material. The first nest is lined much more substantially than those that harbour later broods, and it is obviously a protection against the more inclement weather.

Birds with the gayest feathers and those that require long brooding

build domed nests or lay their eggs in holes in order to conceal both themselves and their young. Dull-plumaged birds usually have a much more
open nest, their colouring acting as camouflage. Ground builders sacrifice
depth to concealment.

Nests that are apparently loose in structure and carelessly built of grass,
leaves, sticks, or roots are in reality meticulously put together, though
they may be open to the sky. Such is the woodpigeon's nest. In contrast
to this type of building is the perfectly finished chaffinch's home, the little
roofed-in nest of the chiff-chaff, and that of the plover who favours the
bare earth.

Birds certainly haunt sites with which they have become familiar: they
often become conservative to a locality, though they rarely use the same
nest twice. As always there are exceptions, for I have seen swallows, martins, blackbirds, tits, and nuthatches repairing their old nests. Some birds
are naturally selective, taking both time and trouble to obtain a site which
they fancy and, more important still, a mate who particularly appeals to
them. Year after year a starling perched at the top of a silver birch just outside my bedroom window; I am sure he was the same bird because of a
certain malformation of claw. He was some time before deciding to mate
and even then appeared to be searching for a particular hen who would
satisfy his fastidious taste. After the momentous decision was made, I
watched him obviously instructing her to build a nest in the eaves of my
cottage which he had come to regard as desirable. He would fly to the spot,
voice his call-note, and when she followed him there would be chatter between the two. I am convinced that with many birds it is not just any hen
that serves his mating instinct, but he makes a definite choice.

At my cottage in Sussex I get much the same community of birds every
year, blackbirds in particular. They come into my sitting-room, perching
on my desk and even on the edge of my breakfast tray. My favourite hen
blackbird has a white hood and wings and, contrary to the belief that the
unusual bird is not approved by the rest of the species, she has an impres-
sive array of suitors; when she has chosen a husband she insists that he
shall love, cherish, and obey. She usually rears three broods every year
and I think changes her husband every time. Her favourite nesting site is
a climbing rose tree just outside my kitchen door.

I am also proud of the visits paid to me by a pair of turtledoves, who even venture into my kitchen, which is, I think, unusual, as they are proverbially timid.

Pigeons nested for six years in a tree within sight of my garden hut. The seventh year I noticed only one. In sorrowful fashion he perched for several days, lonely and disconsolate on the edge of the old nest. This happened for two successive years, then he never came again.

I am pretty certain the same woodpeckers have chosen my cottage garden for the last three years. I am not so certain about the finches and tits as they are more difficult to distinguish, but collectively they return year after year, choosing much the same sites for nests. Swallows certainly return every year: how these birds find their way over miles of forest, desert, and sea to the same barn, no one has yet been able to discover.

Friends of mine in Sussex acquired a house with an old tithe-barn adjoining, where swallows had apparently built for generations, quietly brooding their eggs during the Norman invasion and centuries later when Hitler's bombers roared overhead. Norman William and Austrian Hitler have passed into history, but the swallows still return. My friends fitted windows to one side of this fine old barn, making a very delightful room, all unaware that swallows had regarded it as their ancestral home. When they came to realize this fact they at once inserted an opening high in the old masonry, so that the birds could fly in and out in all weathers both to build and later to feed their young even though the room was in constant use. The birds have now become at home with their human companions, even perching on the beams in spite of the unfeathered bipeds beneath. When last I saw them the mother and father were on one beam and five of their offspring on another. I thought it most engaging to watch the parents flying in and out on their excursions for food, finally coming home to roost. I think it shows both consideration and interest on the part of my friends that they do not permit any artificial light in this barn in the spring and summer after dusk, in case it should disturb the birds. They tell me the swallows build three nests during the season, hatching out each brood successfully.

I have found that birds are immediately aware of any bits of wool, combings of dog, horsehair, and the like, and it has always been my perhaps childish pleasure to feel that I help them a little in their arduous search for nesting material. I have noticed, when they use grass for their building, how particular they are as to the exact length, often discarding several pieces before getting one that is to their satisfaction. I have frequently known birds to use flowers as love-offerings and even, it would seem, as decoration for their nests; this may sound fanciful but I have seen it; maybe the colour and sweetness attract them. This year, sparrows building over my kitchen added to their untidy nesting material white alyssum flowers, and I watched starlings bringing blossoms of sycamore and sprays of forget-me-nots to their family residence. Long-tailed tits building in my hedge collected bits of coloured wool and flower-petals, which were woven with rainbow effect into their wonderful nest. In the Philadelphia Academy of Science, a robin's nest may be seen made entirely of blossoms and white stems of the everlasting flower. Birds often do appear to take particular delight in building among flowers and blossoming trees; I know few more lovely sights than tits just out of the nest perching in a row on a twig of an apple tree in bloom.

I find it interesting to notice small things about birds that are not to be found in the valuable ornithological books. To me these little things make the whole vast subject of feathered life more absorbing and mysterious. There can be no doubt that birds have a preference for certain colours; others they will avoid. There are particular smells they favour and those they will back away from, showing obvious distaste. I have noticed that the male and female do not come by the same route to their nest; they follow their own chosen way meticulously, obviously having special air routes and traffic regulations to which they strictly adhere.

It is estimated that about a hundred and twenty million birds nest in England and lay more than two hundred million eggs. It is of course impossible accurately to count birds but these are approximate figures made by careful watchers. Blackbirds and chaffinches are the most frequent nest-builders; it is said there are about ten millions of each; starlings and robins tie with seven millions, house-sparrows somewhere around three millions. But the numbers of all English birds are decreasing with the disappearance of suitable nesting sites.

Birds gather the material for their nests in ways varying according to their beaks and capacities. Eagles drop on branches to break them;

A. Mann

Very special Garden Robin

John Markh[

Long-tailed Tit at nest in hawthorn bush

sparrow-hawks dive on a branch for the same purpose and if this does not succeed they will hang upside-down until it cracks. Woodpigeons pick up their sticks from the ground, rooks break twigs with their beaks, which is not always an easy task. Sometimes a bird gets into difficulties and becomes entangled with his own nesting material, and in these distressing circumstances I have often noted how they are given first-aid by their own kind. One day I saw a sparrow flying over my head carrying a lengthy piece of string presumably for the nest; a strong wind was blowing and the string made the bird's flight difficult. He was obviously trying to reach the eaves of the house, but this was not a simple matter. Not only was the string (about two yards) a difficult burden, but the wind was blowing dead against him. Just as he reached his objective a gust twisted the string round his body and legs, rendering him helpless and suspended. I wondered what I could do to help, but he was sending out his own vocal S.O.S. and it was not long before he was answered. One sparrow after another darted for the suspending end of string nearest him, pecking it with their beaks always at the same place; in about three minutes it was severed and the part that remained he easily shook off with a few body movements and a pull of his beak to the portion round his feet. He then again picked up the piece of string and proceeded undaunted with the building.

When nesting material is dropped in the immediate vicinity of a nest, it is almost invariably removed; probably the birds are trying to avoid anything by which the site might be located. I have actually watched a golden plover and a goldcrest carrying away unwanted material lying near the nest. They will not tolerate dirt, often carrying away excrement from the nest for some distance, and I have seen them eat their own eggshells. Birds are very particular about the sanitation of their homes and meticulous with their own cleanliness. Water-hens will have a bath and preen their feathers before going to bed and all birds enjoy a water or dust-bath. The mother birds are equally careful in keeping the fledglings clean; once when I was watching a little family of bearded tits I saw the mother gently combing their head-feathers with her bill.

This book is almost wholly concerned with the sites chosen and special methods adopted by birds to build the nest that will best serve them for

B

laying their eggs and rearing a family. Nevertheless there will be readers who do not know my other bird books and it might be thought that not to mention bird-music shows a lack of appreciation and is a conspicuous omission. Therefore I include a record made at my cottage of a dawn chorus and evensong. Only once have I made meticulous notes of the time that each particular bird voices its morning greeting: this was for my own interest and to compare on more casual occasions when I made no notes, and I think perhaps some readers may be interested. It does give the variety of bird-song that can be heard even from a cottage garden. I am very fortunate that mine is situated in close proximity to the Downs woodlands and scrub; therefore I have perhaps greater opportunity for observing a variety of birds than many amateur bird-watchers and am probably more favoured with the particularly rich gift of bird-song.

A.M. *First Song*

4.10	Tawny owl	5.03	Bullfinch
4.22	Lark	5.11	Jackdaw (call-note)
4.24	Cock-crow	5.16	Linnet (pair; nuptial flight
4.26	Blackbird		and call-notes)
4.32	Robin	5.17	Whitethroat
4.40	Wren	5.27	Partridge (call-note)
4.41	Mistle-thrush (alarm)	5.31	Crow
4.45	Pheasant (call-note)	5.39	Green woodpecker
4.46	Woodpigeon	5.51	Lapwing (field adjoining)
4.47	Great tit	6.11	Yellowhammer
4.47	Song-thrush	6.28	Cuckoo
4.48	Nightingale	6.30	Chaffinch
4.49	Hedge accentor	6.36	Jay (alarm)
4.54	Yellowhammer (call-note)	6.40	Chiff-chaff
4.55	Magpie (alarm)	6.43	Blackcap
5.02	Willow-warbler	6.43	Stock dove

P.M. *Last Song*

6.16	Great tit	6.40	Chaffinch
6.22	Chiff-chaff	6.48	Hedge accentor
6.28	Blue tit	7.01	Wren

7.20 Partridge (call)	7.34 Pheasant
7.28 Magpie (alarm)	7.34 Blackbird (song and alarm)
7.30 Song-thrush	7.36 Robin
7.32 Nightingale	7.42 Lapwing

N.B. Swallow seen flying close and low 6.56 p.m. and Pipistrelle bat 7.22 p.m.

I have often been asked where birds sleep during the night. I think they like to keep their roosting-places as secret as possible and it is rare actually to locate them. There is no doubt that when light flows from an uncurtained window on to a hedge it will disturb them, often inducing protesting notes; therefore I try never to draw back curtains if I think they may roost nearby. The smaller birds sleep chiefly in hedges: even in winter the twigs and branches crossing each other hide them, and no marauder can so easily seize his prey in a holly or hawthorn hedge.

It is a matter of surprise to many that birds should remain secure on their perch when asleep. This capacity is one of the numerous safeguards Nature has given her children, for when a bird relaxes and squats on the perch the grasp of the claw appears to react on the muscles of the knee-joint and so tightens those of the toes, thus giving a sort of safety-grip which is not released until the bird straightens his legs and sets the claws free. No doubt a much more technical explanation has been given but there can be no question that its muscles serve the bird's need in this wonderful way.

They keep themselves warm by tucking their heads under their shoulders and puffing out their feathers. The air penetrates between, settling in the soft down close to the body; this warmed air, unable to escape, prevents the bird's body from becoming chilled by the atmosphere.

Birds naturally seek the warmest spots in which to roost: one often finds holes in haystacks made by the smaller birds who have chosen this site for their bed. The owls choose holes in a tree or the interior of buildings; wrens cluster together in old nests; ground birds like the partridge always lie in a circle on the ground with their heads outside and tails together—usually a parent bird remaining on the outside on sentry-duty. Birds that

favour woods sleep in the trees: sea birds will often roost on the sheltered
ledges of the cliffside, the smaller varieties finding cavities in the rocks or
hollows in the sand.

Parent birds will guard their young regardless of their own danger; a
brooding hen seems oblivious to everything but the duty of motherhood,
steadfast at her post even when the nest is invaded. Rooks will remain on
the nest when trees are cut or blown down, refusing to desert though this
would mean safety for themselves. Mother birds often give their lives to
protect their young: if the gorse or scrub in which they nest is set alight,
they will be burnt alive rather than leave their post. I have found the
charred body of a linnet still covering her young.

2

THE FAMILY ARRIVES

'I think, if required on pain of death to name instantly the most perfect thing in the universe, I should risk my life on a bird's egg.'
T. W. Higginson (1863)

OOLOGY is an interesting branch of natural history, but I fear those who study it are more often than not destructive of bird life. My father, who was a great lover and observer of birds, used to say it was infinitely more interesting to watch one pair of birds in their natural haunts, marking their ways, needs, and habits, than to fill a cabinet with dead and labelled specimens.

Birds' eggs vary both in shape and colour and we cannot fail to be confounded by the diversity in the spotting, scribbling, blotting, mottling; Nature never seems to repeat herself—she is infinite in her capacity to vary and this remains and will remain a hidden mystery. As Omar Khayyám wrote:

> Myself when young did eagerly frequent
> Doctor and Saint and heard great argument
> About it and about; but evermore
> Came out by that same door as in I went.

It does not decrease my wonder to know that 'the colouring matter of the egg is deposited during the passage down the oviduct—a long coiled tube leading from the ovary or place where the eggs are formed—to the outer world.' The texture of the egg varies; it may be smooth, greasy, polished, or rough. All this is for a purpose hidden from our understanding. I have found the deeper I look into nature, the more convinced I am that nothing lacks purpose; it is only we who lack knowledge and understanding.

It is strange that the swallow and housemartin, so much alike, lay such very different eggs, yet the owl and woodpigeon, so dissimilar in appearance, lay two eggs each, having close resemblance in size and colour.

Birds who nest in the dark as a rule lay eggs very light in colour. Certain ornithologists believe that birds sometimes actually whiten their eggs from the powder in their plumage so that they can be the more clearly seen when they are laid in dark places; even plants that are fertilized by night-feeding insects usually have white flowers. It is also a provision of nature that the mouths of fledglings are brightly coloured, thus showing more clearly to the parents. The lapwing or peewit egg is blotched, probably because the bird nests in the open and requires the camouflage markings as protection.

The ways in which birds try to protect their eggs, whether by instinct or by reason, are interesting; when game leave the nest they cover them with dead leaves; dabchicks paddle on their white eggs until they resemble mud. Water-fowl finding their nest in danger by reason of flooding lift the level of it and if necessary remove the eggs until the water subsides, when they carefully carry them back.

Birds have many devices for keeping their eggs warm when it becomes compulsory to leave the nest for feeding purposes; ducks cover them with down plucked from their own breasts, partridges with leaves. Owing to the heat drawn from the earth the eggs of ground-building birds keep warm for a considerable period when the parent is driven off the nest; perhaps it is the security plan of nature that their chicks leave the home very soon after the hatching so that they may find cover. The only eggs I know that are not brooded by a bird are those of the brush-turkeys of Australia; they are left by the parents in a mound of decaying vegetable matter for the heat to hatch them.

One of the first things about birds and their eggs I personally noticed was the fact that the hens turn their eggs so that they may be kept at an equal warmth. Those laying pear-shaped eggs, smaller at one end than the other, carefully place the pointed end inwards so that they can be more conveniently brooded.

The guillemot's egg is laid on the bare ledge, but as one end is much smaller than the other it turns round when disturbed but does not fall off in spite of the continual coming and going of the parents. The nests of pigeons and doves have little protection; perhaps that is why these birds lay only two eggs so that they can the more easily be covered during brooding.

I believe the smallest egg is laid by the humming-bird and the largest by the ostrich, though it is said there was once a bird in Madagascar who laid an egg infinitely larger. It is sometimes found with the skeleton of a chieftain. Its girth was twenty-eight to thirty inches, the length about thirty-six inches; no doubt the chief had hoped to be sustained on his long journey.

The whole life of a fertile egg is wonderful; indeed, to the uninitiated like myself, nothing short of miraculous. I have been told there is a pocket of air between skin and shell and that but for this formation the chick would not be able to break out, as it breathes this air before hatching, thus gathering strength to peck a way through the shell. I have actually heard the chick tapping with the egg tooth, a little chalky knob on the end of the bill which drops off after doing its work. This tapping sometimes continues for nearly forty hours until the hole is drilled: the warning note of the parent bird will actually stop the chipping of the shell when danger is abroad. So marvellous is the provision of nature to protect life.

Another wise precaution is that the mother bird, whose natural instinct is to rear the young she has produced, usually has less conspicuous plumage than her mate.

In some cases, however, the male takes this duty, or pleasure, upon himself; the emu, bustard, quail, and phalarope are four such birds. With pigeons, the cock takes day duty and the hen night duty; perhaps she feels she is more reliable. On the other hand the female ostrich, usually laying fifteen eggs each weighing about three pounds, broods for six or seven weeks assisted by the male who takes the night watch. There is often a sort of engaging ceremonial which accompanies the change-over: the woodcock, for instance, goes to meet her mate as he comes to relieve her; they cross beaks and hold the position for an appreciable time before the relieving bird goes on duty.

The faithfulness and patience of all brooding birds must command respect and admiration. The albatross will remain on her eggs for a month without food; she is enabled to do this by coming to her nest with a reserve of fat which sustains her while sitting.

I have heard it said that boys will never be cured of birdsnesting, but I know from experience that the damage they effect can be very considerably lessened if they are encouraged to take an interest in watching.

Few children realize what the theft of eggs and the ravaging of a nest means to the bird: home destroyed, deprivation of family, and all the consequent suffering. Boys are by no means the only offenders: commercial dealers are equally guilty; the often inconsiderate photographer or sometimes even the ornithologist in the eager pursuit of data fails to regard the consequent distress to his subject.

There are certain laws against the theft of wild bird's eggs and penalties under the Wild Bird Protection Act but I do not think myself these laws are sufficiently stringent or far reaching; perhaps one day there will be a stricter legislation to protect wild life even as there is for our own kind. The preservation of crops and growing foodstuffs has been well instilled into the people; surely something should be done to stop the continual destruction of birds, their nests, and eggs. All birds are menaced by the collector, while those having food value suffer continual depredation. The plover and gull yield eggs nutritious to man and therefore they are taken in ever-increasing numbers. If such ravage is allowed to go on unchecked many birds that delight us will disappear from the countryside and sea-shore. How much interest and beauty we should lose, not to mention the material value birds may have, for often they are a very real help in keeping down the onslaught of grubs and insects.

The birds have little devices for dealing with their natural enemies, rats, stoats, weasels, and cats. Some of these are supplied by nature, many by instinct, others acquired by experience and, it would seem, even wisdom; but birds are powerless against their enemy man and his weapons, the destruction of hedgerows, the oil discharge from his ships, his modern mechanized farming. The man of yesterday with his scythe had more time; he could observe and spare the feathered creatures if he were so minded. I remember when I was a child the regret of an old man who was scything at having killed a young pheasant and his care that the rest of the brood should escape.

The habits of young birds are as variable as is the construction of their homes. Some run almost directly they are hatched: partridges, peewits, and wild ducks often run off with an eggshell still on their backs. Some fledglings feed themselves readily, provided the hen is near to encourage, but even they will almost invariably come back to the mother bird at night to be kept warm and protected. Some young birds fly very successfully though they have never been in the air before; swifts are specially endowed with this power of flight directly they are fully fledged, indeed it is absolutely necessary to their existence, as a fall to the ground would mean death. Ducks have not this power of flight, although when born in the morning they can find their way to the water and can swim in the evening. Moorhens can swim and dive immediately they are hatched, although they seem unable to feed themselves: I believe this to be the case with all water-fowl. There are young birds who are carried by their parents: swans convey their cygnets on their backs, the chicks of the woodcock are often held between the parents' thighs with the lower tail feathers. Curlews will guard their fledglings when they attempt to leave the nest too soon, the mother bird manipulating their movements with the aid of her long beak.

One summer when I was convalescing at Cliftonville and listening to the band from the enforced confines of a wheel-chair, I was attracted by a twittering which grew louder and louder until the whole audience was interested. A baby sparrow with too adventurous a spirit had evidently fallen from the nest. Anxious parents were immediately beside it and after continual manœuvring managed between them to lift the fledgling and carry it back to safety. The whole audience applauded and the band that had temporarily ceased playing in order to watch the incident resumed. Experience has taught me that if I find a young bird outside the nest it is wise to leave him where he is and then stand at a short distance on guard against enemies, for usually the parents will devise some means of conveying their offspring to safety.

Much of our own time is occupied in preparing food, eating it, and clearing up afterwards; the birds in addition have to seek and acquire their food, and the greater part of their life is spent in the process. A robin will eat fourteen feet of earthworm a day, and a pair of barn owls will account for ten thousand mice in a year. It must be a matter of interest and wonder to all watchers to see how the bird's bill is perfectly fitted to the food required. Seed-eaters have short, stout bills; those who require insects have beaks much more pointed; the hawk's bill is eminently suited for tearing flesh, the pouch of the pelican for storing fish; the humming-bird is supplied with a long probe with which he can suck the nectar; the nightjar has a very small bill but a large mouth enabling him to gulp the insects;

the long bills of the curlew and snipe are practical for poking into the soil; the beak of the crossbill serves him well for opening pine-cones.

The collecting of food for young birds demonstrates untold self-sacrifice and forbearance on the part of parents; indeed the feats of food-finding and feeding by them are almost unbelievable: fledglings often consume more than their own weight every twenty-four hours. Dr Arthur A. Allen by careful watching has found that a mother wren makes one thousand two hundred and eighteen journeys between dawn and sunset when feeding her brood, which gives a little idea of the energy and patience needed. I have often watched a little wren feeding her young; she will poke the food into one of the many open beaks and then watch anxiously. If it does not go down immediately she plucks it out again and pops it into the next beak, knowing full well that the fledgling who swallows it promptly is usually the one with an empty stomach. Insectivorous birds are often brought food more than a thousand times a day. In the case of cormorants and gannets the young ones put their beaks well down their parents' throats and take out the necessary food.

If a fledgling abandoned by fate or circumstance vainly flutters his wings and continually voices the cry for food, the persistent appeal is rarely ignored even by birds of another species. Blackbirds are very considerate in this way. I have noticed that with some birds the elder brood of a family will help to feed the younger. Blue tits will sometimes do the same for a robin and robins for a thrush. I have a photograph of a robin proudly feeding a fledgling great tit who had left the nest a little too soon; a cock chaffinch has been photographed rendering this service to young thrushes; a cock sparrow to a nestful of greenfinches. All this redounds very much to the credit of the birds who are often not content with fostering their own species but will extend this valuable service to others. Housemartins and swallows will sometimes join together to feed a brood: to me it is always very moving to watch this consideration for the young constantly exhibited in bird life.

The parents have the arduous task not only of seeking the necessary food but of keeping their nestlings dry in rain and guarding against their sometimes dangerous exposure to the sun. The body and wings of the hen often provide this protection. Some baby birds require water and I have observed the parents flying to the nearest supply and soaking their breast feathers, then returning to the young who suck the moisture still clinging to them.

Those birds who are resident with us during the winter have much to contend with and whenever possible I feel they should be given every help in return for the joy and service they render in the spring and summer. It is not within our power to serve all, but some can be fed and given water consistently, the early hours of the morning, after the birds have endured a bitter night, being the most important. I have found that they welcome the digging of even a small patch of ground where they can get grubs. In whatever way help is given it should be regular.

3
HOMES OF STAR ARTISTS

Nightingale; skylark; woodlark; blackcap

TO make any special selection of star artists from all the sweet and varied songsters of the winged world seems almost ungracious and ungrateful. The three usually chosen are the nightingale, skylark, and blackcap, all of whom make homes which, though doubtless desirable residences to their owners, do not suggest to the uninitiated human that they are models of neatness or examples of fine architecture. But it is perhaps significant that these birds, who surely reach the very pinnacle of song, whose magic notes penetrate far into the mystery of space, should be reared with their breasts to the earth, rather than amid the whispering loveliness of tree and bush. Is it that Mother Earth from whom all life is drawn thus suckles in particular her favoured children, giving them direct contact with her goodness and wonder, which they in turn carol forth to an often indifferent world?

NIGHTINGALE

It would seem that Nature did not intend any particular child of hers to have all that is beautiful. Everyone is given something. The nightingale, acclaimed as the king of song, does not take precedence as an architect. To the human eye the nest is fashioned in a somewhat careless manner, loosely put together with bents, fine roots, and dead oak-leaves, and lined with hair or some other delicate material; though it serves the bird satisfactorily it is impossible for the human to remove it without its falling to pieces. One nest discovered and described by an ornithologist was composed entirely of skeleton leaves. The bird in this instance must have taken an infinity of trouble to gratify its particular taste. Such individuality is not rare, though unusual.

If undisturbed the cock always sings near the nest, but if an intruder is suspected he will change his platform, thus enticing away the unwanted trespasser to a safe distance from the cherished home. From my childhood I remember newly-hatched nightingales in a nest among the undergrowth of a little wood which my father kept as a bird sanctuary and how grieved I was when I found the nest and birds had been destroyed. Though I was very young at the time I knew that something had been lost that was beautiful and precious and something done that was wanton and cruel.

Everyone must feel a thrill at the realization that he has the honour of harbouring a nightingale's family on his own land. For two successive years I have experienced this delight, a pair building in my beech hedge. But on neither occasion did I actually discover the nest until after the young were hatched and flown, though I suspected it by the nearness of the marvellous singer. I preferred to enjoy his song rather than seek the exact whereabouts of the nest and cause anxiety, if not distress, to the birds. The nest was revealed at the base of the hedge only when it was clipped after the nesting season. I always wish that those who own gardens with hedges would leave the shears alone until the young birds are hatched.

It is said that the nightingale arrives from Persia seven days before his future mate who comes from Abyssinia. He greets her with song and the nest is begun almost immediately. The building takes five days from start to finish. From this time until the arduous task of feeding the family begins he sings, thrilling not only his lady-love but the human listener too.

I find this enchanting singer something like a robin in manner and form, though more sedate, while both have the same trick of looking sideways at the ground, the same-shaped head and eyes; both have spindly legs and bob and flirt their tails but the nightingale's movements are more deliberate and he is as shadowy in colour as the dimness he often seeks.

The Prussians are usually considered to be hard hearted but trees that were scheduled for felling outside Cologne were spared solely because they were especially favoured by nightingales. The joy of inimitable song bestowed by the unobtrusive little brown bird was valued more than any sum the timber would have realized.

> Thou wast not born for death, immortal Bird!
> No hungry generations tread thee down;
> The voice I hear this passing night was heard
> In ancient days by emperor and clown:
> Perhaps the self-same song that found a path

> Through the sad heart of Ruth, when, sick for home,
> She stood in tears amid the alien corn;
> The same that oft-times hath
> Charm'd magic casements, opening on the foam
> Of perilous seas, in faery lands forlorn.

SKYLARK

This bird's nest is often spoken of as being carelessly built, but with even a slight knowledge of birds one realizes that it is cleverly fashioned to escape observation, seeming to be part of the stubble or bent, just a circle of grass among grasses though the inside lining is of finer material.

The skylark will rise singing from a cornfield and his song seems part of the glory of limitless space. 'Hark! hark! the lark at heaven's gate sings.' The wind blows the corn backwards and forwards, one wave looking like another to the human eye, but the lark knows exactly the whereabouts of his nest.

It is a sad fact that many larks' nests are destroyed by modern machinery. These birds are very much attached to their young, and though timid in the ordinary way the male becomes bold during the time his mate is sitting. The hen is equally courageous and will sometimes place herself in the path of the human who comes too near her home, calling attention to herself and diverting interest from her brood. Her nest is very often unobserved because she sits so close. A farmer I know records an instance when a field was being cut; the top part of the nest was shaved off and he found by a seeming miracle the bird was uninjured and still sitting on her eggs. He told me that, returning in the evening to see if all was well with the bird, he found to his astonishment she had gathered a heap of the cut grass, making a sort of dome on the top of the nest in order to provide a shelter previously given by the standing grass. I have been told of several instances of skylarks who removed their eggs and even their young in times of danger. I have myself actually seen a lark succeed in conveying one of her young ones in her claws from the threatened nest to a place of safety.

WOODLARK

Although the woodlark is not often thought of as one of our star artists, yet he is so nearly related to the skylark that I feel he should be mentioned with him. The woodlark does not soar so high but sings longer and his notes are more flute-like and unbroken; some have even compared them to those of the nightingale. He sings perching and soaring, also on the descent; and I have heard him at night.

He is very much like the skylark but smaller and with a shorter tail and bill. He builds a neat little nest, which is sometimes quite exposed, at others sheltered by grass or bracken.

BLACKCAP

The cock arrives in April, always before the hen, and immediately voices his glorious song; again like the nightingale he sings by night as well as day. It is said that these birds sing their best in dull weather; perhaps we are then more gratefully aware of their song. I think blackbirds are certainly most musical on wet days, thrushes favour thundery weather, but yellowhammers and larks seem most eloquent under unclouded skies.

One of the many joys of the lovely month of April is the song of the blackcap, so perfect of its kind, not divided like that of the thrush or nightingale, but a short melodious warble. Every year I always hope that a pair may decide on building in my garden; they have made their home more than once in the honeysuckle which has festooned itself on one of my trees. I like to hear the cock singing on the top of his chosen tree, pouring forth his gladness. He is often called *mock nightingale*. But he has distinct individuality, though he can imitate the strains of most other songsters. He is generally agreed to be the ace singer among the warblers. I have heard him spoken of as the contralto of the woods; his notes are flute-like, pouring forth easily, and though the strain is repeated, it is always varied.

Blackcaps always choose a secluded habitat and their nests fortunately are not easy to find; they usually build low among brambles, creepers, or bushes and are very pernickety about the actual site. They will often begin building in two or three different places before being finally satisfied. As with the nightingale their nest is very slight, made of dried grass lightly put together, and lined with horsehair. The cock assists during the incubation period, very often singing on the nest, which I think most unusual. The hen never sings as she broods her eggs, being probably wise enough to know that this would betray the whereabouts of the home. The male bird, however, cannot refrain from expressing his jubilation; it seems he must rejoice audibly in the possession of nest, mate, and a prospective family.

No bird is more tender towards his mate, and any casual watcher can observe his constant solicitude for her well-being and that of his family. I think it is a lovely sight to watch the young ones following the parent birds, hopping about the branches of the tree they have known as home, and at night I have seen them all roosting together on a branch, a parent at each end guarding their fledglings.

Surely this wonderful singer should be saved from destruction. Even if he does eat a few currants he also destroys an immense number of injurious insects; moreover the fruit usually consumed grows wild and should justly be the birds' larder.

Wren brooding her young in a bundle of fishing nets in a shed

Chaffinch at nest in a pear tree against a wall

4

ARCHITECTS AND FELTERS

Long-tailed tit; greenfinch; goldfinch; chaffinch; hawfinch;
chiff-chaff; wren; golden-crested wren; willow wren; siskin

SOME nests in particular seem to suggest the work of a skilled artist. I have chosen ten of these and placed them in the category of architects and felters.

LONG-TAILED TIT

In the county of Worcestershire where I was born, the long-tailed tit is often called *mumruffin*, no doubt because the loose feathers round the face rather resemble a muffler. These tits are probably the tamest of all wild birds, and to watch the building of their nests has given me enormous pleasure and filled me with admiration for their patience and artistry. The nest is a veritable miracle of construction. Many naturalists have been so amazed and interested in it that they have carefully counted the number of feathers used for the lining. Macgillivray found the nest he examined contained well over two thousand feathers. I have seen long-tailed tits alight even on the back of a farmyard fowl in their effort to obtain the material desired. I once made my children try to find a hundred small feathers near our garden; they realized the energy expended by these birds in building.

The walls of the nest are thin but elastic, moss being skilfully threaded together with lengths of spiders' webs, whilst wool and countless specks of silver lichen are also used. The whole is wrought into a felt nearly a quarter of an inch thick, so closely woven that it is difficult to pull it apart. The nest is windproof, sunproof, and waterproof, the tiny entrance being near the top of the dome-like structure.

The wonderful cup having been gradually built, I have watched the birds turn round and round, paddling with their feet and pressing with their breasts to make the interior round, soft, and desirable. This lining required indefatigable labour to produce; each feather had to be carried and placed in position. The work and time entailed seems almost incredible; a pair of long-tailed tits may travel something like seven hundred miles making ceaseless journeys to wood and field gathering that which they feel necessary. I am confounded, indeed humiliated, when I think what these little birds, weighing less than an ounce, achieve by their industry and perseverance. How is their sense of art and beauty conceived? We are taught our crafts; who teaches the birds?

It always puzzled me to imagine how the long-tailed tit disposed of her tail when brooding; it would be easy enough with a round, flat nest, but with the wonderful, oval, bottle-necked structure possessing so small an aperture it appeared to me a problem. At last I was fortunate enough to observe a little hen sitting and I saw that she had lifted her tail above her head, which protruded out of the tiny opening.

These birds have numerous enemies. There can be no question that the magpie is one, for he enjoys the eggs and too often kills the baby birds. Natural tragedies also occur, as long-tailed tits lay many eggs in so small a cavity that some of the nestlings may be suffocated, yet fourteen or more are often successfully reared within this marvellous oval ball.

The pair I watched stayed together at night, but when the nest became too full of fledglings the parents slept outside. When the little birds ventured out they clustered together on a branch and thus, when the nights were cold, helped to keep each other warm, all the tiny heads being turned inward.

The family keeps together during the whole of the remaining season, indeed until pairing time returns, seeking food and relaxation in each other's company. Their incessant calls and constant movement among the branches suggest the joyous restlessness of children. They appear like fairy arrows, and anyone who observes them, even casually, must be entertained by the sight of the little inseparable family.

A long-tailed tit built her lovely nest in the midst of a rose hedge at the bottom of my garden but I found it torn down when only half-finished, lying on the path beneath. On examining it carefully, I counted over one thousand tiny soft feathers, mostly those of the partridge and pheasant, doubtless collected from the Downs and near-by woods, as no one kept fowls in the vicinity. The feathers used by the birds were obviously carefully chosen to make the desired cosy bed and would often have to be sought at a distance.

It is a very difficult thing in these days to preserve the safety of a nest, at least so I find. For two years running I found a long-tailed tit's nest in a gorse bush on the other side of a wire fence which leads from the lane passing my cottage into a path of rough downland. Last year I watched over this nest for days, but naturally there were times when I was absent and so the eggs were taken and the nest destroyed. This year I am trying another device to protect the winged artists' home. I have gathered branches of prickly hawthorn and wild rose that were torn down in the lane by a tractor; these I am threading through the barbed wire and hope they may be a sufficient obstacle. Surely the long patient industry of the little bird should appeal to the most callous nature. If only it were possible to make boys realize that a day will come when they will regret destroying, in one minute of wantonness, weeks of concentrated work. Teachers, parents, films, and television could bring home more certainly, to young and old alike, the care and toil necessitated in building a nest. Then I think the work of the birds might be held more in regard.

The law which now prevents, to a large extent, the capture of wild birds does not seem to be effective in stopping the destruction of nests or the thieving of eggs, yet the harm done is equally serious to bird life.

There is no doubt that many feathered creatures, even as humans, have deadly feuds. The long-tailed tit can be a relentless fighter when occasion demands. My gardener once brought me a pair of these little gladiators on the palm of his hand, still continuing the clinch in which he had picked them up off the path. They were separated with difficulty and we put one through the window, the other out of the door, hoping they would forget their own grievance, only harbouring resentment at our interference, and I was delighted that the plan succeeded.

GREENFINCH

I cannot imagine a more apt description of the greenfinch or green linnet than Wordsworth gives in the two lines:

> My dazzled sight he oft deceives
> A Brother of the dancing leaves.

It is lovely to watch this little bird preening himself at the end of a blossoming spray in spring, singing his small, sweet song, maybe with pride in the knowledge of his beauty. As the spring colours are to me primarily yellow and green, so his plumage suggests leaf and flower.

The greenfinch builds rather low in bushes and favours a thick hedge or hazel bush. The foundation of the nest is formed with small twigs, moss, and rootlets, felted together with scraps of wool. The lining is soft with thistledown, willow-cotton, and feathers.

The hen is responsible for the building, the cock feeding her while she is sitting and being assiduous in bringing food for the young. I have often seen him, after the family has flown, still perching near the empty nest voicing maybe regret or possibly relief! Again I think of Wordsworth's lines:

> Amid yon tuft of hazel trees,
> That twinkle in the gusty breeze,
> Behold him perched in ecstasies,
> Yet seeming still to hover.

Greenfinches evidently like companionship and will congregate during the day, twittering together. Perhaps they are indulging in reminiscences which must be well sprinkled with regret for the good old days when hedgerows were plentiful and the present sparseness of food was not so harassing. During their talks over these ever-increasing problems I have noticed many other small birds join them, mainly sparrows and yellow buntings, but though obviously enjoying these social gatherings, at night they will seek out some sheltering thick growth in which to roost solely with their own kind.

GOLDFINCH

The goldfinch is not at all stereotyped in his choice of a building site, placing his perfect nest high or low in trees, gardens, shrubberies, or orchards. It is deftly built with bents, moss, and lichen, cosily lined with down, wool, or hair. The whole is woven into a compact felt with infinite skill. The down used for the lining is usually gathered from early coltsfoot or if later in the year the thistle, and every one of these seeds has to be collected separately. I found a nest in one of my fruit trees and watching the building was impressed by the skill and care the lovely little bird exercised. Knapp has well described this tiny architect as 'that inimitable spinner, that Arachne of the groves'. The nest certainly shows an appreciation of form and colour almost suggesting a sense of beauty.

An incident that occurred when I was watching these birds induced me to think that they possess intelligence. The pair I was observing nested on a very frail branch, and when the young birds were hatched the parents evidently realized that the weight of the growing family was becoming dangerous and that the slender support might break, so to save the nest they intertwined stronger near-by twigs with the bending ones.

The goldfinch is particularly blessed by nature in having not only beautiful plumage but the gift of song. I have a friend who was able to rescue one of these lovely little birds with a broken wing. Very reluctantly he was kept in a cage and though never able to do more than flutter down from his perch, he settled there contentedly. Any upward flight was impossible to him but he retained his capacity for song, and favoured certain music. There was no question that he had a preference for Mozart, for whenever this composer's work was played, his response was particularly vigorous. It would seem almost that the bird recognized a kinship with that light-hearted quality which this music possesses.

The goldfinch to me always adds to the joyousness of spring, the most vocal of all seasons for the feathered creatures. He not only gives the delight of his song but also serves by consuming many weed-seeds that we do not want; he specially favours dandelion, groundsel, coltsfoot, hawk-weed, and thistle. In my wild garden I preserve a little patch of thistles to attract him and am rewarded by having a near sight of his beauty and the pleasure of his singing. The French call him *chardonneret* (*chardon*— a thistle). In some countries he is called *thistle-finch* and in Scotland *gold-spink* or *goldie*.

This little bird has many enemies among the winged creatures, who are only too ready to slip into the nest and peck out the tiny eggs, crushing and sucking up the contents.

CHAFFINCH

The chaffinch's nest is usually found not far from the ground, in either bushes or trees. If the latter are chosen it is fixed, like the long-tailed tit's, securely in the fork of a bough, so that it is almost impossible to remove it without cutting off the branch. This wonderful little home is skilfully made of moss, roots, grasses, and lichen, woven together (sometimes with spiders' webs) and lined with hair, wool, and feathers. A nest in my neighbour's garden was lined with coltsfoot down, the airy material being wonderfully kept in place against the nest wall by a long black horsehair cunningly carried round in a spiral from top to bottom. I was intrigued by wondering whether the down or its internal supporting spiral had been laid in first, but that I have never been able to discover. The rim is beautifully rounded as if turned by a lathe and decorated with white and green lichen picked from the bark of trees.[1]

It has been recorded that when the bird fails to get the lichen desired, she will collect scraps of paper or cotton wool. I have seen a nest thus decorated in a flowering blackthorn and I found difficulty in distinguishing it from the blossoms, as was no doubt intended; the camouflage effected by the chaffinch I think perhaps the most remarkable I have seen. Only this spring I was taken to a friend's vinery and shown by the old gardener a wonderful example of this, which almost suggested the thoughtful working out of a plan to baulk discovery; the bird had built on a vine, the nest perfectly merging into the stem as if it were one and the same. The gardener was evidently not unmoved by the bird's patience and ingenuity, for he said: 'Aye, if these 'ere town-plannin' folk were wise, they might learn summit regardin' buildin'. By castin' an eye over this 'ere job of work, they might think twice and use local material—stone or brick—what blended natural; then we shouldn't be 'avin' the like o' these eyesores what besmirch the meadows and this village of ourn.'

It seems this particular little bird had built two nests, the first in another glasshouse; but there she had been splashed with liquid used for spraying and so decided to evacuate. But she still favoured building on a vine, and it was the second nest that impressed the gardener and induced my wonder and admiration. The vine had been pruned rather severely and the wounds treated with white-lead paint; the chaffinch had not only copied

[1] In the mountains of North Borneo there is a bird called Whitehead's broadbill who makes his nest in much the same exquisite manner as our chaffinch. The nest is in the shape of a purse, the lichen being carefully woven into it and around the branch from which it is suspended. The nest ends in a sort of pointed tail which looks exactly like the many streamers of moss which hang from the trees on every side.

the exact colour of the stem but, most amazing of all, had woven into her nest little scraps of white wool to resemble the paint markings. The bird must have made hundreds of journeys to procure the material for her camouflage and must also have noted the time when the glasshouse was opened and closed, so that the building and subsequent feeding of young might be accomplished.

The hen chaffinch will keep her eggs dry even in the most terrible storms; though her own outer feathers may get soaked, the soft down on her breast keeps the eggs both dry and warm. It is strange that the cock dislikes the sun and will seek out a dark, cool place, while his hen loves heat and when not brooding will lie with outstretched wings enjoying a sun-bath.

These birds are useful, eating the larva that often lies within the bud; if those who condemn them would look more carefully they would find the concealed worm, which is sought by the bird but is the pest of the grower. Few will remember that a pair of finches can dispose of four thousand caterpillars a week when rearing a nest of young.

The song of the chaffinch is the very essence of spring, joyous and fresh, almost rollicking, finishing with a flourish. Their slate-blue caps, wings barred with white stripes, and rose breast enhance the attraction of the hedgerows where they still exist.

HAWFINCH

He is the largest of the finches but is a very shy bird, not often seen. At the slightest sound he flies off and hides amid foliage. His conical beak is particularly strong and well-suited for breaking the stones of fruit to extract the kernel; though he does not care for the actual plum or cherry he does enjoy the laurel, holly, juniper, and hornbeam. His beak serves him well in opening a beech-nut to which he is very partial, and is a useful defence against cats.

He favours a bushy hawthorn or holly for his nest but also builds in high branches of other trees. I have found only one nest and that was in my orchard; it was shallow and not very compactly built—nothing to be compared with the wonderful artistry found in the nests of the other finches—composed largely of twigs and fibres mingled with grey lichens. His song is rather harsh but I have heard him in winter uttering sweet, plaintive notes.

CHIFF-CHAFF

This little bird is among the very earliest of our spring visitors. When I hear him in March it is difficult to believe that he has travelled four thousand miles through the wind and storm of late winter; but then all things connected with birds are remarkable. Eighty-five per cent of our singing-birds return to their breeding haunts after completing vast migratory flights; it is almost incredible that they should return to some quiet little bush, tree, or crevice they have known.

I look forward to the chiff-chaff's two characteristic notes which no doubt are responsible for his name. His colouring always seems to me so much in keeping with the catkin, and he is with us at the time when these lovely tassels hang from the hazel. Gardeners must welcome him, for neither apple, cherry, nor plum tempt him to plunder; he is satisfied if allowed to clear the tree of insects.

I do not think any description of the nest of the chiff-chaff, or *dark-legged petty-chap* as the bird is sometimes called, can be more graphic than John Clare's, and so I quote the poem:

> Well! in my many walks I've rarely found
> A place less likely for a bird to form
> Its nest—close by the rut-gulled wagon road,
> And on the almost bare foot-trodden ground,
> With scarce a clump of grass to keep it warm!
> Where not a thistle spreads its spears abroad,
> Or prickly bush to shield it from harm's way;
> And yet so snugly made, that none may spy
> It out, save peradventure. You and I
> Had surely pass'd it in our walk to-day,
> Had chance not led us by it! Nay, e'en now,
> Had not the old bird heard us trampling by,
> And flutter'd out, we had not seen it lie
> Brown as the road-way side. Small bits of hay
> Plucked from the old propt haystack's bleachy brow,
> And wither'd leaves, make up its outward wall.
> Which from the gnarl'd oak-dotterel yearly fall.
> And in the old hedge-bottom rot away.
> Built like an oven—through a little hole,
> Scarcely admitting e'en two fingers in,
> Hard to discern, the birds snug entrance win.

'Tis lined with feathers, warm as silken stole,
Softer than seats of down for painless ease,
And full of eggs, scarce bigger than peas!
Here's one most delicate, with spots as small
As dust, and of a faint and pinky red.
Stop! here's the bird. That woodman at the gap
Frighten'd him from the hedge: 'tis olive green.
Well! I declare, it is the Petty-chap!
No bigger than the wren, and seldom seen.
I've often found her nest in chance's way,
When I in pathless woods did idly roam;
But never did I dream, until to-day,
A spot like this would be her chosen home.

WREN

Some of my earliest recollections are associated with watching wrens building in the crevices of the red sandstone caves, a feature of Kinver, where I was born. I have been fortunate in having many opportunities of observing these endearing little birds, so perhaps I may be forgiven for writing of them at some length.

It was well said by a poet that the nestlings 'are fed in the dark, not one forgot'. The nest is so deep that very little light can enter and that is probably why the ancients call the wrens troglodytes—dwellers in caves. The cock sometimes arrives ten days or a fortnight before the hen and I have often watched him—this little feathered ball of energy—constructing a nest; he may even build as many as four of these cock-nests. Whether this is to encourage or entice his chosen mate, or merely for future use, who can say? But it is almost certain that he uses them later for bachelor quarters or for roosting or for bringing up his young. Only one of them is wholly completed and lined with feathers and this is the work of the hen. No doubt for some reason best known to herself she considers the other cock-nests not sufficiently concealed for the safety of her family. This favoured nest is fashioned with the utmost care; it is dome-shaped with a tiny entrance and composed of moss, grey lichens, twigs, and dried leaves. The cock sings to the hen while she works and though appearing to take great interest in the proceedings, he does not usually occupy himself with any subsequent building after he has offered his original selection. Probably he feels that he has done sufficient work in that direction and that his energy should now be concerned with entertaining his mate by song and with the all-important search for food. The little hen works indefatigably and carries bundles of dry leaves as big as herself to reinforce the foundation; in the space of ten minutes she will bring quite six bundles of leaves, examining them carefully and dropping all those she does not find suitable.

There can be no question that wrens deliberately try to avoid detection. If they should build in a tree, thickly covered with ivy, then green will always predominate in the nest, thus achieving an effective camouflage. If a cosy hole in a hayrick is selected, dried grass is used in the composition of the nest. I once found a wren's tiny home among litter in a yard and it was cunningly fashioned to resemble the debris with which it was surrounded. Wordsworth, who wrote so many lovely poems about flowers, describes in one of them how the wren chose the shelter of a clump of primroses for her home, the leaves assisting to hide the moss-built cell.

After a serious illness, when my capacity for sleep was temporarily suspended, I had the pleasure of watching a wren at work on her nest; she was evidently one of the exceptions who was given assistance by her cock. At the end of the first day, when the foundation of the home was finished, she pressed the nest into shape with her breast, turning herself in all directions, and after this had been effected to her satisfaction she began to raise the sides. This often necessitated longer flights, and absences of about ten minutes. Felting together the sticks, leaves, and moss, she rounded them carefully, giving the necessary firmness by continually pressing with her breast and wings. She was at work all day and again at dawn while her husband cheered her on with his song until eight a.m., when he gave her some assistance. They then worked together until eleven bringing in building materials. Their 'elevenses' lasted until nearly one o'clock, this period evidently being set aside for rest and refreshment. Then they continued, both toiling together until four, when the hen again worked alone. This time-table was faithfully repeated and on the tenth day the nest was finished. It was about five feet from the ground, concealed in an ivy-clad tree-bole; there was the customary small entrance and an unusual additional opening below, covered by a large ivy-leaf.

After the eggs were hatched, I watched my parent wrens feeding their babies from forty to sixty times in an hour. The fledglings' hunger was immense and the parents had to provide an unceasing supply of worms, spiders, grasshoppers, etc.

My little hen descended along the ivy-stem to remove excrement after feeding the nestlings, thereby revealing that the nest had been elongated owing to the stretching and straining caused by her large, hungry family. While one was being fed at the upper entrance, another pushed his head through the thin wall and still further enlarged the opening in his persistent clamour for food. Both parents fed them continually; mother never made a sound, but when father brought his supplies he voiced evident satisfaction with each contribution; I noticed he made about one trip to every ten or more of the mother bird's. After carefully watching, I saw two of the little fledglings leave the nest by the upper opening and a third from the lower; the last baby to leave, finding himself alone appeared to deliberate, then with a determined effort he too faced the unknown.

My neighbour, who is an indefatigable bird-watcher, told me that with his wife and son he kept a particular wren under close observation for fifteen hours of daylight and during that time the bird fed her young one thousand one hundred and seventeen times. It would seem, therefore, taking an average of only fifty visits per hour and twelve hours during which the young birds are fed, that the parents clear from plants at least six hundred insects in the course of the day—this on the supposition that both birds take but a single insect each time, though from my observation I should say they certainly carry off more than one at every flight.

One afternoon when I was convalescent and had been sleeping in the sun on my verandah, I was awakened by my wren's high, clear note almost in my ear and found to my astonishment that she was on the arm of my chair, evidently determined to attract my attention. Looking down, I saw her four babies were on the verandah; so also was a cat coming stealthily towards them with crouched body. One clap of my hands and the cat had vanished but not the birds. Intense anxiety had given my wren such boldness and she had undoubtedly become accustomed to me and realized that I was friendly. After the cat's departure she obviously wished to convey to me that I was to remain on guard while she hunted for food. I must confess to having been rather glad when their bedtime arrived and they were all conducted up the stairway to their nursery and tucked up safely for the night; a wren will always call her young back to the nest in the evening.

Wrens often appear to seek companionship at night or in cold weather, frequently in a bush, sometimes in the eaves of a stack or even of a house. As many as ten may occupy an old nest; this habit of gathering together may be for safety, as one of them is sure to be awake when danger threatens, but I am sure the chief reason is to keep themselves warm; in spite of this attempt to preserve heat, they are frequently found dead, rolled together in a ball. It is distressing that during a severe winter wrens suffer disastrous casualties and there seems little one can do to help them.

I have never seen a wren morose or sad; he is bright and perky and hops along with his short tail jauntily raised at right angles.

> When Christ was born in Bethlehem
> There perched beside His crib a wren
> Who by the little Saviour laid
> Two feathers close beside His Head.
> This did he many times until
> The softest pillow he had made.
> The Christ-Child smiled most lovingly
> And touched the brown tail tenderly
> And that in very truth is why
> The small bird bears his tail so high![1]

The wren's song is sweet. Indeed, in the whole insectivorous tribe there is hardly a finer musician. It is a marvel that so diminutive a bird can pipe so loud and clear a strain, persisting with it even when the snow is lying deep on the ground. I like the Dutch name for him—*Little Winter King*.

GOLDEN-CRESTED WREN

The fir trees which border my garden furnish these lovely little birds with desirable sites. They particularly favour the fir and the pine, though one may see them hovering about the birch trees, where they go a-hunting for the minute grubs which are their food. The nest is such as a fairy might conceive, slung like a tiny hammock, often on the high boughs of a coniferous tree, concealed by an overhanging branch which protects the fledglings from sun, storm, and prying eyes. They are careful to make the nest fast; it is built in such a way as to resist the prevailing wind, and is fre-

[1] Author unknown.

quently bound firmly to the supporting twigs with lengths of bast. The nest is a combination of neatness and beauty, surely one of the most marvellous in our island, not excepting the long-tailed tit's. Deep and cup-shaped, it is surprisingly large in proportion to the builder, the outside being as well finished as the inside. It is composed of moss, leaves, and fir needles and is woven with wool, cobwebs, and a generous supply of feathers into a compact felted mass, providing the softest imaginable bed. The whole is closed at the top with only the tiniest possible entrance at the side.

This wonder builder, so exquisite and minute, is sometimes called the *marigold-finch* and is I believe the smallest European bird, only three and a half inches long from head to tail and weighing no more than two and a half ounces. No bird is more entertaining to watch; he seems to indulge in acrobatics for his own amusement. In the winter of 1957, which was unusually mild, I saw several of these birds feeding on the wing, which I had never seen before. So rich is their colour that when they are amid the spruce they love, their fiery crests gleam like tiny tongues of flame.

WILLOW WREN

The willow wren's tiny nest is as soft as silk, sometimes built on the ground, usually hidden in the grass of a bank. The country people call it a 'ground over'. It is domed, composed of grasses, moss, and dried leaves, cosily lined with feathers, with an entrance near the top. Willow wrens, or willow-warblers as they are sometimes called, once built in my garden, choosing somewhat surprisingly a lupin plant. It was delightful to watch these little birds through my glasses and I noted their colouring blended perfectly with this chosen site. The hen fed her young with five caterpillars every few minutes, so it is no wonder that they are canonized by gardeners and are sometimes called *Saint Wren*.

These little birds have a simple liquid cadence of notes which is repeated some five to eight times a minute and which I always rejoice to hear, as they are to me true harbingers of spring.

SISKIN

I have often seen nests of the siskin in the pine-woods of the Highlands, always on the topmost branches looking like little pine-cones. Here they find a larder provided not only by the tree seeds but by the insects which infest them—thus they render the tree valuable service in addition to satisfying their own needs. They rarely nest in the south, but much to my delight and surprise I found this spring a pair had built in a fir tree at the end of my garden. Though the nest is smaller, it is built something like that of the goldfinch, being composed of twigs, moss, lichen, and wool, lined with roots, down, and hair. This tiny bird shares with his handsome cousin the crossbill the liking for the end of a pine branch and also his taste for seeds.

The hen incubates her eggs for about fourteen days, never leaving the nest; both parents exhibit immense patience, industry, and affection. They are a great delight to watch, appearing continually gay and quite content with life. I have never seen them quarrelling with any other birds and they do not appear to want anything that is not their particular portion. They thoroughly enjoy all work and play and when not concerned with family affairs are constantly twittering, singing, or preening their lovely plumage.

5

PLASTERERS

*Swallow; housemartin; swift; nuthatch; mistle-thrush;
song-thrush; redwing; fieldfare; blackbird; magpie*

SWALLOW

THE plasterers that everyone knows best are the swallows, martins, and swifts. The swallow's long, slender, forked tail is probably responsible for his Gaelic name '*gobhlan-gaoithe*' (fork of the wind). He is a lovely bird with his chestnut throat and forehead and the beautiful blue sheen on his back and wings. He usually favours for his nest the interior of buildings, particularly sheds and barns, fixing it on rafters, angles of a wall, or even inside a chimney-stack. The nest is lined with feathers; it is saucer-shaped, open at the top, and formed of minute particles of mud cemented together, partly with his own saliva and partly with water from puddles or a near-by pond. I have watched him lifting his wings and tail so that they shall not get soiled as he mixes the mud carefully; it would seem that he cannot tolerate a speck of dirt on his lovely plumage. It is probable that the mud is swallowed and regurgitated later, for I have watched the birds arriving at the nesting site with only grass stalks in their bills. It would seem therefore that the mud is brought up when these stalks are in position, one layer only being fixed at a time and then left to dry before the next is plastered on.

That the swallow's taste for a site does not always run on the conventional lines laid down by centuries of ancestors is apparent. Gilbert White writes of swallows who built for two years on the handle of garden shears in an outhouse. Another pair built on the wings of an owl which was hanging dead from the rafters of a barn, and they have been known to build among the branches of trees, though I have never seen this myself.

Most people eagerly look forward to the arrival of the swallow from sun-scorched Africa, his advent always being regarded as the beginning of summer, though it is only too true that 'one swallow does not make a summer.'

Swallows and martins will return year after year to the same nesting site, greeting it with evident delight. They will fly continually around the old home, sometimes for days, before they begin again to renovate and set it in order; this may be to make quite sure there is no mistake or perhaps to prolong the enjoyment of homecoming.

To watch swallows is always a delight. I like to see them perching on a branch, preening themselves, sometimes shaking off the early morning dewdrops, then carefully lifting their wings and breaking into song. How amazing to watch their zigzagging flight when with such dexterity they capture their insect food!

Most country people, myself included, believe that it is good fortune to have a pair of swallows build on their houses. In Scandinavia the swallow is looked upon with affection, his cry is called by the people *scvala* meaning *console*, and they consider it unlucky to injure or to destroy a swallow's nest, the bird being still regarded as sacred to the Penates or household gods. Laplanders augment their eaves by nailing narrow planks beneath them, leaving just enough room between for the swallows to nest; no doubt this particular welcome is afforded the birds on account of their capacity to deal with the gnats which are so troublesome during the summer. A swallow destroys a hundred times its own weight in insects in one season.

I had never known anyone to disturb a swallow's nest until recently, when I found that a certain vicar, who perhaps should be nameless, had destroyed all the swallows' nests in his vicarage and church porch. His excuse was that they made a mess; I wished that he could as effectively have removed the litter which was an all-too-deplorable evidence of unfeathered bipeds.

Unlike the vicar, many saints seem to have found birds congenial companions. Guthlac, the hermit-saint of the eighth century, who was of the royal family of Mercia, particularly favoured swallows; it is recorded that they sat unafraid on his knee. Attributed to him are the two lines:

> He who lives his life according to the Will of God,
> To him will the wild birds draw more near.

There is no question that even as the robins' friendship and the rascal cuckoos' arrival are welcomed, so the swallows' advent is awaited and recorded and we are always reluctant to say goodbye to them in October when they leave. To live, swallows must continually pursue the sun; the mystery of their migration is baffling, for when with us they make but short, darting flights. It is still believed by some that they do not migrate but rather become comatose. This is a possible theory in relation to those who hatch late and are forced to hide or hibernate during the winter, for they have been found when part of a building or sometimes a cliff has collapsed. Olaus Magnus writes: 'In the northern waters fishermen oft-times draw up in their nets an abundance of swallows hanging together like a corrugated mass.'

Gilbert White certainly inclined to the theory of hibernation, and in 1797 Bewick quoted a Mr Klein who stated that swallows 'assembled in numbers on the reeds at the edges of rivers, clinging to the stems until they broke with the weight, when the birds fell into the river. Their immersion,' he said, 'is preceded by a song or dirge which lasts for more than a quarter of an hour.' Though Klein discarded the theory that swallows spend the winter under water, yet he could not reconcile this conclusion with the fact that they had been taken from the water and had lived.

Though the hibernation of certain birds was accredited by the earlier ornithologists, it has been repudiated by the moderns. Yet, as in many ways, there comes a reversal of thought; there are still those who contend hibernation does take place. Seton Gordon tells us how a bird has not only been observed during hibernation but has been weighed and its temperature taken and other records made.

In 1946 a bird was watched and investigated. It was one of the nightjar family and was found in the crevice of a cliff in the Colorado Desert. This bird remained insensible and without food for eighty-eight days, during which period it lost only one gramme in weight. The Hopi Indians' name for it is *holchko* (the sleeping one). Swifts have been found in Scotland, dormant in a cranny of the rocks; so who can actually deny that hibernation may be possible?

HOUSEMARTIN

The housemartin's tail is forked like that of the swallow but lacks the long outer feathers; there are few who do not admire his glossy dark-blue back and head, his immaculate white rump and under parts, and his

D

daintily feathered toes. Unlike the swallow he prefers the exterior of buildings for his nest, and the pellets he moulds are finished where the material is collected and then brought to the nesting site. The mud required for the plastering is now scarce: muddy roads and lanes are disappearing and there are few puddles; there is a consequent decrease in swallow and martin life which is to be deplored, for they are of great value to man as they not only gather insects from the air but also rid the fruit-trees of these pests.

In company with the swallow and swift, martins seek both building material and food in the air, for they experience great difficulty in rising from the ground. I have often been fascinated watching them feed their young, catching an insect on the wing and partially digesting it before ejecting it into the mouth of a hungry fledgling. This process takes place not only at the nest but when the young are actually in the air.

Housemartins usually arrive after the swallow and sing from April until the end of October, but they have been seen in November at Oxford and chicks have been recorded in October. This late breeding is, however, generally disastrous, as their migrating instinct is strong enough to compel them to leave even their young.

A housemartin building under the eaves by my bedroom window enabled me to observe the skill of this bird architect and plasterer and to wonder at the dexterity with which the desired lining of feathers, fluff, and wool was gathered in the air. There was even a sort of ledge added to the nest which I imagined was in order that the young could be moved to this extension. The nest was so close to the window that I could put my finger into it, but the birds soon discovered this possible danger of molestation and stopped up the entrance accessible to me and opened another on the opposite side!

When martins leave their work of nest-building or renovating, even for a few seconds, to seek further material or food, sparrows may immediately take possession, though they have already a nest of their own. This practice usually means a fierce battle when the rightful owners return and unfortunately the victory is often with the marauders.

I have frequently been asked what can be done to circumvent this unfortunate habit of the sparrow, and the question has even been raised on the radio. I have personally found the most effective measure is partly to destroy the old nest of the martins before they return. This means that in all probability the sparrows will have had their families while the repairs are being completed, but this year my martin visitors came very early and so the sparrows were already in occupation of their nest; I then relentlessly broke it down, the martins repaired it and successfully reared their brood.

Gene Stratton Porter tells of a martin who succeeded in outwitting a molesting sparrow. Probably realizing that a fight at the door of his nest would damage the structure, he decided on giving the sparrow a taste of his own medicine. He flew to the sparrow's nest, which was near by, and in an obvious fashion took from it a large beakful of straw, then a second and a third. This resulted in bringing the would-be marauder back in haste; the martin returned to his own nest and doubtless enjoyed the joke with his wife. The author tells us that both couples then reared families in their legitimate and respective homes without further trouble.

Housemartins are believed by many to give a more reliable weather-forecast than swallows, but there can be no question that all the swallow tribe are particularly sensitive to the elements. When there is humidity and chill in the air the slight wings of insects refuse to carry them high; therefore members of this family guided either by sensations or by power of sight come down to hunt for their prey; this may be an explanation of why flying high or low denotes certain weather-conditions.

The following delightful story of a martin was told me by the late Admiral Mark Kerr when he was serving in the brig *Martin*:

On a very cold day when it was blowing a gale, a martin bird flew on board our 'Martin' Brig for shelter, evidently blown out of his course and exhausted. Perhaps he thought he would find shelter in the great floating nest, perhaps it was desperation. I enticed him down below and put him in a box of cottonwool near the stove. When he was well warmed up I caught a fly on the beams and, opening his beak, pushed it in. The result being satisfactory I presently gave him another and shortly afterwards he would stand on my finger, fly off, pick up a fly by himself, and return to my finger. My messmates were so delighted that they all took a turn at catching flies.

I had always heard that martins were untameable, but never did a bird become so tame in a few minutes as our little friend. He actually took mouthfuls of food from between my lips. He flew around in the ward room giving a chirp to each of us before he turned in after his own fashion, which was sitting on the back of a chair with his head under his wing. When the fury of the storm abated and his strength was restored he continued his lonely flight. All the crew cherish the memory of a most friendly little so-called 'untameable'.

SWIFT

The swift has narrow scythe-like wings equal to his body in size, and all four toes are directed forward, his sharp claws helping him to cling to a wall or rough surface with as much aptitude as a fly.

This bird appears to have complete understanding and companionship with the air, a union of bird with element that perhaps no other creature possesses in quite the same way. Swifts actually live on the wing, and it is said they fulfil their amorous rites, and even sleep, in the air.

Any patient watcher may see the male bird in flight from soon after three in the morning until nine at night, feeding his mate and young. It is estimated that he must travel at least one thousand miles in that time. Some naturalists have described his flight as more like that of a bat than a bird; he will sometimes circle very high in the air, skimming the eaves of a house with terrific speed. When these birds are catching insects they are supposed to achieve the staggering rate of one hundred miles an hour.

They can neither walk nor stand on the ground, their legs being so short that it seems impossible for them to take off again. Materials for their marvellous nests are either caught in the air or gathered from a thatch, then stuck together with the saliva from their mouths. When once their home is established they will return, like the swallow and martin, to the same site for many years, and this homing instinct is inherited by their descendants, who in some unknown way are drawn back to their ancestors' chosen site when their miraculous journeys from the Sudan, the Cape, or Madagascar are accomplished.

Nothing save the cruelty of caging will stop swifts, swallows, and martins from migration; no one who has the misfortune to see one of these birds battering himself in a cage at the migration period will ever forget it.

I have only once heard of humans successfully fostering a swift; they lived in a top-floor flat in a London suburb. They found a young swift crouching in a drain-pipe, wounded in neck, leg, and wing, having been badly mauled by a cat. They fashioned a temporary nest, dressed the wounds, and frequently fed the bird with a mixture of scrambled egg and raw meat, using tweezers. As his condition improved he gradually helped himself, then began watching for his natural insect food until, in order to catch flies, he was forced to attempt short flights about the room. The wing healed and grew strong, until at last at the call of migration he was able to fly back to his natural habitat, free of houses.

NUTHATCH

The nuthatch is a valued visitor to my garden in the spring, running up and down the trees in the manner of a woodpecker. It is entertaining to watch these birds fix a nut in the crevice of the bark, then, with their short, stiff tail to give them added support and a firmer stand, neatly extract the desired kernel.

Architects and plasterers among bird builders, they show much wisdom in choosing a site. Both male and female build the nest and are very careful that their home shall be entirely free from draughts, meticulously cementing every crack and crevice with clay. They usually choose a natural hole and collect dry leaves and flakes of bark for the interior. As many as six thousand six hundred and ninety-five separate scraps of building material have been counted in one nest. They plaster up the entrance, leaving only a tiny hole, something after the manner of the hornbill. The nuthatch often has desperate battles with other birds, particularly the starling, for his nesting place; that is doubtless why the hole to the entrance is made so very small.

He is sometimes called the *mud-stopper*, *mud-dabber*, or *nut-jobber*, all names very suggestive of his work. I find it enthralling to watch him when he flies to a tree or telegraph-post and clings to it. Both he and the woodpecker in this respect approach the confounding achievement of a fly on the ceiling! He always descends the tree head first, a feat which is accomplished, I believe, by no other English bird; his claw seems almost out of proportion to the rest of his body but no doubt this provides him with his astounding grip. The young climb even before they can fly.

I am pretty certain that the same pair have taken up their abode for some years in an old elm tree in my garden—no doubt an adjacent hedge of Kent cobs is the particular attraction. I have observed nuthatches collecting mud at the margin of a puddle in the roadway and working it into a bolus the size of a hazel-nut; they then fly off with it in their beaks to the chosen nesting site, twenty feet up an old elm tree, where they proceed to plaster the entrance. I noticed the hen seemed to do most of the plastering whilst the cock stood about on various perches near by whistling his encouragement; after adding the bolus of mud the hen pecked it with rapid blows of her beak until it had been worked into the desired formation.

I was not the only watcher of this particular pair; starlings were interested too, and one attempted to enter the narrow opening. I was not sorry to see him become stuck midway. Having nothing against which he could plant his feet for purchase he kicked out into the air and, by a process of wriggling, finally fell head foremost into the cavity, from which he rapidly emerged with the nuthatch's nesting material in his beak. Later the same day the disgruntled owners plastered up the enlarged hole. Two weeks elapsed before I saw the starlings again return to the cavity with their own nesting material and later the nuthatch was once more replastering. The following day the starlings were still interfering, all attempts to drive them off being only temporarily successful. Two days afterwards I discovered the dead body of the hen nuthatch on the ground near by, with her bloody, almost featherless head affording evidence enough of the violent struggle to the death in this losing battle for a nesting site which had lasted over seventeen days.

These birds suffer very much in winter and many do not survive, but some at least can be saved if sufficient patience and persistence are exercised by the human. I have only once had a nuthatch at my bird-table and there is no question that it was sheer desperation and lack of food that brought him there. Starvation will overcome timidity and suspicion.

MISTLE-THRUSH

The mistle-thrush is the largest of our song-birds and although the plumage of cock and hen is alike there is an obvious difference between them, the cock being more aggressive and having a challenge in his aspect which the hen lacks. In the West of England this thrush is called the *holm-thrush* because he feeds on the berries of the holly or holm. These birds also enjoy the berry of the baleful yew and of the mysterious mistletoe; indeed it is believed that the name 'mistle' came about because the young are often fed on this berry. It was thought by early writers that the seeds of the mistletoe were transplanted from one tree to another by this thrush.

The nest is an elaborate structure with grass walls, the inside being plastered carefully with mud and lined with dry grass and various bits of soft material. All birds naturally resent their nest being the subject of prying eyes and they will very often forsake it when the home is no longer private. The mistle-thrush is no exception to this rule. A friend of mine told me of a curious incident which occurred when he was using his telescope to look at a steamer far out at sea; it seems he left the instrument on its stand, pointing directly at the nest of a mistle-thrush where the hen was sitting, ten or a dozen yards away. She deserted, but before doing so pierced a hole in each of her eggs.

The bird is often called the *storm-cock*. When winds blow strong from the west he likes to perch on the top of a lofty tree and pour forth his challenge to the elements, for he sings best in wild weather. His song is loud and clear, one phrase being often repeated, but it lacks the variety of the song-thrush. This valiant singer is courageous in defence of his young and his property, attacking the jackdaw, magpie, and crow when they come to steal the eggs. Oliver Pike gives an example of their valour when protecting their nest against overwhelming odds. The particular incident he observed was in a wood not far from the sea in south-west Ireland. A pine-marten was beginning to push his way through the undergrowth when Oliver Pike immediately heard the harsh alarm notes of the birds ringing out. The pine-marten came to the thrush's tree and began to climb: the male thrush became more and more perturbed, continually voicing his protest; again and again he swooped at the marten as the animal approached. The hen, who had not yet left her eggs, at last flew off and joined her mate in the attack. The marten was now standing on a broad branch forty feet from the ground. As the two birds swooped past he raised his head and snarled; his long back was arched and he made ready to spring but the birds were undaunted and the cock struck him. The marten almost lost his balance and before recovering received a stinging blow from the hen. With an angry cry he tried to turn, lost his foothold, and crashed down. As he fell he clutched at the branches but missed, turned over, struck a thick bough with a heavy thud, tumbled to the grass, and lay still. Above, the mistle-thrushes still called, but the quality of their note had changed, for their enemy lay lifeless on the ground beneath.

SONG-THRUSH

The song-thrush is architect, plasterer, mason, felter, and basket-maker; the nest is similar to that of the mistle-thrush, but without the soft lining. It is usually made of twigs, roots, and moss, plastered on the inside with mud which is often composed of rotten wood and even cow-dung. This is made as smooth as if it had been patted down with a spoon, the hen turning round and round smoothing it with her breast. When dried the nest is a shelter which is impervious to air and water.

The birds work industriously to make the nest, and harder still to feed the young, for beaks are always open waiting for more food. Many of the mothers obviously become worn out by their unflagging devotion; a young thrush is said to eat four yards of earthworm in a day. If death from man or cat takes the mother, the father will continue to feed the young, often killing himself by the double work entailed.

A one-legged thrush frequented my garden for two successive seasons. In the mating season he and his wife built their nest and hatched out young, but one morning I found the mother lying dead on the ground. The father had now all the responsibility of feeding and bringing up the fledglings; he worked hard throughout the day, acting as father and mother to the brood during the ensuing weeks and managed, though handicapped by the loss of his leg, to rear two. I put bread soaked in milk for him out on the verandah and he collected it hour after hour. But he had to rest frequently while carrying the food in his beak. At last he brought the young birds on to the verandah, obviously with pride, also doubtless to show them where food could be found. It was evident that he was exhausted for that same evening he crouched on the usual tree, too weak to perch in an upright position. But he lifted up his head, and opening his beak, voiced his joyous note and sang until after dark. It was his last song.

I like an extract from the Gaelic, which roughly translated runs thus:

The thrush is in the still morning, sweetly, sweetly singing:
The thrush is in the still morning, whoever there be to hear it.
It is the bird of all sweetest voice, sweetly, sweetly singing, whoever there
be to hear it.

Thrushes are certainly becoming rarer; they suffer casualties from the fast motor traffic and are often victims of severe weather. Their death is a loss to us, not only because of their beauty and the delight they give with their song but because of their value to agriculture. A hundred thousand song-thrushes will consume during the months of April, May, and June three thousand million caterpillars and other insects, yet the birds are not protected by law. Probably no one knows the many varieties of food birds eat, but I think it interesting that the root of the cuckoo-pint (called in our part of the world 'lords and ladies') is scratched out of the ground and eaten by the thrush in severe weather.

The migration of birds always has been and always will be mysterious and wonderful. I have never been fortunate enough to see any vast quantity of thrushes migrating, but a watcher from Ireland, in County Clare, reports that in January he saw approximately thirty thousand flying at a height of thirty to sixty feet. This vast exodus began at approximately half past nine in the morning and lasted till noon: the number being estimated by the fact that in the two and a half hours no fewer than two hundred birds passed in just over a minute. These included some plovers, green and gold, and a few snipe, but the main body of the migrating birds was thrushes. This suggested the advent of a cold spell, which did indeed follow.

All birds certainly have a hard fight for existence; they are affected by weather-conditions, and many things that serve man are to them a menace. Even our lighthouses, particularly those on the north coast of Scotland, the Outer Hebrides, Orkneys, and Shetlands, are responsible for the deaths of countless birds, many thrushes among them. The weary birds, almost at the end of their long journey, are attracted by the light of the great lantern and striking the glass fall bruised and dying. I know more than one keeper who is distressed by this; some even make an effort to keep the birds off the lantern by tying on it strips of material which, blowing in the wind, they hope may scare the birds off, but I hear it is not very satisfactory. The remedy for the appalling toll of bird life taken by these great lanterns has not yet been found.

REDWING

The redwing is among the birds who would appear not to be aptly named, for the red of his plumage is not on the wing but on the flank; in the land of vineyards he is called the *wine-thrush*. He is the smallest of the thrush family and an infinitely shyer bird than the others. He builds his nest in scrub near the ground with grasses carefully fixed over a mud cap and he may well be called a plasterer.

He spends only the winter and early spring in the British Isles, and must often regret this, as he succumbs to severe weather very quickly, being unable to get food. It is always distressing to see these lovely birds struggling against starvation in the bitter weather, particularly being so utterly unable to help them. During the months redwings spend with us they are slender, but in France they grow plump feeding on grapes and thus, alas, become desirable for some palates.

Some people think the redwing's song is suggestive of the robin's; it certainly ripples in much the same way. He is often called the *nightingale of Norway* and I have heard him in full song in that country; he usually favours the top of a high tree for his platform, though he does indulge in community singing before going to roost.

FIELDFARE

The fieldfare is sometimes called *herald-wing* and is a larger bird than the redwing. Like all the thrush family he has the speckled chest, but one can recognize him because of his grey head, chestnut mantle, and black tail; I have seen him in company with other thrushes but can always pick him out by his light-coloured rump. Both sexes are alike in plumage though the hen is rather paler.

He is only a winter visitor and the last of the thrush family to arrive— we see him from late September to about April. He very rarely breeds in our island; I have seen only one nest and that was not very high up in the fork of a birch tree, but occasionally he will choose rocks or even the ground for his nest which is constructed with grasses and moss, solidified with earth, and has a lining usually of dry grass. Though he builds fairly low he seeks the highest branches in which to roost, in contrast to the red-wing who favours the thicker growth beneath.

Fieldfares seem fond of community life. I have seen a flock almost cover a field in the Fell country where they are frequently netted in large quantities when feeding on the wheat stubble. They are among the few birds I know who enjoy the yewberry and they particularly like the berries of the hawthorn.

His song is not often heard in this country, our climate probably being not sufficiently cold to encourage him. Sometimes he tries to warble but more often one hears only his harsh note which might be described as 'chacking'.

BLACKBIRD

The blackbird appears to be increasing in numbers, and shares with the chaffinch the distinction of being the most abundant of our British birds. And that is as well, for there are few who do not appreciate his wonderful song. He has a delightful habit of singing triumphantly during his courtship, as if display is not enough and he must also voice his rapturous love.

Blackbirds build the same kind of mud-lined nest of sticks and roots as the song-thrush but add a final lining of moss and dried grass, and the birds take the greatest care to keep it scrupulously clean.

> The overarching boughs between
> Of some selected evergreen,
> Of laurel thick, or branching fir,
> Or bed of pleasant lavender,
> To lodge secure their pendant home,
> A well-wove frame, with moisten'd loam
> Within cemented; and without
> Rough but compactly, all about
> With moss and fibrous roots entwined,
> And wither'd bent grass softly lined,
> Where may repose, in season due,
> Their pregnant balls of chalky blue,
> Besprent about the flatten'd crown
> With pallid spots of chestnut brown.[1]

They build very early and the hen sits when there is a good deal of cold weather; perhaps that is why the nest is very substantial. It would seem they often favour the same site. I had a blackbird's nest for four years in succession immediately over my kitchen door, which is by no means quiet owing to constant callers. I could never understand why the birds should choose this place instead of some more secluded spot in the garden; perhaps it was because they knew that constant titbits were forthcoming from

[1] Bishop Mant.

the kitchen. When the first nest was in process of building I watched with great interest. The cock fussed round the site for a considerable period before he definitely decided upon it. He was equally particular about the material that he chose, discarding many grasses not to his taste. Then he whistled for his mate, obviously telling her to help him with the nest-building. Whether she approved I rather doubt for there was a good deal of discussion, but she evidently put up with it for the sake of peace and joined her mate. Once the hen had accustomed herself to the site she found it desirable, probably because a generous, bird-loving housekeeper is not always to be found so handy. Certainly the pair raised three broods in this nest the first and the following three seasons, always meticulously renovating the same old nest: then in the fifth year the kitchen-door site was abandoned and the hen built under my bedroom window in an old rambler-rose which has sheltered many a bird. She was piebald, having a completely white head and tail, and has provided a number of piebalds to the district, much to the interest and delight of its inhabitants. Though it is believed that piebalds are shunned by their own kind, my hen is much in demand each season and can pick and choose between the cocks who sue for her favour. Age certainly does 'not wither her, nor custom stale her infinite variety'. She is obviously a coquette but a good mother, and I have seen her assiduously feeding, not only her own family but also an apparently famished young starling.

There are many peculiar instances of blackbirds' building; my neighbour had a pair who built seven nests in a shed at intervals of a foot. The hen laid one egg in each but deserted all seven. Later in an adjacent bush the same pair built a nest and hatched a brood successfully. I once saw a baby chicken in a blackbird's nest which was seven feet from the ground; I never discovered how the chicken got into the nest and I felt this almost equalled the mystery of the cuckoo's egg.

There have been many conjectures among ornithologists as to who is the earliest riser among birds; I have come to the conclusion that it is probably the blackbird; he often lands on my lawn while he is still half asleep. I have watched with amusement the characteristic manner in which, when more fully roused, he runs over the ground a few steps, pauses, runs on again until he is suddenly arrested, then with head on one side obviously listens. After intense concentration he gives a sharp peck at the earth: the hidden worm has not escaped his unerring capacity for detection. I have seen him on a branch between thirty and forty feet high, always with head on one side intently listening; then he will pounce on the exact spot where the worm is concealed.

They love to bathe and do this constantly even in heavy rain; equally they enjoy the sun. In the early days of my bird-watching I was often perturbed by seeing a blackbird crouching on the ground with wings outspread and bill agape; I imagined that he was in distress, not realizing that this was actually sun-bathing. Unlike the human, a bird cannot divest himself of his garments, but he can spread his feathers and so experience much the same advantageous pleasure.

MAGPIE

Originally *Magot pye—Margaret's pie* or *crow*, from the Latin *pica*. I have heard him called *chatterpie* in some places. There is no doubt he is not generally regarded with favour, yet it should be remembered that in spite of his wicked habits he consumes countless worms, slugs, mice, and young rats. His nest is visible from a long distance when branches are bare. It is floored with mud, sometimes so firmly that it will withstand a bullet from a rifle. I have heard him described as one of the Grand Masters of bird masons, though he may also be placed among the weavers, weaving thorny sticks together with great skill. The nest is dome-shaped, substantially constructed, securely interlaced on the outside with sharp thorny twigs, the inside cup of mud lined with grass. Only one small hole is left undefended, round which are twined the strongest thorns for protection.

While other birds are so often beset and robbed magpies usually hatch out their broods successfully, and a legend is told that a deputy from the feathered world asked a magpie to explain to them her plan of building.

'If you listen patiently I will tell you,' she said. 'I begin by taking a stick and laying it thus, then I take another stick and lay it thus, then another stick I lay so.'

'But that is what we all do,' chirped the anxious listeners.

'Then I take a fourth stick,' continued the magpie.

'We all know that much,' voiced the impatient assembly, 'and if you have nothing newer to tell us, we may as well be off.'

And so they all flew away and to this day they have never learnt to protect their nests because they had not the patience to let the magpie teach in her own way by beginning at the beginning.

It has always interested me that magpies build not one but several nests. These do not serve as the cock-nests of the wren for they appear never to be occupied. I believe they are rather built to serve as a possible decoy.

A magpie is one of the most entertaining birds to watch. When he sees something which attracts him he approaches cautiously with a few hops: becoming assured that it is harmless his gait becomes majestic; he holds his head slightly to one side and investigates the object which fascinates him.[1] Few things escape the keenness of his eye. He is difficult to approach and exceedingly suspicious, but he becomes confiding in countries where he is left unmolested. In Norway it is remarkable that he is rather a favourite bird and builds his nest beneath the overhanging eaves of the houses.

[1] This habit of holding the head to one side is very noticeable in all birds and very natural considering the position of the eyes, but I have been particularly interested in noticing that nearly all birds when looking intently at something on the ground incline their heads to the left, always seeming to inspect carefully with the left eye; but when they are looking upwards they will incline the head to the right and use the right eye. I wonder if it is possible that the sight of each may vary.

6

TUNNELLERS

Kingfisher; sand-martin

KINGFISHER

I HAVE seen a kingfisher's nest which was tunnelled horizontally three feet deep in the clay bank of a stream but I am told it is sometimes bored even deeper. This entrance ends in a rounded cavity pressed into shape by movements of the bird's breast. It seems amazing that he can drill such a tunnel in clay, gravel, or sand baked hard by the sun, but the bird's beak is evidence of his arduous work, being scarred from tip to base.

From the human point of view the nest is by no means desirable, being a mass of regurgitated fish-bones, and excessively smelly; perhaps this is just as well for it discourages the curious. It is remarkable that the birds fly in and out to feed their young, with no mark or smudge on their wonderful plumage.

Doubtless he is king of bird-fishers; the name itself is from the Saxon *cyning* meaning king or chief. In olden days he was called halcyon. Montaigne wrote: 'While Halcyon rears her young, God has ordered that the whole ocean should be stayed.' It was believed that the birds made their nest, hatched their eggs, and brooded their young on the great waters. Pliny wrote: 'They breed in winter at the season called Halcyon wherein the sea is fair and calm for navigation.' Both Drayton and Milton refer to this belief. The ancients firmly believed that the birds nested on the sea, waterproofing their home in some miraculous way, and that it drifted to and fro on ocean currents, creating calm for a considerable distance around it in order that the family should be in peace. We still talk of 'halcyon days'.

Whether the bird is reared upon a mass of half-digested fish-bones or on the ocean wave there is no question that he is a creature of great beauty. On the wing he appears bright blue and there are few things more dazzlingly brilliant than his plumage; there is scarcely anyone who is not peculiarly moved by its exotic radiance. I am always thrilled by him in sunshine or shadow; whether on the nest when his eyes are like two searchlights or when seeking food or preening his lovely plumage.

> His are resplendent eyes;
> His mien is kingliwise;
> And down the May wind rides he like a king,
> With more than royal purple on his wing.[1]

On the banks of the river Eden in Sussex I once saw five kingfishers sitting in a row waiting to be fed. I have also watched these exquisite birds in the mating season, flirting together and rising high in the air, and I shall not forget the day when I saw a kingfisher perch at the end of a fisherman's rod; I may add that he got his fish first! He is a wonderful angler, watching patiently and silently, at times almost appearing to sleep but in reality ever intent and alert. When he catches his fish I have seen him smash it and then toss it high in the air before swallowing.

SAND-MARTIN

The sand-martin and his mate will bore for their nest a cavity of three inches in diameter at the mouth, widening along its probable six feet in length, and all this in a couple of days. While thus engaged their activity is prodigious; to watch them is almost exhausting. Not only do they carry out the arduous work of excavating but they may be seen collecting with their claws the sand which they have thrown aside and removing it from their habitation. Sometimes they will abandon their work even when completed and begin again, elsewhere. There is no apparent reason for this as far as humans can see, but it may be that they find the presence of a stone or some hard substance which they cannot remove; or perhaps some special sense which birds seem to possess causes them to feel the place is either unsafe or undesirable for the rearing of their family, and they waste no time moaning but start again undaunted by misfortune. Often during the excavating operations there will be no sign of a bird but if the watcher strikes upon the ground with a stick, immediately a rush of wings will be heard from every tunnel. These burrowings may sometimes be vertical and always the nest is a little higher than the entrance to the hole—prob-

[1] Author unknown.

Song Thrush at nest with young in a wych elm tree

Green Woodpecker feeding young

ably to guard against the moisture. Here is deposited a pile of dry grass and soft feathers on which the eggs are laid.

I do not think the birds undertake the laborious task of excavating in a quarry if they can find a more suitable locality where the sandy soil is loose and pliable yet tolerably tenacious. They will then use their legs as a kind of pivot, working away with their beaks as if they were drills until an almost cylindrical hole is made. I have watched them grasping the perpendicular surface of a bank with their claws and pecking small holes, which they patiently enlarge by moving round and round, edging off the sand with the side of their bills, which they keep shut. Progress is slow at first but when they can stand in the excavation they get on quickly.

E

7

EXCAVATORS

*Woodpeckers; great spotted woodpecker; lesser spotted wood-
pecker; willow-tit*

WOODPECKERS

HOW truly Richard Jefferies wrote: 'To wander out into the
brake, to creep from tree to tree so noiselessly that the woodpecker should not cease to tap—in that there is joy.'

In many parts of the country the woodpecker is called the *yaffle*, probably because of his call, which country people say foretells rain. Perhaps
my favourite name of all for this bird is the Gaelic *lasair-choille* (flame of
the wood), but he has many other names: *rasin bird, hew-hole, wood-spite,
jar-peg*; in Manx *Philip of the hemp*; and by the Welsh, more aptly, *Augur
of the woods*. Alike with kingfisher and jay, the bird is blessed, or perhaps
cursed, with exotic plumage which attracts and makes man gape, then
provokes him to avaricious desire to possess.

The best-known varieties are the green and the greater and lesser spotted. There can be no doubt the woodpecker has certain qualities which
arrest both ear and eye. Perhaps no bird uses its body to greater advantage
in the fight for existence. Owing to the formation of his breastbone he can
press his body close against the tree, while his claws are formed to secure a
firm grip, two forward, two backward. He can cling like a fly to a wall, incessantly tapping with his beak to reveal the desired insects. This wonderful beak serves as drill, hammer, and pick. The feathers of his tail have
stiff spines pointing downwards and inwards, which help to steady him
when occupied in the work of excavating for a home or searching for food,
serving almost as another claw. Nature serves him well with an invaluable
long tongue, twice the length of his bill, which he can keep rolled up in a
special cavity at the back of his skull and shoot out when desired. It is
coated with sticky saliva and tipped with barbed bristles, and to the insect
is like the hook to the fish. Under a chosen piece of decayed bark, which
the bird has removed with his serviceable beak, lies the desired food; out

comes the tongue, the insect is secured; in the same way he deals with the innumerable ants he pecks out of the ground. I am grateful to the woodpeckers who so industriously search my lawn; though I am filled with admiration for insects, I cannot bring myself to desire their near company.

Woodpeckers are not ground birds, save when they seek ants' eggs; they live with trees and know them as do few other birds. Experienced foresters realize that though a tree may look healthy it is unsound when the pied and green woodpeckers favour it. I have always been interested to watch them selecting a tree for their nest and pecking a way into it. They never throw good labour after bad, but if at first an unsuitable tree has been chosen and proves not rotten, they immediately leave it for another that will meet their requirements. Their excavations sometimes take many days, the birds drilling into the tree until a circular hole is chiselled out to their satisfaction, boring horizontally for some distance, then turning downward where the cavity is enlarged and rounded at the bottom; about one foot below the entrance will be the nesting place. It takes a pair of green woodpeckers at least fourteen days to make their desirable residence. I have a neighbour who has made a study of these birds for over thirty years and he informs me that he has never known the measurements of one of their nests to vary by one-sixteenth of an inch; it would appear that they work almost to a careful scale. The chips that fall to the ground during the work involved in the building are conveyed to a distance; it seems the birds are instinctively aware that these might give dangerous information to a possible marauder.

The arduous work of making their nest is often of no avail owing to the plundering nuthatch and starling, who, in spite of all efforts at prevention, are only too frequently successful in dispossessing them.

I like to think that the same pair of green woodpeckers have visited me for some years; they certainly seem to know the place and for shy birds have become very tame, though I realize they are never as fearful as the great or spotted woodpecker. I think it is quite remarkable that my pair take a bath in the bird pool, which is only about six yards from the house, and they evidently instruct their two young ones to do likewise, demonstrating the pleasure of bathing, but this instruction I was amused to see received little response. This evidently annoyed the parents and they decided on a more provocative method. Coming out of the pool, they attacked their reluctant offspring from the rear with gentle pecks until at last they were compelled rather than tempted to take their bathe; this was followed by much chittering and yaffling and then all flew away over the fir trees, doubtless to discuss the merits and demerits of a bath.

GREAT SPOTTED WOODPECKER

The great spotted woodpecker, when undisturbed, will nest in the same tree year after year, drilling a new hole below the old one; I find this to be usually two inches in diameter and fifteen deep. More cautious than the green woodpecker, they are seldom seen on the ground. The female shows such attachment to her eggs that it requires more than ordinary interference to disturb her; in fact, she will not quit unless a hand is introduced into the nest. Owing to this, my gardener reprehensibly secured a female who was sitting on eggs, taking both eggs and bird home, a distance of at least a mile and a half. The bird then escaped and flew straight back to the tree where she had been nesting. There she found her disconsolate mate and laid another clutch of eggs, which so impressed the man that he has never molested a sitting woodpecker since.

LESSER SPOTTED WOODPECKER

My experience of watching woodpeckers in Sussex is that the lesser is the rarest of the three; and that he is more streaked than spotted! This may not be so in other districts. The female is less exotic than the male, having no red cap, yet the male is the more devoted in spite of his finer feathers. Their nesting apartment is almost spherical and not much below the entrance, with an approach of some few inches; the hole excavated is one and three-quarter inches in diameter and eleven and a half deep. I have found them more partial to the topmost branches of tall trees than the other two varieties, and perhaps because of this they are seldom seen.

Last winter a friend of mine in Blackheath found a lesser spotted woodpecker on her window-sill. She lifted the bird gently and brought him inside; he was utterly exhausted and starving. Having three cats she dared not keep him and asked me if I would take him to my cottage. I was very dubious about this as I felt the journey would be too severe a strain in his weak condition and, alas! this was only too true for the bird did not recover. I was dreadfully distressed as it was the only failure I have had with a wild bird that has come under my care.

In the winter I have seen a lesser spotted woodpecker constantly on an apple tree by my kitchen window and have known him burrow to a depth of several inches through the snow to reach food. He is among the birds for which I dread the cold winter, for it takes from them a heavy toll.

WILLOW-TIT

The willow-tit is another bird who excavates, boring a hole in the rotten wood of an alder or willow stump, very much after the manner of a wood-pecker and utterly unlike the working of a tit. The nest itself is not a very elaborate affair and is composed of fine fragments of wood and a mixture of fur or willow down.

8

STICKLAYERS (PRIVATE ENTERPRISE)[1]

Turtledove; ringdove or woodpigeon; passenger pigeon;
jay; crow; crossbill; waxwing; golden eagle

IN this section of stick-laying builders I think first of doves and
pigeons, perhaps because I have enjoyed them all my life. My
own pigeon-houses and dovecot have been to me a never-ending
source of interest and pleasure.

TURTLEDOVE

I suppose however much we may deny it there is always one bird which
has for us some personal special appeal. We may say we like them all the
same but this is never true. There is one flower, one tree, one person that
consciously or unconsciously reigns supreme because we are naturally
selective, and though every bird contributes something to my pleasure
and interest because every one is different, I think for me the turtledove
is a little to the fore. I find with these gentle birds so much that appeals—
their soothing note, their harmonious plumage, their unfailing devotion
to mate and young.

Solomon is accounted wise and he chose this bird for one of his loveliest
descriptive passages: 'Lo, the winter is past, the rain is over and gone; . . .
the time of the singing of birds is come, and the voice of the turtle is heard
in our land.' It is rather as if he felt that above all others this bird completed
a beautiful and satisfying picture of sight and sound. To me their soft
woo-true-oo is one of the most soothing sounds in nature, suggesting a
quiet tenderness which in itself is a benediction. I cannot think of anything
more desirable or restful than to lie in a wood in spring with the miracle
of fresh green around me and the sound of the turtledove overhead.

Upon the dove was conferred the highest honour ever given to any living creature; the bird's capacity for love, purity, and gentleness caused it

---

[1] For other sticklayers see Chap. 15.

to be chosen as a symbol of the Holy Spirit. In some of our churches there is still the figure of a dove high above the font, and the chain which raises the lid induces the descent of the bird, typifying that the Holy Spirit descends upon the child in baptism.

With the cooing of this lovely bird I feel myself surrounded by saints. A dove bearing a ring is associated with St Agnes; St David is shown with the bird on his shoulder; St Dunstan and St Gregory the Great with one at the ear; St Enurchus with a dove on his head, and St Remigius with the bird bringing his holy chrism. The dove is sometimes represented as whispering in the ears of saints, no doubt teaching the wise counsel of love and forbearance, and sometimes flying out of their throats after death, symbolizing the spirit which rises. The Swedes say it was the dove that perched on the cross and stayed there through the hours of Christ's agony, continually cooing '*Lord! Lord!*' in a pitiful desire to give some sympathy and comfort to that tortured body.

I think it interesting that Picasso, whose work is by no means gentle, should have acquired the companionship of a turtledove who had lost her mate. The bird flies through his studio window or makes her way up the stairs to perch on the artist's hand, even being permitted to interrupt his work; she will follow him about almost like a dog, free to come and go at will, always welcome.

The dove has the distinction of belonging to the ancient mother goddesses of vegetation, gardens, courtship, and increase. Doves and swans together drew Aphrodite's chariot and were her messengers of love. At Dodona in the famous oak tree favoured by the gods two doves dwelt among the leaves, and pilgrims who came to question the oracle were answered by these two birds.

There is still a belief that woe betides the man who kills the turtledove because this gentle bird has always been associated with God and His Holy Spirit. Geoffrey Grigson mentions other superstitions, 'that doves protect you from lightning, murder, and sudden death (which perhaps explains the dovecot on the house—or at any rate, tame doves of one species or another in cages on the wall). If you dream of doves, it brings happiness. If you wish three times (you might remember this for next May) when you hear the first dove in the hedge, your wish will come true.'

There is no doubt that the thoughts of the dove are linked with thoughts of peace and this association will probably exist as long as man and bird endure.

These gentle birds are almost the last to arrive in this country after wintering in the Mediterranean and North Africa. They come in May and this loveliest month of spring is well called by many country people 'month of the turtledove'. The soft colouring of the birds' plumage, blue-grey, lavender, and fawn, the blush-coloured breast, even their tender notes, the soft rolling of *r's*, seem in harmony with the sweet of the year.

There is no question that love is essential to their existence. It is evident from the time the male's flight display is over, when, after circling round his desired mate, he descends to remain ever close beside her in faithful companionship. While the nest is being built I have often watched a pair fondling each other's beaks and uttering their love, 'billing and cooing' as it is well called, and when the female is brooding her mate croons continual endearments. Indeed so persistent is he in demonstrating his love that sometimes she is almost pushed off her eggs until he takes his turn on the nest. He feeds her with unfailing vigilance, making of this necessary service yet another opportunity to demonstrate his affection, for after giving her food he will gently stroke her wings with his beak and then the pair will again lock their beaks in a caress. After the mating and rearing of young the pair keep together all day, rarely more than three yards apart even in flight, and when they roost they press close against each other. Though love occupies so great a part of their life they are most courageous and will fight to the death to protect their home and young.

It may appear to the casual observer that turtledoves concern themselves little about the architecture of their nest, but its construction serves them as probably no other building would, for though apparently but a handful of coarse twigs the whole is so formed that it becomes almost a part of its surroundings and thus escapes detection.

WOODPIGEON

Woodpigeons also voice the lovely soothing *coo* and have an equally gentle disposition. I have often heard them described as blue-grey birds but this is not quite correct for their feathers vary from grey to wonderful shades of purple and bronze; indeed their breasts and necks reflect all the colours of the rainbow. They build a loosely fashioned twig house which again appears to be carelessly constructed. There is a Nottinghamshire rhyme:

> Coo-coo
> Me and my poor two
> Two sticks across
> With a little bit of moss
> And it will do, do, do.

They are exceedingly jealous of their home and family, guarding these with a vigilant courage even in the face of death; yet strangely enough, if through unlucky chance their eggs are touched by any other than themselves, they will desert.

The hen constantly evades the pursuit of her ardent lover but whether she is reluctant or practising 'tricks of delay' is problematical. In any case once mated their joint building is accompanied by every evidence of affection and they appear to be faithful for life.

For the first ten days all young pigeons are fed on what is called pigeon's milk. The crop glands become enlarged and the mucous membrane which lines the interior of the crop peels off in the form of a milky secretion with which both parents feed their young. The squabs insert their beaks into that of the mother or father, sucking this valuable food down much as a baby draws milk from its mother's breast. From my observation pigeons appear to be fed only three times in the day. When they are a month old the parents begin to feed them with seeds, always softening these first in their own throats. After a fortnight it is father who looks after the two young ones with the greater care and attention, the mother appearing to lose interest. I have a friend who rescued, at different times, two pigeons who were very much injured; they subsequently mated and had two eggs. The male was a most devoted parent but the female seemed to feel no sense of responsibility; she did not even cover her eggs with care. One therefore became cold and was ejected from the nest. The male then decided to sit on the remaining egg, which he did continuously, only very occasionally coming off for a stretch and always rushing back as if fearful that his precious charge would suffer.

Pigeons certainly have a great capacity for food consumption; it is said that their crops can hold sixty acorns, which seems incredible, and that a bird has been known to swallow a surprising number of crab-apples one after the other! The damage they do to crops is always remembered, while their immense destruction of harmful insects and grubs is forgotten. Shakespeare might well have been thinking of these birds when he wrote 'the evil that men do lives after them; the good is oft interred with their bones'. I well remember talking to an old man who lived what is called 'rough' on the Westmorland Fells and I shall never forget what he said about woodpigeons: 'The shootin' o' birds does mair harm nor guid if things git levelled oop; ah offen thinks if t'Almighty sights us and oor distructful ways, He mun be mighty fed oop and it be powerful strange He gees us as mich chance o' livin' as He doos.'

Being unprotected, pigeons are relentlessly shot; I know a man who boasts that he has killed fourteen thousand, six hundred, and seventy-one, his average being more than two thousand a year, killing more than forty in one evening (usually taking birds coming in to roost) and sometimes shooting over one hundred and fifty in two hours. Sitting birds are shot, and also thirsty ones coming in to drink. I read in a sporting paper recently that 'they give the sportsman something against which to pit his skill when the game season is closed.'

Both the turtledove and woodpigeon can live to a good age if not molested. I know of two instances which I think rather remarkable; both birds were rescued, badly injured, and were cared for by a young couple who were bird-lovers. The woodpigeon lived happily with them for twenty-nine years, the turtledove remained with them for thirty years, so though the limit of age for both is usually about twenty years, it can evidently be exceeded.

It is said that the woodpigeon is originally of the plover tribe but since he became vegetarian the habit of perching in trees grew upon him, and he developed a large crop capable of holding leaves, seeds, and berries which he usually digests.

The woodpigeon and the domestic pigeon seemingly have to a slight extent interchanged habits, for sometimes the woodpigeon will build on a house and now and then feed in the street, while I once saw a pair picking about in the goods yard of Baker Street station. On the other hand, domestic pigeons have taken to trees in Hyde Park; I have never seen this elsewhere save in a few places where trees are exceedingly close to a dovecot. I knew one pigeon in my young days who benefited from the inventions of civilization, for a nest made in one of the London parks was composed almost entirely of ladies' hairpins.

The days are gone when every country house had its columbarium or pigeon-house. These were usually square or octagonal, with gabled roofs and a weathercock. Evelyn mentioned a pigeon-house, 'a most laudable example' at Godstone in Surrey, and in an old picture of Sundridge Place, Kent, in 1720, a dovecot is shown standing in the centre of a fish-pond; the upper part of the cot was pierced with holes and perched for the birds, the water floor was evidently used by the ducks as there were steps up from the water. An octagonal dovecot on a wood trestle is also shown in Logan's view of St John's College, Oxford. There is a large seventeenth-century dovecot at Beddington Hall, scheduled as an ancient monument. It still has the potence intact together with nesting holes for a thousand birds. The finest cot remaining in Essex, still in sound condition, is at Loft's Hall, Saffron Walden, where the number of nesting holes is fifteen hundred.

There is no question that our ancestors valued and favoured the pigeon. Bulwer Lytton, in a letter to Lord Durham, mentions d'Orsay's pigeons: 'D'Orsay is installed in a cottage ornée next door and has set up an aviary of the best-dressed birds in all ornithology. He could not turn naturalist in anything else but Dandies. The very pigeons have trousers down to their claws and have the habit of looking over their left shoulder.'

In Persia, pigeon-towers have always been a feature of the outskirts of towns. Vast flocks of the birds may be seen returning to their sites in the environment of Isfahan. The annual revenue from these towers is considerable, the value being in the pigeon's dung upon which the melon thrives. The fruit is indispensable to the Persians during the hot summer.

It is possible that the Jews had pigeon-houses; in Isaiah, chapter lx, verse 8, is the passage: 'Who are these that fly as a cloud, and as the doves to their windows?' The Egyptians too, as their old paintings, still preserved, bear witness, evidently possessed pigeon-towers. The ancients must have realized the capacity of these birds for rapid flight and their unerring instinct for finding their way home. In a domestic condition they were kept in Egypt about 3000 B.C. and the art of training them as carriers of news was known a few hundred years later. Centuries before Christ they were employed by the Greeks for carrying messages, and it was by this means that the names of the winners of Olympic Games were sent to their home-towns.

I believe Decimus Junius Brutus to be the first captain who harnessed homer pigeons to his war chariot; when besieged by Mark Antony's forces he despatched the birds with messages to Octavian for reinforcements and with their help he corresponded with Hirtius at the siege of Modena. During the siege of Paris in 1870 the French sent communications by pigeon post out of the city and the Germans used hawks to kill these dangerous and valorous messengers.

In India the art of domesticating pigeons goes back thousands of years and her bird fanciers have contributed two particular species, the fantail and the pouter. The unquestionable love of a pigeon for his home serves man in good stead; because of this the mated homer is found to be the most valuable as carrier or for racing. One bird flew, in a test race from Rome to his loft in County Durham, a distance of one thousand and ninety-three miles. Storms slow down but cannot stop these birds; they may pause for a sip of water but food will not tempt them to loiter. Electricity is the only thing that beats the homer; he may well be described as 'man's courier of the air', or again as 'the sinews of war'. Surely such a bird deserves to enjoy his natural lease of life.

In the last war well over two hundred thousand pigeons were used by Britain and the U.S.A.; two thousand were used on daily duty by Coastal Command. Air, Sea, and Land Forces, all have profited by pigeon-service. The more that is learnt of the manner in which they worked during the war, the more does amazement grow. When Europe was ringed with for-tifications impassable to man, pigeons flew backwards and forwards from Allied to enemy soil, touching land from which no airman could return, bringing details of enemy movements, gun-sites, ack-ack batteries, and V-bomb emplacements. Nothing stopped this service and it has been the means of saving countless lives.

PASSENGER PIGEON

Passenger pigeons are, alas! now extinct, which shows what man can do with his ravage. Wilson in 1808 estimated the number in one colony at two thousand three hundred million, and now there is not a single sur-vivor.

A pigeon of to-day who might be given the descriptive adjective of 'passenger' is one who for some months has been strutting into the garage of the London Passenger Transport Board at Sutton, Surrey, where he flies on to the top of a single-decker bus and takes many rides, sometimes breaking the journey half way and returning to the garage, always by bus.

JAY

The jay is called in Sussex *keeper's watchdog*, and indeed there is no winged creature in the world more alert, but this does not prevent the keepers from slaughtering them remorselessly. The locality of the nest varies, sometimes being in undergrowth, though I have known the birds to build in a tree fifty feet from the ground. I had a jay's nest in my own garden, high up in a conifer; it was open and cup-shaped, composed of small twigs and lined with rootlets. The nestlings have dark-coloured mouths with no particular markings, because it is not necessary as with birds who breed in dark holes.

Few will deny the beauty of the jay, whose lovely colouring is not surpassed by any bird of the wood that I know, and the sight of him, although he is on mischief bent, invariably gives me a thrill of pleasure. I was delighted to find a pair in Hyde Park during the coldest days of winter in 1956 and again in 1958, and though still wary, as always, they were eager for food I had brought for the sparrows and pigeons. I found them still about this spring and with four of their young ones. Unfortunately for them they are easy to recognize, not only by their colourful plumage, but there is no mistaking either their curious mewing note or their high-pitched harsh call, which they repeat two or three times.

CROW

The crow, unlike the rook, is a lover of solitude, always avoiding man's dwelling; he will not even tolerate any other bird near his selected territory, not excepting his own offspring. Neither will he desert the locality he has chosen for his home unless compelled by an adverse fate.

They do not build so high as the rook, though they usually choose the fork of a tree that is difficult for man to climb. The hen does most of the nest-building, but I have seen the cock laboriously breaking off green twigs; this is unlike the other sticklayers, who invariably choose their nesting material dry. The nest is formed with roots and twigs cemented with mud and lined with hair, fur, or sheep's wool. They are acquisitive birds and surprising oddments are often found in their nests; in one I saw were a cigarette packet, three bus tickets, rabbit bones, a crab's claw, a shell, some string, and a piece of leather.

The young are hatched very early, usually in February or the beginning of March, when other birds are only thinking about laying their eggs. They are very solicitous over their young and when they are fledged the family keeps together for a time; then they separate and it is rare to see more than a pair together.

Their habits are not desirable; they rob the nests of ground game, also those of the blackcap, whitethroat, wagtail, and many of our finest song-sters. Being both clever and cunning they doubtless realize that their re-prehensible practices make them feared and hated. I have been intrigued to watch them craftily carry away any evidence of their savage raids to some distance from the vicinity of their own nesting place. I should say that the crow's intelligence equals that of the community-building rook, though I find it much less admirable. They also appear to share with the raven the secret of longevity. Shakespeare refers to the 'many-seasoned crow'; probably their shrewdness is partly responsible. They are also obviously blessed with a wonderful sense of direction and always fly straight to their destination, 'as the crow flies'.

CROSSBILL

Crossbills particularly favour a high branch in pine woods for their building. The nest is apparently loosely built on a foundation of twigs, lined with grasses, hair, feathers, or scraps of wool.

As suggested by the name, this bird's striking characteristic is the pecu-liar bill, which has two horny shields crossing one another obliquely at the tip, and is used for knife or scissors as required. As their beaks become worn by long use they are continually replaced by new growth. Buffon wrote that this little bird's bill was 'a useless deformity and an error and defect in nature' but surely it is an implement perfectly adapted to the work of splitting open and securing the seeds of fir-cones and fruit. I can see they have been in my garden by the stripped cones under my fir trees; we probably owe their increase in many parts of England to the plentiful planting of conifers, for they feed principally on coniferous trees, extracting the seed in an amazing fashion by beak and tongue. They can pick up and shell anything, however small, and I have even seen them pluck and enjoy the delicate seeds of the thistle.

I read an interesting account of crossbills written in 1593:

> Great plenty of strange birds, that shewed themselves at the time the apples were full rype, who fedde upon the kernells onely of those apples and having a bill with one beak wrythinge over the other which would presently bore a great hole in the apple and make way to the kernells.

A record of the years in which these birds have made noticeable visits to this country shows them always to have been prolific apple years.

It is interesting that while the young birds are in the nest the unique, crossed mandibles are not visible, indeed with them they could not well receive food from the parents. The unusual beak never appears until the need to procure their own food makes the formation a necessity.

They have the same claw as the parrot tribe and can cling in all sorts of positions, holding on with bill and claw usually on the under-side of the bough. Their characteristic method of extracting seeds gives them not only food but exercise and entertainment, which keeps them continually interested. Birds must be fed but they also require constant occupation.

Crossbills always seem imbued with the spirit of good fellowship even when seeking their food. 'Live and let live' is evidently their motto; they often sing together with their peculiar little *zip-zip*, and all are very voluble and appear to enjoy incessant chatter. I found I could come quite close and they still remained happily confident on the bough, looking at me with no apprehension; I have been told that until they have realized the menace of a gun they show no fear at the report.

There is a great variety of plumage exhibited by these birds; it seems continually changing, perhaps with age; sometimes being a brighter green, red, or orange, and when the birds are in full feather it is often a rich crimson; or a mottling of all these colours may be seen. Some crossbills are dark green, even sober grey, very dusky in appearance, and this can be very confusing to a watcher.

They are more frequently seen in Scotland than in England, probably owing to the greater abundance of fir trees, but I once counted twenty crossbills in a rowan tree growing by the side of Broughton Road, Worthing. They presented a memorable picture with their varied and exotic plumage among the red berries.

It is wonderful to watch them banding together for the mysterious migration. They start this hazardous journey at the beginning of summer, their destination being principally determined, it is thought, by the wind's direction. I have never seen them flying very high but it is almost certain that they fly with the wind, which would conserve their strength.

WAXWING

The waxwing is also a sticklayer, usually making his nest from twigs of birch and pine, the trees he favours for his food and pleasure when he visits this country. But our climate has never tempted him to nest here as far as I know.

He is often aptly called *wandering waxwing*, for no one seems to know exactly where and when he comes and goes. Indeed he rather suggests the gipsy's nomadic habits having no dwelling place in particular. It would seem that, like the crossbill, he journeys more or less as the wind listeth.

I have been fortunate enough to see quite a number in close proximity: more than one flock alighted in the bushes which bordered the house where I was staying in Cockermouth. I also saw a company feeding on the red hawthorn berries so plentiful on the banks of the Cocker. Waxwings bring a gay note to any area favoured; their plumage is exquisitely silky, and there is no mistaking the scarlet wings and tabs on secondaries, white flash on wings and yellow fringe to the tail, black bib, and characteristic tuft on the head which stands up straight when alarmed. Both sexes are alike save perhaps that the female has less noticeable scarlet tips on her wings. The sight of them is always to me a festive occasion.

GOLDEN EAGLE

The golden eagle has been threatened with extinction chiefly because he is regarded as an enemy by keepers, but at present the bird is holding his own in the Highlands and Hebrides. I was told by a ghillie who often talked to me that a pair build two or three nests one of which they patch up and use annually in turn. Though of huge dimensions[1] the nests ap-

---

[1] An eagle's nest, which blew down near Lake Eire, weighed nearly two tons; another was found, which, when carted away, filled several wagons with sticks and leaves; some branches six feet long had formed the breastworks.

H. Morrey Salmon

Turtledove

C. P.

Carrion Crows

pear to be put together in a very elementary fashion: actually the framework is serviceable enough, being made of stout branches sometimes as thick as a man's arm; then comes a layer of fine twigs with a lining which is always soft. The eagles gather materials for their nest in February and March and begin to sit at the end of that month or the first week of April. The period of incubation lasts about five weeks, after which the young are in the nest nearly three months and are still being fed by the parents in August. The eyrie never becomes foul with droppings from the young, as does the nest of the raven, for the eaglets when they wish to evacuate will back unsteadily to the edge of the nest and eject over the side, clear of the eyrie.

I always longed for the thrill of discovering an eagle's nest for myself and at last I found one in Sutherland. In rain and mist I was scrambling down by the side of a burn when an unusually dark mass between rocks caught my eye. Looking through my glasses I knew at once that it was an eyrie though there was no sign of life. Clambering over to it I found to my immense disappointment that it was empty. Many of the twigs and branches of heather of which it was composed were thicker than three of my fingers put together; a quantity of moss was on the top of the nest, bones of birds and jaw-bones of rabbits and hares lay about, and just below was a broken white eggshell.

Though naturally crestfallen I decided to go on searching and to my delight, high up in a cleft on a rock face, a short distance from the old eyrie, I saw another mass of heather-stalks. I managed to climb round the precipice and look down into this nest from about three feet above. Inside were two white chicks about the size of bantams; they were very immature but had a few dark-brown feathers among the white down and yellow eagle beaks tipped with black. One chick never moved a muscle and continued to frown down on the world below, the other looked up at me curiously and made little piping noises; there was no sign of the parent birds near at hand. But circling above me with motionless outspread wings I saw a golden eagle, and another great bird was watching me suspiciously from an adjacent pinnacle; this was evidently the female as she was the larger of the two. I was thrilled but still possessed of a certain amount of sense, so I reluctantly left the eyrie and watched from a discreet distance, hoping the parents might return to their young. Instead, I saw the 'sailing'

F

bird swoop down the side of the mountain, yelping and screaming after some prey it had sighted. He flashed past me like a thunderbolt and I flattened myself against a rock; I never saw that eagle again but the female was still watching me, perching motionless, silhouetted against the sky. Discretion is the better part of valour and withdrawal sometimes the wisest strategy, so warily and slowly I descended, leaving my golden eagles to their chosen solitude.

It interested me that both nests were built facing north and were completely sheltered by rock from the south, west, and east. It occurred to me that if this was deliberate, the purpose would be protection of the young from hot sun and prevailing winds. I carried back with me two very inadequate photographs, some saxifrage which was growing out of the side of the first nest, a few pieces of eggshell, an eagle feather, and a thrilling memory of these great birds whom I liked no less for their resenting my intrusion upon the splendid isolation in which they chose to carry on their family affairs.

There is no question of the strength of an eagle; though his own weight seldom exceeds twelve pounds, the span of wing exceeds that of a swan and he can inflict very severe injury upon the human who attempts to molest him. I have been told the lovely wedge-tailed eagle of Australia can kill a kangaroo and that he has a wing-span of ten feet and a length from beak to tail of forty inches.

There is a remarkable account given by Sir William Dugdale, Garter King of Arms in the seventeenth century, as to how the Stanley crest originated:

> There is no doubt, but that these, whereof I am now to speak, were much enricht by that fair inheritance which came to them by the marriage of Sir John Stanley, Knight, with Isabell, the Daughter and Heir to Sir Thomas Lathom of Lathom in Lancashire, Knight; of which family, there was a former Sir Thomas de Lathom, Knight; of whom, by credible Tradition, it is thus reported: That he begot a Son called Oskytel, on a woman, who lived not far from thence: And, that having no child by his own Lady, he designed to adopt this Oskytel for his Heir; but so, that he himself might not be suspected for his Father. Observing therefore, that an Eagle had built her Nest, in a large spread Oak, within his Park at Lathom, he caused the Child in Swadling-cloths, to be privily conveyed thither; and (as a wonder) presently call'd forth his Wife to see it:

representing it to her; that, having no issue, God Almighty had thus sent him a Male-child; and so preserv'd, that he lookt upon it as a miracle: disguising the truth so artificially from her, that she forthwith took him, with great fondness, into the House; educating him with no less affection than if she had been his natural mother. Whereupon he became Heir to that fair inheritance. And that, in token thereof, not only his descendents, whilst the Male Line endured; but the Stanleys proceeding from the said Isabell (the Heir Female) have ever since borne the Child in the Eagle's nest, with the Eagle thereon, for their Crest.

9

HEDGERS

Bullfinch; hedge-sparrow

BULLFINCH

THE spring would certainly lose some of its glamour, as far as I am concerned, without these handsome birds, with lovely rose-vermilion breast, black cap, steel-black bill, lustrous purple-black tail, white rump, and blue-grey back. A country name often used for the bird is *coal-hood*; in Wales he is called *red one of the orchard*. I have had a pair nesting for many years low in my hawthorn hedge, which is within convenient reach of the apple trees. I am convinced that it is owing to their work clearing these trees of insect pests that I get such a marvellous crop of apples. I think the bird is blamed unduly by farmers and fruit-growers; personally, I have found the good they do infinitely greater than the harm. I am very willing that they should take a fee of fruit in return for their work and the pleasure that their beauty gives me. A man once told me he had killed over thirty in his garden during a period of two weeks; I have avoided this acre ever since, deciding there were other men whose company I preferred.

Bullfinches are certainly rarer than they were when I was a child and I find my neighbours are very keen on coming to see my pair. The nest is built of twigs and moss lined with fine black rootlets; they have two broods, the hen alone incubating, sitting tight on her eggs. They are usually exceedingly shy birds, but my pair have come to realize that I intend them no harm and to my great delight the cock often takes a bath in the bowl on my verandah.

An invalid friend rescued a bullfinch with a broken wing; the bird has now been her greatest treasure and friend for many years. Ornithologists are sure that birds never dream and it seems presumptuous to differ from this opinion, yet my friend is quite certain that her bullfinch does dream, and experiences mental activity when asleep; with eyes closed and his head comfortably tucked under his wing he will suddenly voice quick alarm notes and then dash himself against the cage: when this occurs she lifts him gently and strokes his lovely plumage, crooning a lullaby as she might to a baby. He then returns to his perch and sleeps contentedly.

HEDGE-SPARROW

Hedge-sparrows never fail to build every year in the lane outside my garden. I fear I am not the only one with eyes to see his turquoise blue eggs which mean so much to this little hedge-bird. It would seem that nature here has not been kind, for in early spring, when the first eggs are laid, the nest is much too exposed not to suffer from the acquisitive eye, and the eggs are temptingly conspicuous to the young collector; also they are within easy reach—rarely more than about four feet from the ground. Probably only the fact that these birds have several broods saves them from extinction. They themselves are unobtrusive enough in their plumage, gentle song, even in the way they creep about under the hedge almost like little mice; indeed when young, both in shape and colour they might well be mistaken for them. As the spring advances the nest is concealed with a thick veil of foliage and so it is usually the later clutches which survive. The nest itself is composed of moss, twigs, and roots, with lining of hair and wool. It is much more carefully formed than that of the house-sparrow with whom the bird is so often confused, although he is only a very distant relation. All the other names of this bird are much more appropriate—*hedge-warbler, hedge accentor, dunnock,* or *shufflewing.* I am personally very fond of this latter name, as there is no doubt it refers to the continuous shake of the wings which is so particularly characteristic. The little song he voices is short, clear, and cheerful, but not so joyous as that of most birds, and it is given pretty well all the year round. It is usually sung from hedge-top or bush, and is heard to best advantage early and late in the day. The usual call-note is a rather plaintive pipe but it has a special appeal of its own.

This is one of the nests that the cuckoo favours for her egg; it is commonly said that the hedge-sparrow is the cuckoo's best friend.

10

BUSHRANGERS

I. GROUND FLOOR

Yellowhammer; cirl bunting; corn bunting; stonechat;
whinchat

YELLOWHAMMER OR YELLOW BUNTING

I BELIEVE it is more correct to call this bird yellowammer; the 'h' appears only to have been added from the days of Dr William Turner. The Germans still call him *goldammer, ammer* being their term for bunting.

Age certainly does not seem to affect the beauty of this bunting, as his plumage becomes brighter and more lovely with length of days. The female is not so conspicuous as the male, being more streaked with brown; one of her outstanding features to me is the dark moustache line. The young ones are brown practically all over, save for the head.

I often find nests of the yellowhammer in Sussex, all either on or very close to the ground, usually under the shelter of a bush. In many ways they are similar to that of the greenfinch, being composed of grass, roots, and moss woven together and lined with hair when procurable. I have been interested to notice that usually they have something that serves as a landmark, to which they will fly directly on their way to the nest with food for the young. Their eggs have so many markings that the birds are sometimes called *scribes* or in Cambridgeshire *writing larks*.

Probably one of the bird notes most frequently recognized is that of the yellowhammer because of the country belief that it suggests the words *a little bit of bread and no cheese* and these are continually repeated with great emphasis on the last two notes. It might almost appear that he wishes to impress upon the hearer that his needs are but simple.

One of the bird pictures that I treasure in my mind is the sight of them looking like little yellow butterflies as they assemble in flocks on the hedges which still border certain tracks of the Downs.

CIRL BUNTING AND CORN BUNTING

The cirl buntings resemble the yellow buntings in appearance and the notes they voice are much the same; they also favour hedgerows and bushes but build rather higher. The corn bunting is the largest of the tribe and builds something of the same nest, low in a bush, but evidently prefers a site in open country or downland.

All buntings can be recognized by a knob on the upper part of the bill which fits into a cutting-angle in the lower jaw. This has the useful purpose of giving these birds a marvellous power of abstracting the kernels from the husks of corn or other small seeds which constitute the main part of their diet.

There are many who feel that their contribution to bird-music is not great, but I always listen eagerly for their notes; there is something, to me, pleasant and homely in them which more spectacular bird-song lacks.

STONECHAT

The stonechat is also called *stonechatter*, probably because of his chattering as he perches on a stone, and sometimes *stoneclink*, no doubt owing to many of his notes, when the nest is approached, sounding rather like stones knocking together. I very much like the Icelandic name *stonedapple* for he certainly dapples the stones with life and light.

I have also heard him called by country people *black head of gorse*, possibly because of his little black head and the habitat he favours which is usually the common or open gorse-clad downland. Here it is that stonechats will build their nest and rear a family, though in the autumn they seek the shelter of more enclosed ground.

The birds are early home builders and the nest is cunningly concealed at the bottom of a gorse bush or heather clump very close to the ground. It is composed of dried grasses and weeds, lined with hair, bents, and sometimes a few feathers. The cock sings while his mate is sitting; he will hover round but never directly enter the nest and is always careful to avoid detection when bringing food. Both parents are solicitous for their young and even when the family have left the nest they all keep together. The young are continually called and evidently instructed not to wander; this constant vigilance persists until they are able to fend for themselves. Having once chosen a building site that is to their taste they are very conservative and appear to possess no roving instincts.

I have watched the cock and hen taking the young for their first excursion into the gorse; the chestnut-pink breast and white collar of the male is unmistakable. I like their dainty, sprightly movements as they hop from bush to bush, the constant flirting of their wings and quick runs on the ground. This unceasing agility and apparent habitual gaiety is infectious, giving even the watcher a sense of well-being.

The cheerful little song when in flight seems inspired by a gay heart. I have noticed the cock always seems to voice pleasure, or perhaps thankfulness, after food.

WHINCHAT

The whinchat is sometimes called *gorsechat*. He certainly favours the gorse bushes, as do many birds, doubtless regarding them as places of safety. I have heard country people call him *blackberry eater* though he leaves us before these berries are actually black; he eats them with evident relish when red.

With summer's departure he flies south to seek his food, for he cannot withstand our winter, but I am fairly certain he comes back on his return from South Africa in the spring to practically the same nesting site, for I have found a whinchat's nest for several successive years in the same bush. This desire of birds to return to a chosen site is, I think, understandable, but the ability to do so is amazing and utterly confounding to the ordinary mortal.

The whinchat's nest is usually on the ground and not easily found, being always carefully concealed among tangled branches, brambles, or low bushes; sometimes, not being satisfied with nature's covering, they will collect dried grass or material which corresponds to the surrounding undergrowth, arranging this to further hide the nest.

The nest I was able to observe most closely was certainly that of a recurrent builder, as I found it for several seasons in the same spot among the bilberry bushes that abound near my old home in Worcestershire. It was in close proximity to bracken and cleverly camouflaged, composed of moss and dead leaves, lined with fine bents and hair. The cock was always near his brooding mate, hanging on a slender stem of bracken, constantly singing; and his song suggested to me his pride of home and family. He often let me come quite close without giving the slightest sign of fear and I was able to enjoy the sight of his pink-chestnut breast shading to nearly white. He lacked the black head and white collar of the stonechat but had a white streak at the edge of wings and white at the base of tail. The female is duller in colouring, though in autumn the cock becomes rather similar.

The particular cock I was watching never flew very far up into the air but hovered with whirring wings just above the tops of the grasses, darting backwards and forwards; perhaps that is why in many of the southern counties he is called *vuzzchat*, a name no doubt suggested by the sound of his rapid wing-beats.

His double clicking note is similar to the single click of the stonechat. The song, which has been compared to that of the goldfinch, he gives continually, often even at night, from April to the end of June.

2. FIRST FLOOR

Shrikes; red-backed shrike; great grey shrike; linnet;
mountain linnet or twite

SHRIKES

Shrikes are more frequently spoken of as *butcher birds* and I have heard them also called *mountain magpies* and *murdering pies*. To the average lover of feathered creatures, their habits are revolting but then perhaps the birds might well cry, *No worse than yours*. It is rather strange that their song should be sweet; they also possess the gift of mimicry which serves them well in securing their prey. There is little doubt that, thereby, small singing-birds are often lured to an untimely end, imagining themselves called by one of their own kind.

Turberville wrote of the shrike:

She doth entrappe and deceive by flight, for this is her devise. She will stand at pearch upon some tree or posts, and there make an exceeding lamentable cry and exclamation, such as birds are wonte to doe being wronged, or in hazards of mischief, and all to make other fowles believe and thinke she is very much distressed, and stands needfulle of ayde; whereupon, the credulous sellie birdes do flock together, presently at her call and voice, at what time if any happen to approach neare her, she, out of hand, ceazeth on them, and devoureth them, (ungrateful subtile fowle!) in requital of their simplicity and pains.

From the *Book of Falconrie and Hawkinge* published in 1611, I see that the shrike was frequently used by falconers.

These butcher birds will impale their victims on a convenient thorn or spike. A German described them to me as *ninekillers* because, he said, each kills nine singing-birds a day! I do not know if this be true, but it is an accepted fact that shrikes will consume at least three a day. In addition to the feathered creatures, they will devour a quantity of beetles, grass-hoppers, and other insects. They appear entirely carnivorous and, as far as I know, never take seeds, buds, or fruit.

RED-BACKED SHRIKE

I cannot pretend the red-backed shrike is a favourite of mine, though he has chosen to nest for several years in a thick hawthorn hedge which borders my cottage garden. The nest is about eight feet from the ground; the materials used are moss and grasses, the result being rather untidy and bulky. I noticed the cock did most of the structural work but the hen evi-dently did not consider her mate had the ability to cope with the interior. She alone gathered the pieces of hair and fine roots required for the lining, never permitting him to choose any part of the desired material. I could not help thinking she regarded him in very much the same way as many women their menfolk, assigning to him the rougher work of the builder and the unsavoury business allotted to the butcher. The hen will, how-ever, visit the larder and take what is provided and also, when brooding, permit the cock to feed her. Yet, if disaster should overtake the pair and one of them be killed, the living bird, male or female, will keep the larder supplied and also fight ferociously any marauder who comes near nest or food-store with thievish intent.

The appearance of this bird is rather hawklike, because of his strong hooked beak which serves well his cruel method of acquiring and preserv-ing food. I am rather surprised that the poet Thompson wrote:

> I like a shrike
> Because with a thorn for a guillotine
> He does his work so well and clean.

Sometimes the larder is chosen and started before the nest is built, but the birds are not always content with one; I have seen four used by one pair and I believe that even more have been noted. These are not as a rule very close to the nest, being even a hundred yards or more away and always well stocked; in addition to small birds I have seen a frog or even earthworms, beetles, cockchafers, moths, voles, shrews, and bumble-bees impaled on thorns.

The birds are assiduous in fostering their young and a lost clutch is invariably replaced. The broods are often unruly and contentious among themselves in the nest, yet immediately they leave it they cease quarrelling. How well I understand their feelings, as any form of congestion and lack of space induces similar irritation in me.

GREAT GREY SHRIKE

The great grey shrike does not nest with us but is an occasional late autumn or winter visitor, usually driven by adverse winds on to our coasts. I have only once seen this bird; it was December and he was voicing his song, which was interspersed with a harsh note that sounded to me like *shrike*, suggesting the name given to him.

He is at least two inches larger than the red-backed, but his grey, black, and white plumage is very different from the richer colouring of our better-known variety. He has the same revolting habit of fixing his prey on thorns and trees.

LINNET

It is my early morning walks that yield me the richest harvest of song; then it is that I hear at its best the linnets' sweet community singing. I share with them their evident love of the sun. If a cloud passes over they will suddenly become silent, but immediately the sun reappears, they once more voice their song. Only at midday there is an interval, when all nature seems to pause as it were before getting a second wind.

Linnets were at one time plentiful on the South Downs but now, alas! they are more rare. I always look eagerly for the small cock with his crimson forehead and breast, for to me these gentle little birds will always be among the most welcome of our songsters, indeed an integral part of the sweet gorse and quiet downside. No bird seems happier in sharing with all feathered creatures the delight in that which life offers; I have never seen any contests or quarrelling among them.

Linnets' many changes of plumage often cause confusion to the amateur watcher. During the first year of life the male has no red on the head and only a very slight tinge on the breast; at this time the bird is often known as the grey or brown linnet. When older, and particularly during spring, always the birds' most colourful and joyous period, his forehead becomes a richer rose which spreads over neck, back, and sides of breast, even the white under part being tinged with blush-red; he is no longer the grey linnet. In autumn the rose-colour is less conspicuous, white predominating on head and breast, but in winter the lovely rose feathers again appear. These little birds are exceedingly fastidious about their appearance, not a single feather is allowed to escape attention and they love bathing; even the young ones preen as soon as they are able to indulge in any movement.

The cock helps in selection of the nesting site but does not seem to have any skill in building, though no bird could attend more faithfully upon his mate. On each journey that she makes, gathering her nesting materials, he flies to and fro in close attendance and much twittering may be heard; the hen probably feels this denotes interest and it will spur her on to even greater industry; also perhaps it may give her an assurance that he will not interfere with something that she does so much better.

The birds usually build in some quiet spot, often in a gorse bush, and the nest is composed of twigs, moss, and roots, lined with feathers, wool, thistledown, and willow-down. The male guards his mate very carefully; if he suspects danger his lovely little song changes to a cry that is full of distress and he flits about in evident agitation. When the young arrive both parents look after them most assiduously; though naturally timid neither will forsake the nest when on duty, whatever the consequences.

I find few things of greater interest than watching the building of a nest and feeding of young, for both I regard as remarkable evidence of the bird's persistence, ingenuity, and a certain intuitive knowledge of suitability of site and material; also of its amazing patience. The pair of linnets I watched observed a certain procedure at the nest which appeared agreeable to both and certainly nourished their family. I knew of course that linnets had two broods in the year over their five months' nesting period and that both sexes took part in the brooding, which is by no means the case with all birds. At the end of the male's session, he rose very carefully to greet the returning female, then stood on the edge of the nest, extending and fluttering his wings while voicing happy twitterings. I was surprised that the hen did not appear to have brought any food in her beak, but I saw she emitted a liquid something like milk which was carefully given to each fledgling in turn. If she had sufficient each bird was fed three times, then after this partly-digested food was consumed she settled down on the nest while the male flew off, it being his turn to search for the next meal. He probably found relief and refreshment in the change of occupation. When he returned with his contribution she did not go through his greeting ceremony; perhaps she felt that no time should be wasted in such pleasantries—food and quickly was the order and she was careful to pre-digest all he brought before feeding the fledglings. The cock looked on with evident pride, sometimes voicing this very gently and then he would again take his place on the nest.

MOUNTAIN LINNET OR TWITE

The mountain linnet, heather linnet, or twite also builds in low bushes, though he favours a variety of habitats and might come under the category of 'hole-and-corner' builders, being fond of making his little home in the shelter of an upturned clod or even among stones.

I first heard him singing high up on the Fells in Westmorland and I did not immediately recognize him as the mountain linnet. It was an old dalesman who enlightened me: 'They birds likes to live in the open country here'bouts same as me, tho' we mostly calls 'em twites, maybe name be given count o' their note, tho' I sometimes thinks they be sayin' "chat-chat", tellin' us what they be adoin' on. Many a nest I find allus close to ground, it be kep' 'markable clean; female feeds young 'uns from her crop wi' green stuff an' insects; allus cleans nest an' 'tis evident as she teaches young 'uns to get on't edge so as their droppin's fall ower; if you finds nest fouled it's sartin sure summat's happened to hen. They pretty well knas me now but i' general they doant let foalks come anyways nigh, they kips runnin' forrard so's you be inticed to follow till you gits proper wore out, then bird flies back home.'

11

DOWN TO EARTH

Pheasant; golden pheasant; partridge; woodcock; ptarmigan;
corn-crake; dottrel; curlew; stone-curlew; plover; grey plover;
ringed plover; golden plover; lapwing or peewit; dunlin; meadow-
pipit or titlark; tree-pipit; tawny pipit; nightjar; hen harrier;
marsh-harrier; Montagu's harrier; short-eared owl

MANY birds choose to make their nests on the earth. This is probably for reasons of camouflage and it may be that they draw something of their strength from the Mother of us all.

PHEASANT

I have always thought game birds must be puzzled and suffer perhaps greater disillusionment than any other of the feathered tribe. Thomas Hardy wrote words that might well be spoken by them; perhaps they are if we could understand their language:

> They are not those who used to feed us
> When we were young—they cannot be—
> These shapes that now bereave and bleed us?
> They are not those who used to feed us—
> For, would they not fair terms concede us?
> If hearts can house such treachery
> They are not those who used to feed us
> When we were young—they cannot be!

Frances Pitt reports that a hen pheasant shot in Shropshire proved, upon examination, to have one hundred and fifty-three beetle larvae in her crop: the grubs were a species of wire-worm dreaded by the farmer, so the pheasant, far from being a foe, can be a friend to agriculture.

Pheasants have become so much a part of our bird life that they are now styled residents. They even appeared on Anglo-Saxon bills of fare, yet they originally came from Western Asia bringing with them something of its colourful splendour to bejewel our English woodlands. They lay their eggs in a hollow on well-sheltered, covered ground; but the hen often gathers a mattress composed of dead leaves and grass. I have known the pheasant upon rare occasions to build her nest in a tree. She may have as many as eighteen chicks in one clutch, this large number probably being a provision of nature, for pheasants are subject to high mortality. Like the cuckoo, she will sometimes drop her egg in the nest of another bird, but she does not seem to have the same sense as the cuckoo in choosing the right nest, for when she deposits her egg in the nest of a water-bird, although it may be brooded and hatched, the chick will most likely drown.

Though the cock pheasant is very assiduous in his wooing, after the hen has laid her eggs he leaves her to brood them, showing no further interest. Indeed he is by no means a worthy mate, often collecting for his entertainment quite a harem.

In the heart of Clapham Wood adjacent to my cottage in Sussex is a certain cock pheasant that I regard with interest. He roosts high in a sycamore tree in the keeper's garden. This handsome fellow is singularly tame and will even take food from the hand if it is offered, seeming devoid of either fear or suspicion, though his wives on the other hand are all wild and suspicious and never venture out of the wood. The Alsatian bitch resident at the cottage causes 'Cocky' no alarm though she often noses into his rations; in fact I have seen them eating together from the same dish and he shows no resentment when a robin, or indeed any small bird, comes for a share; he is even on friendly terms with the cat! As I watched him I could not help thinking of the utopian promise that 'the lion shall lie down with the lamb.' It would seem this is an actual possibility providing always each creature knows the other's intentions are not maliciously destructive.

GOLDEN PHEASANT

The pheasant's exotic cousin, the golden pheasant, has plumage more gorgeous than that of the gayest parrot. One of my earliest recollections is that of a beautiful, stuffed, golden pheasant which had been a great companion to my mother when she was a little girl. She told me he had been scrupulously clean in his habits and had been allowed to wander about the house and perch upon the backs of chairs.

She said how depressed and apparently ashamed he had appeared during the moult when he had continually tried to hide. I believe the moult is felt very keenly by all birds and not solely physically; they are probably aware of their appearance in addition to being much more vulnerable to inclement weather and suffering a loss of activity. It always seems to me a pernicious habit to shoot birds during the moulting season when they are easier prey. There is no doubt birds realize the disadvantages of their condition at this time and try to speed up their moult in order to get it over quickly; any watcher can see them constantly plucking out their own loose feathers.

PARTRIDGE

This is another bird who favours the earth, scratching out a hollow in the ground and lining the nest with dead leaves and grass. The clutch is usually about fourteen eggs, sometimes even twenty-two, and the hen will brood them for eight hours at a time without a break. It was to me a strange sight to find two hen birds on the same nest, though I believe this practice is not uncommon and is sometimes followed even by the more pugnacious pheasant.

Both the male and female partridge are wonderful parents, the cock attending continually to the wants of the hen, who sits so closely on the nest that she is sometimes decapitated by the harvester. I have known instances when her habit of close and faithful brooding has, however, stood her in good stead and actually has saved not only herself but her family.

The cock shows great excitement and pleasure when the first-born comes out of the egg, peeping at his offspring several times as though he can hardly believe his eyes, returning continually to see if the other wonders will appear from the remaining eggs. The birds preserve their home life, keeping together even after the family is reared, and they roost on the ground in a circle, as do quails, for safety.

In *Testament of Beauty* Robert Bridges writes:

> It is pretty to mark a partridge, when she hath first led forth her brood to run among the grass-tussocks or hay-stubbles of June, if man or beast approach them, how to usurp regard she counterfeiteth the terror of a wounded bird draggling a broken wing, and noisily enticeth or provoketh the foe to follow her in a vain chase; nor wil she desist from the ruse of her courage to effect her own escape in loud masterful flight, untill she hav far decoy'd hunter or blundering hoof from where she hath bid her little ones to scatter and hide.

A wonderful example of the manner in which nature protects its creatures is found in the fact that during the nesting season partridges, and indeed all game birds, lose their scent, and a pointer may pass within a few yards of a sitting partridge without discovering it.

I think few people realize the good work they render man. I once picked up a partridge, still warm; it had apparently collided with the telephone wires along my lane and had broken its neck in the fall. A neighbour of mine asked if he might examine its swollen crop, to which I agreed. The examination revealed it to be tightly packed with nine hundred and three wire-worms, four small snails, a woodlouse, and a number of grass-seeds; the total weight of the contents being three and a half ounces. I have no idea how long a bird would take to fill its crop to this extent or how frequently it would do so, but the total number of pests destroyed by a covey of these birds in one season must be colossal. So they also serve!

With the French variety of this same bird (the red-legged partridge) it is usually agreed that the hen lays two clutches in separate nests, one for herself and one for the cock who will devote himself to the eggs in his allotted nest.

WOODCOCK

The woodcock often nests in a hollow on the ground at the foot of a tree, usually in damp woodlands. I have seen the hen, when she finds it necessary if danger threatens, or when on her evening journey in search of food, carrying her young by pressing them closely against her body, between either the thighs or feet. I have never seen any other bird carry its young in this manner.

Woodcocks leave the shelter of their woods every evening to feed on fields and marshlands, returning before dawn. I have been in a wood and have seen them take off on these foraging flights, uttering their characteristic croak or sometimes changing to a sharper, higher note. They always follow certain tracks aptly called 'roading'. I have even been instructed by a keeper to cross a glade at a given angle which he said was a 'cock-road' and the most direct way to my destination.

In addition to their characteristically long beaks and large prominent bead-like eyes, which often betray them, I have noticed with interest and surprise that their ears are below their eyes. In bitter weather, the cover-

G

ing and freezing up of feeding grounds is to them disastrous. I have seen starving woodcock, barely able to fly, perishing miserably, and have been utterly helpless to save them.

The unfortunate woodcock is regarded as a dainty dish. The peasants of the Roman Campagna have a simple method of snaring the bird which they described to me with pride; they were surprised when I did not applaud. They tie a bell to their waist-belt at night and set out with net in hand. The cattle which graze on the marshes carry bells and the birds, in time, become used to their tinkling; so the peasant has an easy time of it, for the woodcocks make no attempt to fly off, believing themselves to be safe. When the peasant is near enough, he puts his net over the bird as she squats on the ground.

PTARMIGAN

I have seen the ptarmigan brooding her eggs on the high slopes of the Scottish Highlands, in a hollow on the ground among the stones and lichen which she favours. If the mother is disturbed when sitting she will endeavour to attract the intruder, shuffling along an uneven course, away from the nest, croaking and strutting in order to gain attention and distract the watcher from the newly-hatched chicks, who will be lying quiet in the shallow depression, probably obedient to instruction. These birds are active almost from the hour of their birth: a good thing, for their father has departed for the time being, to lead a bachelor existence with other shirkers of family cares. He knows by some instinct when the family is full-grown and then always returns to rejoin his no doubt rather weary mate, to enliven her perhaps with stories of his adventurous doings.

Nature has a way of safeguarding these birds, for they have three moults and each time their new plumage takes on the colour of their surroundings. Favouring rocky heights and mountains for their habitat, they descend rather lower in winter, though they can survive severe cold; often I have known them to burrow in tunnels under the snow.

CORN-CRAKE

The corn-crake or *landrail* is often called the *daker-hen*. Alas! his voice is rarely heard to-day though I remember, as a child, holding my breath listening to him, for his crake possessed something of the eerie quality which is conveyed by the hoot of an owl. The voices of both these birds impressed me, particularly in the stillness of the night, and when I went out with my father to hear the dawn chorus I sometimes saw a corn-crake running through the grass, voicing his strange cry as he went. My father told me this cry ceases when the young are hatched unless, by some mishap, the first clutch of eggs is destroyed. Then a second clutch is laid and the craking recommences; he told me he once heard the bird more than thirty times in a minute.

I also remember my thrill and pride on finding a corn-crake's nest among thick mowing-grass in a meadow near a stream; it was composed of a mat of withered herbage. I would often steal down to see how the birds were getting on. The male was fussing around, obviously hardly liking to leave his wife for a moment; if she left the nest he would watch her anxiously to see that no harm befell her. I remember my excitement at the first sight of their fifteen little black chicks looking curiously about at the great world in which they suddenly found themselves. This was too much for me to keep to myself so I showed the nest and the chicks to my father. He told me that corn-crakes also build in clumps of flags, nettles, or rank vegetation, particularly favouring thick grass, making a deep scrape which is always hollowed by the cock and lined by the hen. Probably their choice of site accounts for their rarity nowadays; the destruction of eggs and brooding birds by machinery, and the use of insecticides which destroy their natural food, have been disastrous. Of late years I have found the corn-crake only where the scythe is still used.

The French call this bird *roi de cailles* from an old belief that quails chose him to lead them on their migration. He is a powerful flier but once he lands he is rarely seen on the wing again, remaining under cover as far as possible.

I was interested to see a corn-crake at the Zoo, brought there by misadventure which had terminated in his present good fortune. Unable to make headway in the teeth of a raging gale, he alighted on the deck of a naval landing-craft off Cherbourg. By lucky chance a sub-lieutenant aboard had once been employed at the Zoo, so it was left to him to feed and care for the unusual guest. When the ship berthed, the corn-crake was taken to the Zoo where surprisingly he settled down comfortably almost at once. Worms and other insects were placed in a patch of loose soil and the corn-crake dug for them quietly, apparently unruffled by his experience and seemingly quite content in an aviary.

DOTTREL

When climbing in the Lake District, three thousand feet up where the vegetation is scanty, I was fortunate enough to find a nest on the ground in a very slight depression, with pieces of moss and lichen round the edge. I have been told that dottrels take an infinity of trouble in selecting their nesting site and will try many places before being eventually satisfied. The cock incubates as faithfully as the hen, sometimes even more assiduously, but in the nest I found the hen was brooding; she looked at me with a gentle, interested eye, utterly unafraid. Birds who haunt the less-frequented places where man seldom intrudes exhibit a certain curiosity but rarely fear; they have not yet learnt to recognize in us an almost certain menace, and perhaps that is why I was able to approach this nest. The hen's colour was so much in keeping with the surrounding heather that she would never have been located had I not first heard her mate's low, monotonous whistle. This song or note is eerie, having an elusive quality difficult to describe but which, once heard, is never forgotten.

CURLEW

The curlew is a strange and interesting bird not only because of its distinctive, peculiarly long, curved beak, but also for its mournful yet musical note. Few are not held enthralled by its haunting quality, yet perhaps it is not on the lonely moorland that this cry makes the deepest impression, but rather on a July night in a London street when I have been fortunate enough to hear them passing over to or from their breeding grounds. Then the eerie but lovely sound is more poignant because so utterly unexpected; but this bird has other notes; I have heard it when angry, utter a sound that rather resembles the barking of a dog.

They do not rise easily from the ground but when once airborne they are swift in flight, observing the chevron pattern. I have heard it said that, like plovers and godwits, they are able to fly at the terrific rate of two hundred and forty miles an hour! They have a catholic taste in habitat and feed by night as well as by day but are very nervous on the ground, invariably sleeping with one eye open, which makes them the wariest of all birds in avoiding the gun; in this they are probably helped by their protective colouring.

I have never seen them indulge in much preening, though they stand for lengthy periods on one leg with their peculiar bills lying along their backs. They can swim and it is entertaining to watch them, usually in small companies of twos and threes, investigating any ooze, inch by inch, with great care.

They often favour the ground for their nest, which is just a hollow lined with dry grass, being usually found amid the ling on moors or in rough pasture on the hillside.

STONE-CURLEW

The stone-curlew also lays her eggs on the ground, thus sharing with the lark the likelihood of death from tractor or harvester. Again, like the little 'pilgrim of the sky', she practises the same nest-approach, a series of zigzags obviously employed to preserve the secret of the site. When eggs are laid on the ground in little or no cover birds are particularly watchful and careful of their young.

That the stone-curlew builds among flints may be instinct or design, for nothing could produce so perfect a camouflage. The nest, which to our way of thinking may appear sketchy and uninviting, is desirable and precious to them. This rough 'home' will always be a magnet to the pair and they will return to the same spot year after year, travelling, between nesting seasons, many thousands of miles to winter in South Africa.

These birds have a characteristic walk, bending the head low and stretching the neck forward. I am not sure that this is not purposeful, for it adds to the difficulty of seeing the birds, whose whole appearance harmonizes so perfectly with their chosen site. The young run immediately they have emerged from the egg, even as the partridge and other birds who make no nest and therefore have no sort of cover.

Stone-curlews were at one time plentiful on the Sussex Downs not far from my cottage; at night, when they fly high, I have often heard their haunting cry, and have been possessed by a desire to share their acquaintance with limitless space and their capacity of expression so in accord with the hour.

PLOVER

I have always had an affection for plovers and their plaintive note, which I yearn to hear when 'long in city pent'. Most people who read Sir Walter Scott's poems will have noticed how often the plover's cry is mentioned; it is not surprising that it should have appealed to the unsatisfied heart of the poet.

To-day I miss the flocks of plovers feeding in the fields; owing to modern machinery they are almost as rare a sight as horses on the road. It is of some consolation that even in this mechanized age there are some who respect a plover's nest. I found in the middle of a field adjacent to my cottage a short stick standing, cleft at the top to hold a small white card; this puzzled me for some time, then I found that it marked the site of a plover's nest which had been exposed when the field was harrowed in early spring. The tractor driver, who nearly drove into the eggs, had placed it there so that he could turn a little each time he went near the bird, thus leaving the nest undisturbed. His care was rewarded, and the young plovers were safely reared. It gladdened that particular man to see them in flight, for plovers are among the best friends of the farmer. They are fairly selective feeders, liking wire-worms and other grubs that bode no good to a field of wheat.

An ornithologist who was seeking for the nest of one of the plover family in West Africa, was surprised at being unable to obtain assistance from his boy, who was usually a willing informant and helper on such expeditions. When questioned he explained that his religious beliefs did not allow him to rob any bird which nested on the breast of mother earth.

GREY PLOVER

This bird does not nest with us and probably he is the shyest of all this large and fascinating family of waders. The sight of him and his fellows in the early winter on our Sussex foreshore always thrills me and I watch them wonderingly, amazed as they concentrate solely on the search for food, having forgotten, apparently, their long hazardous flight—that marvel of migration. They visit us for a short time during their trans-equatorial flight to the southernmost regions of South America, Africa, and Australia. I think of them taking off from the Arctic wastes where they nested in the Siberian tundra, finding there as desirable residence some depression among mossy peat, lining the scrape carelessly with bits of moss and lichen. Under the midnight sun they have laid their four eggs, both male and female sharing the incubation. They have headed south at the first keen frost, flying in flocks of ten or twenty with strong rapid wing-beats keeping in a line or two lines, at a height of about eighty feet from the ground. They will journey back to their nesting grounds in the spring, when they will be in the full glory of their bridal attire.

RINGED PLOVER

Ringed plovers sometimes line their scrape with small white stones, pieces of shell, and dead grass, but more often than not are content to lay their eggs on the bare sand or shingle, the markings on the eggs serving as excellent camouflage. Plovers themselves, like the curlews, blend so well with their chosen habitat that they are almost invisible when brooding. They are affectionate and courageous parents; if anyone approaches the nest their cries of distress are really pitiful. The young chicks, who have been brooded by both parents, are carefully guarded and never left until able to fly and feed themselves. The broken-wing trick to lure away any intruder is constantly adopted; I remember a ringed plover, evidently alarmed at my proximity to her young, feigning injury. She was obviously determined to attract my attention, running along in front of me: each time I stopped she stopped and glanced over her wing, no doubt wondering what sort of effect her action was having on me. I felt this protective ruse for her young infinitely touching. I have seen these plovers gallantly defending their brood from other birds; even the bold herring-gull will retire before their onslaught. Love, indeed, gives all creatures an infinity of courage and strength.

Like many other birds they appear to return to the same territory year after year. When this is first chosen there is great competition, but when the matter is settled they seek and enjoy each other's company. Large flocks can be seen always feeding together, very often with the dunlins.

It is most interesting to watch ringed plovers circling round on their courtship flight voicing beautiful trilling notes. It was only recently that I watched an actual display by one of these birds; I concentrated upon one bird in particular, focusing wholly on his movements. When on the ground he fanned his tail to its fullest extent, sweeping the mud, drooped and partly opened his wings, and raised the feathers on his shoulders. Then going back to an upright position he pirouetted towards the object of his choice, keeping rather apart from the flock as though he wished to draw more attention to himself. As he displayed every part of his black and white plumage he looked about twice his normal size. This exhibition was repeated several times, then suddenly there was a rush, a sort of rough and tumble as it seemed; whether the female was as excited as the male I cannot say. There is no doubt the birds were eventually paired and ready for spring nesting.

GOLDEN PLOVER

I have found the golden plover's nest in Cumberland where the bird is sometimes called *whistle of the waste*. The site chosen was barren moorland; the lining of the nest chiefly lichens and twigs; the chicks were lovely, their down being flecked with gold.

The plumage and habits of this bird change considerably with the seasons so that he is not always recognized as the same. During the spring and summer his plumage suggests to me a regal form of some monastic order, a black cassock with spotted hood and cloak of gold and black, white bordered. His sombre but grand plumage seems in harmony with his mournful double call-note and the isolated habitat in which he lives. In the winter, however, his plumage is much less regal and he becomes more sociable with his kind, even gathering in flocks. During migration the birds travel close together and before alighting skim along the ground rather like aeroplanes. When any number of a migrating flock is killed the others will circle overhead, disturbed and distressed by something they cannot understand, but when the shock of this loss passes and it is found irrevocable, they continue on their course compelled by an overmastering urge.

The flight of a golden plover is amazing: he can travel in an overseas flight from two thousand to two thousand five hundred miles and it has been verified that he flies at least from eighteen thousand to twenty thousand miles in the year.

These beautiful and rather trustful birds are, unfortunately for them, a tasty dish. Sportsmen will boast that six or seven will fall to a shot. The easiest shooting I have ever witnessed was when watching golden plovers

John Markham

Female Pheasant approaching nest

Woodcock settling on nest. Example of remarkable camouflage

Curlew

John Mark.

Ringed Plover at nest beside a freshwater loch in the Scottish Highlands

wheeling and swirling over a patch of moorland in Devonshire. As I watched I thought how easy it is to kill and how impossible to create even a feather.

LAPWING OR PEEWIT

The lapwing or peewit chooses territory carefully and then forms his scrape. He takes an infinity of trouble in making it desirable, a most interesting procedure to witness if the watcher can escape observation. Having decided on the spot, he rotates, pressing his breast against the earth and scratching with his feet until the depression is satisfactory; he is not content with making one but, like the wren, will often make several on his chosen estate. Before long a female will certainly appear to look appraisingly at the scrapes. She will usually sample one and if it pleases her she will gather scraps of building materials and will place them round the edge; then she will begin to rub round the depression, shaping it with her breast. The male is now encouraged sufficiently to begin his spectacular courtship with its astonishing, rapid revolutions, its toss and twirl, accompanied by those repetitive call-notes that are so well known. The scrapes which have not been chosen by the hen nevertheless serve the birds well, for they often deceive those humans who seek the nest with nefarious intent.

The female sits for about twenty-five days but the male bird takes over the brooding now and then. Their young are able to run out of the nest the day they are hatched; I have seen them with a bit of shell still clinging to their beaks. The parents continue to show great anxiety for them when danger threatens; they have many enemies: not only man, but rooks, crows, and sea-gulls.

Lapwings are good friends to the farmer and they may be seen working together on the land; in company with rooks and starlings their destruction of leatherjackets is of untold value.

DUNLIN

The dunlin is often called *plover's page* and I like to imagine the majestic golden plover having such an active little attendant. They have afforded me many hours of enjoyment, giving, as they wheel and turn, the sudden revelation of their white breasts and under parts. I find this sudden switch-round in flight breath-taking in effect. The continual change of the flock's form and pattern, as it opens out, closes in, and then appears to hang in the air, is executed without the slightest hesitation or confusion. Dunlins are sociable and are usually seen in large flocks; it is wonderful to watch them descend on the mud flats or seashore; the effect is rather as if some tree in space had suddenly showered its white petals on the earth. They doze in the afternoon, all facing towards the wind, beaks tucked away in their soft feathers.

They favour the marsh and wet moorlands for their building and usually nest in a grass tussock, forming their residences with sedge, grass, and twigs of heather, whichever is handiest to the location they choose. I have found more than one nest and always when the hen was sitting; she at once sensed my nearness and voiced her brooding, alarm, purring note. Perhaps this is the reason why the bird is known as *purre*. But the little, joyous, trilling notes are sometimes heard which certain ornithologists have described as a short burst of skylark music. I have myself heard this song only occasionally but it had an individual quality that I could not liken to that of any other bird.

MEADOW-PIPIT OR TITLARK

Meadow-pipits or titlarks are the smallest of the 'down-to-earth' builders and of all pipits perhaps the most frequently seen, as they reside with us all the year and are found on moors, downs, marshes, and rough pastures. When in the Lake District I never heard them called anything but *ling-birds*, presumably because there it is the ling that they favour for their habitat, just as in Scotland the birds are known as *moss-cheeper*, for where the moss clusters they build their nests.

I have mistaken meadow-pipits for larks until I heard their song, for their slim brown and buff little bodies are rather similar to that of the sky-pilot, and both birds have the almost straight, long hind claw.

In autumn they leave the exposed habitat where they breed and congregate sociably with their fellows on meadows and turnip-fields, but their inconspicuous plumage makes them rather difficult to distinguish until later in the season when it becomes brighter and more colourful.

It seems strange that the cuckoo so often chooses the nests of small birds in which to deposit her egg. I have watched with some indignation the meadow-pipit's untiring labour to satisfy the voracious appetite of the young intruder, who having successfully ejected the legitimate fledglings, settles down complacently with an ever open beak; and he does not demand in vain. The extraordinary thing to me is that birds who are usually so devoted to their young, having incubated a cuckoo, appear to become utterly indifferent to the fate of their own brood, focusing all their energy and care upon the alien monster.

The meadow-pipit utters a quiet little note *tit* or *pipit* as he walks sedately through the grass or herbage near his home, but when danger threatens he gives a sharp repetitive cry of *peep peep peep*. During his nuptial flight he descends singing, with wings vibrating, and again when the hen is brooding her eggs and also when the young are hatched he will sometimes hover over the nest singing his song. When he mounts into the air from the ground he gradually rises with quivering wings, voicing his small *peep peep* which is followed by the trill, but as he planes down with wings spread and tail tilted upwards his song becomes most joyous.

TREE-PIPIT

The tree-pipit comes to us during April and leaves late in September, the males arriving before the females. The nest is usually found near bushes or trees and as with the meadow-pipit it is often concealed in long grass or herbage, and formed of dead grasses or bents, lined with a little moss or hair. As with many birds that build on the ground, the eggs are so marked as to be inconspicuous, blending with the soil or gloom of the sheltering grasses. The tree-pipit's are variable in colour but as a general rule reddish brown, spotted or mottled with a deeper tint of the same colour, an excellent camouflage.

The sexes are alike in appearance as with all pipits but the tree-pipits have a curved hind claw shorter than the toe, and a rather less slender beak. They also have a slower gait on the ground than the other more nimble pipits.

His song is very sweet and I listen eagerly for his notes in April; many of these are rather similar to those of the canary and most people consider he is the finest singer among the pipit family. In his ascent, which never reaches a great height, he voices only a few notes, but as he descends with outstretched wings and tail he sings his fuller song.

TAWNY PIPIT

The tawny pipit is rare but perhaps familiar to many people because of the delightful film of that name in which a whole village guarded the precious nest. He has bred on the Sussex coast, and those fortunate enough to have seen a nest record that it was on the ground sheltered by a grass tussock, and like other nests of the pipit family composed of grass and bents, lined with hair. The brooding hen sat very close but when sensing observation she rose and, flying off, endeavoured to lure away the intruder by fluttering and feigning injury, which is a ruse adopted by many birds.

As they are only summer visitors with us they are not well known; I recognized them only by reason of their lighter, almost flesh-coloured legs and delightful wagtail-like action.

I have heard them voice their song in the air as other pipits do, and when in Spain I heard them singing at a height of about ten thousand feet in the Sierra Nevada. I was told the birds sing at night as well as by day but this I have never been fortunate enough to verify.

NIGHTJAR

The handle of my walking-stick is fashioned in the shape of a nightjar: it seems a fitting choice for something that always accompanies me on my night ambles.

The bird has many other names—*fern-owl, goat-sucker, moth-eater, night-hawk.* Any bird-watcher must be intrigued when he is fortunate enough to see the nightjar squatting on a branch of which he becomes almost a part. He is further helped in his wonderful camouflage by the shadows of night which render him almost invisible; he even closes his eyes to avoid detection. Actually he always keeps his eyes half shut, either because he does not favour the light or because he knows they might reveal his position.

I have been fortunate enough to locate one hovering moth-like among the trees in my garden. He is noiseless in flight as the owl, unless deliberately flapping his wings among the boughs, probably to disturb insects which he captures on the wing. His serrated claws serve him to free the hairs and soft silver dust usually covering the bodies of night-flying moths which appear on his menu.

The hen lays her two eggs on the bare ground. She is a faithful mother, guarding her chicks carefully, and continues patiently brooding, even during terrific storms of rain splashing all unheeded on her back. On one occasion, when watching a hen, I saw that her throat vibrated with a faint purr as she gently rocked from side to side in the nest. Sometimes she changed her position and, slightly rising, hooked the eggs under her breast with her beak into a more convenient position. Once I saw her with up-lifted wings; I have never seen any other feathered creature do this while brooding, and for this reason I remain puzzled.

The nightjar's voice is utterly different from that of any other bird; I have heard it described as rather like the tearing of calico, and I can think of no more apt simile for the strange sound. The best time for hearing it is just after sunset or before dawn; it is so penetrating that it can be heard a mile away. The bird also voices a sort of musical churring that has a charm of its own. This is uttered when alighting, or even on the ground, and is often followed by other indescribable notes which sometimes per-sist for several minutes, being among the eerie sounds that essentially be-long to the night. Yet though these birds are always regarded as birds of the night, strangely enough during migration they fly in the day-time.

HEN HARRIER

All the harriers appear of interest to the ornithologist: I think this may be partly because they are among the rarer birds and likely to remain so, for they are regarded as pests since they beat for game as expertly as man who usually punishes any creature that would share the food he desires for his own larder.

I once found a hen harrier's nest on a moor in Wales under a gorse bush; it was composed of a few sticks apparently thrown together with a very sparse lining of heather and plant stems. The nest appeared a crude affair, but well suited to the bird's particular requirements. My appear-ance disturbed the female but I caught sight of her three bluish white eggs marked with spots of yellowish brown. I retreated to a distance, watching until I saw her return to her nest: I went back every day and, as far as I observed, she brooded for thirty days without assistance from her mate.

The first time I ever actually noted hen harriers was on the South

Downs between Falmer and Plumpton; I was arrested by the sight of two birds quartering their prey and was amazed to see them hunting in such close proximity as they were so strikingly dissimilar that I could not imagine them to be a pair. An old shepherd called to me to 'watch 'em' as they 'were not so frequent seen now'. I saw that their flight was slow and wavering; they seemed to halt in the air, their wings remaining rigid, only the tail continuing to quiver; their intention was dangerously deliberate.

Since that time I have become aware that very little comes amiss to the hen harriers as far as food is concerned and I have watched them seize a lizard and even a snake, and eat it; their favourite time for hunting is at dusk or early morning. I have learned to recognize them by their slender build, length of leg and tail, long pointed wings, slight ruff on the side of the neck, and facial disc something like that of an owl, but though I keep a sharp look out for them I am not often rewarded.

The male and female are so different that it is difficult to believe they are of the same species, the female being at least two inches longer than the male and her plumage mainly brown and white. I hear that she is sometimes called *ring-tail* from the bars on her tail and that the male is called by many *blue-hawk* or *dove-hawk*, his plumage being principally slate blue and white with black primaries. Both birds voice a repetitive, quick, rather harsh note, but I have heard the female utter a queer high-pitched wail.

Frances Pitt told me that when she was observing hen harriers from a hide placed near the nest in the shelter of a windblown hillside, she was surprised to see that among the five young ones there was a particularly fine female which was white save for two dark patches. I have never heard any other record of an albino hen harrier.

MARSH-HARRIER

The marsh-harrier is the rarest of the three harriers and is suffering from the intensive reclamation and drainage of marshland, where he finds his desirable residence; modern agriculture is responsible for the disappearance of much wild life. I have never found a nest myself, but I have been told by watchers that it is a very bulky affair, composed of reeds and sedges interwoven, lined with dried grasses. Only once have I heard of a marsh-harrier building in the fork of a large tree; I feel this must have been a bird with very individual taste.

I have seen these birds in the Fen country gliding with rigid wings over the reeds or water. Sometimes they give a peculiar drawn out cry; I believe this is often after securing prey and probably denotes successful hunting. I am told that the female when disturbed voices a shrill complaining note, but the male's protestations at such times are never so loud.

MONTAGU'S HARRIER

The plumage of the montagu is rather similar to that of the hen harrier but he is a smaller and even more slender bird and more uncommon than the hen or the marsh. They are becoming rarer visitors every year, though they still attempt to nest in East Anglia, probably the most valuable English territory for rarer birds. The nest is little more than a depression composed of rushes and dried grass; when one is found there is usually another not far away, for they breed more or less in proximity, indeed, I am told that abroad large colonies may be seen.

SHORT-EARED OWL

The short-eared owl is less of a night bird than other owls. His choice of a district is frequently dependent on the supply of voles, and when it is a good vole year his wife will produce as many as thirteen eggs, laid at intervals of forty-five to fifty hours, during all of which time she sits patiently. Naturally such intervals in egg-production mean that the young birds are in very different stages of development, the last hatched rarely surviving.

These owls appear not to resent other birds in the vicinity of the nesting site, which is usually on the ground in heather or sedge, but they dislike any of their own kind encroaching too near their territory. Perhaps they consider relations more apt to be possessive than strangers.

The male's face is very like that of the barn owl, white and somewhat ghostly, but the female's is softer and buff in colour. The short-eared owl has wonderful eyes, which change from pale yellow to gold and are surrounded by small black feathers. The short upstanding feathery ear-tufts conceal the actual ears, the right and left being differently formed in order to catch sound both from above and below.

The Orkneys is perhaps the best place to watch short-eared owls, because their desired nesting sites and the food they require are there in abundance; I have known them to build, but only very rarely, in the eastern counties among the reed-beds. I found them difficult birds to observe, scared at the slightest noise except the usual sounds of nature and when disturbed very fierce, soaring in spiral fashion until beyond pursuit. When in the air they turn and twist with amazing dexterity, seeming to know every variation of the wind.

12

WEAVERS

Reed-warbler; sedge-warbler; marsh-warbler; willow-warbler;
grasshopper-warbler; garden-warbler; wood-warbler;
Dartford warbler; whitethroat

MOST birds are weavers but there are some I think of as Grand Masters of this craft, especially perhaps the warblers.[1] These birds build exquisite little nests, grassy moss-covered cups, which the hen lashes to the chosen trees with bits of string and hair, sometimes binding them round and round. Cobwebs are festooned on the outside, which is sometimes decorated with tiny, empty seed-pods, the inside usually being warmly lined with hair and feathers; an exquisite cradle indeed. I have noticed there is a sharing of duties between the pairs of this species, the cock taking his shift fairly with the hen in brooding the eggs.

The warblers all favour the proximity of the earth. I have never found any of their various nests very far from the ground. One might almost say the reed, sedge, and marsh-warblers favour a damp site for their building, but though they choose a variety of habitats there can be no question of their dexterity in weaving.

REED-WARBLER

The reed-warbler has many local names, being sometimes called *reed-sparrow, reed-wren, fen-reedling, marsh-reedling, reed-bird, night-warbler, dicky-reed,* and *reed-chucker*—all no doubt chosen as the watcher sees and hears this little bird. I find binoculars the most useful aid in observing these very timid birds, who immediately become aware of a watcher. It is fascinating to see them running up and down the smooth stems; the distinctive pale, buff stripe over the eye is always noticeable. They spend their lives among the reeds where they find their food, choose satisfactory building

---

[1] In the United States about one bird in six is a warbler. The magnolia-warbler and myrtle-warbler are perhaps two of the most attractive.

H

material to make their home secure, and later feed their families. The mouths of the fledglings are deep red with two conspicuous black spots at the back of the tongue, probably to guide the parents when feeding, for the cup-shaped nest is deep and dark, affording security for the eggs and later for the little family.

Being so secretive and shy, also extremely alert, they are difficult to observe continuously. It would seem that the nest is built almost entirely by the hen, the cock giving casual help. It is dexterously woven between three or four reed-stems; these have the appearance of being driven as supports through the outer structure. The materials used are grass, moss, reed-leaves, and seed-tufts, and the whole is lined cosily with hair and feathers. It is built so cleverly that it withstands any amount of buffeting to and fro from wind and weather and even when heavy rain swells the stream I have never seen this fairy hammock submerged. Lorraine peasants even judge the height to which water will rise by the elevation of the reed-warbler's nest.

These birds voice little diffident songs, sweet and changing, always close to their reed-territory, which they will fight desperately to guard. The protective instinct is remarkable in all birds; usually the cock will try to shield the hen as she sits brooding the eggs, even as she will shield the fledglings with her last breath, and so it is with the cock reed-warbler whose devotion is touching. I have actually seen one of these little cocks fly on to the hen and spread his wings over her until a fierce storm was over.

I am filled with profound amazement and admiration when I think of their migration, so stupendous an undertaking for such tiny creatures, only one-third of an ounce of flesh, bone, and feather. Their temerity, courage, and endurance is but another instance of the wonder of wings.

SEDGE-WARBLER

Sedge-warblers choose osier-beds and ditches for their nests but I have also found them building low down in hedgerows, never higher than eight or nine feet from the ground. It is not a very tidy home and is composed of grasses, stalks, and moss but always softly lined with hair or feathers. They particularly favour the cover of reeds or the sword-like leaves of rushes; many pairs often nest in close proximity and are frequently found in company with their cousins the reed-warblers, with whom they seem friendly.

As far as I have been able to observe, the hen is again the builder and the cock occupies himself by entertaining her, but they both brood the eggs. The hen always undertakes the night shift, probably thinking that her mate might take a fatal forty winks; he roosts at a decorous distance. I have been intrigued to see that the hen is apparently stiff after her long night's vigil; she perches on the edge of the nest and stretches herself, each wing being extended in turn.

Naturalists have described the sedge-warbler's song in different ways. W. Warde Fowler hears him 'pitching up his voice into a series of loud squeaks, then dropping it into a long-drawn grating noise like the winding up of an old-fashioned watch'. The song is certainly varied, indeed there can be no question but that the bird delights in mimicry, and I have frequently been deceived by him. He sings not only during the day, but at night, being often called the *fisherman's nightingale*.

MARSH-WARBLER

The 'marsh' is, I think, the rarest of this species. His plumage resembles that of the reed-warbler but is more olive in colour and he has a sweeter song; some think it even equals the blackcap's. The nest is among rank vegetation and the birds seem particularly to favour meadow-sweet; they never actually build over water, always about two or three feet above dry ground. When they choose osier-beds for their home the nest is slung by 'basket handles' between the reed-stems; it is skilfully woven with dry grasses, moss, and seeds. Only once have I located a nest and I noticed with interest that instead of perching on the edge of the nest to feed their young, the parents alighted on its supporting reed-stem and from this convenient angle popped food into the wide-open and expectant beaks.

WILLOW-WARBLER

The willow-warbler, sometimes called the *willow-wren, haybird,* or *ovenbird,* usually builds its domed nest deep among the grasses in ditches, hedge-bottoms, and banks, with a soft lining of feathers. I find it entertaining to watch these little birds skilfully catching insects on the various seeding weeds.

Though so small they are possessed of stout hearts; a watcher in Norfolk reports that one of these birds nested behind some ivy that was trailing down beside a ditch covered in snow. It was an exceptionally cold April and towards the end of the month there was a fall of snow to a depth of four inches; he saw the little bird burrowing through it to reach the nest.

Oliver Pike writing of the willow-warbler relates a delightful incident he witnessed:

The hen had been brooding her young for at least two hours and during all that time had not taken any food herself, passing on all that the male brought to her young. On his next visit he brought a nice plump caterpillar about one inch in length, which he evidently meant for the hen's particular consumption and when he reached the nest he stood outside and called her. He held the food close to her beak, uttering a few low pleasing notes, vibrating his wings. This special beakful of food must have been very tempting to her but though responding with notes and wing vibrations she would not take it. He continued to hold it near to her beak and at last she took it from him but instead of swallowing it she stopped, evidently struggling against the temptation; then, quickly before appetite should prevail, she passed the delectable mouthful to one of her young, who were waiting expectantly with their necks raised and beaks wide open. After the food had been disposed of she went back to her duties of brooding over them.

When I think of willow-warblers flitting about in their dove-coloured feathers, I am once more in the Fell country where I have seen them most frequently. One of the pictures that comes to me is a 'borrowed' day when nature was in golden mood and the Cumberland hills were veiled in soft mist. Every shade of green was about me in woods, fields, and hedgerow, the broom displaying its wealth of gold and the sweet honey-scented blossom suggestive of the white clover. I am again standing on a blue pansy-carpet fit for a fairy queen, a low hedge divides me from the Duddon fields; I suddenly hear willow-warblers and remain very still as I watch them busy with their building. When grey, bleak days are with me, I am grateful for this memory which always brings with it the sight and sound of these fairy-like little birds, surely some of the sweetest among our summer visitors.

GRASSHOPPER-WARBLER

The nest is composed of moss and dry grasses, wonderfully interwoven; it may be found in several places, sometimes among heather, osier-beds, or dense undergrowth, invariably secluded, as all warblers are very secretive builders. Owing to the position of the nest the birds never fly on to it; instead they move mouse-like along the runway they have made, thereby increasing the difficulty of location. The peculiar song—if you can call it so—which I have tried to describe in my book *I Watch and Listen* bewilders by its ventriloquism, successfully misleading the intruder. Gilbert White, in *The Natural History of Selborne*, writes:

Nothing can be more amusing than the whisper of this little bird which seems to be close by, though it is a hundred yards distant, and when close at your ear, it is scarce any louder than when a great way off.

GARDEN-WARBLER

Both sexes are alike in plumage, olive-brown upper parts, pale buff under parts; the warblers' usual stripe over the eye is not very conspicuous. They build a frail nest low down in brambles and bushes; the cock collects the material and carries it to the hen, then stands by watching her, encouraging her with his song. I was once honoured by a pair choosing for residence a clump of lupins in my garden and was able to watch their building, brooding of eggs, and rearing of family. I noticed the construction of the nest usually went on during the first part of the day, and took about five mornings to complete. The cock helped in the incubation, always approaching the nest with a song, a very beautiful warble resembling the blackcap's (some think it is even sweeter—certainly more prolonged). When he was about to take his turn he vocally expressed his readiness and the hen usually replied to this with a few low notes, standing on the edge of the nest fluttering her wings while he settled himself over the eggs in her place. This procedure was repeated when she returned in about a couple of hours; then I actually heard her singing while sitting, which I think is not usual. Later, I noticed she was brooding the young, the cock bringing the rations; their family life seemed exemplary and they appeared to delight in each other's company. I often watched the pair searching for food in my oak tree; apart from the fluttering of their little wings, the quick up-and-down flight made it seem as if the birds were poised in space. I am pleased to say that all the young birds were reared in safety without being found by the prowling cat.

There is no question that migration takes a large toll of birds and I should say from observation that many more males arrive safely than females. Oliver Pike, who has carefully observed the warblers, said that in his garden a male sang incessantly through May, June, July, and August waiting for the female to arrive, and that during this period he built several nests; not the flimsy affairs that the males usually build but carefully constructed ones. I wondered if it were not possible that this was done to show he was a cock worth while and had something more to recommend him than mere physical attraction or gift of song.

WOOD-WARBLER

These birds closely resemble the chiff-chaff and the willow-warbler but are rather larger, their soft green and yellow plumage being lighter and seemingly designed to match the surroundings of their nests. As their name implies they frequent woodlands and I first found their lovely little dome-shaped home on the ground, in a wood carpeted with wild hyacinths; it was skilfully camouflaged by a few dead leaves, but the silvery trill of the little cock's song betrayed its whereabouts; there were no feathers in the nesting material but plenty of hair and grasses.

Wordsworth, who observed birds and wrote of them so sympathetically, says of the wood-warbler:

> The hermit has no finer eye
> For shadowy quietness.

DARTFORD WARBLER

The nest of this bird is a rare discovery. My neighbour in Sussex was proud of the fact that he had found one in a gorse bush; it was composed of stalks and bents, lined with fine grasses and horsehair. On the edge a feather was sticking up almost ostentatiously as if it were a house sign. He was puzzled that this should be so obviously placed, as though for some definite purpose, enigmatical to man.

Alas! this warbler is now rare. I read that one hundred pounds was offered for a living specimen. I have seen only one of these little birds: he was enjoying himself on a furze bush and did not seem to resent my coming quite close to him; perhaps he realized my intentions were not dishonourable but merely those of admiration and interest.

It must be difficult for these small creatures to exist in the winter, requiring as they do insects, butterflies, moths, flies, and spiders for their food. Perhaps most tragic of all is the fact that in company with other small birds they favour heaths, and in consequence suffer from the firing of gorse and undergrowth which, it seems, is almost invariably practised in the nesting season. This is surely an unnecessary cruelty, as then all birds will guard their nestlings even unto death.

WHITETHROAT

Sometimes called *paddling-warbler* or *little miller*, this bird also favours bushes and builds low, though I have found more than one nest tucked cosily in among the nettles; perhaps that is why he is also called *nettle-creeper*. The male often begins the nest himself but as the hen always supplies the lining probably the cock knows it would be useless to try to furnish the house to her satisfaction, so he wisely leaves this until her arrival. The nest is freely lined with horsehair and vegetable down stuffed cleverly into the interstices as if to keep out the draughts. I always think of whitethroats as weavers because of their clever basket-work of grass bents, which though apparently sketchy is really amazingly, substantially, and skilfully woven. It remains stable and resistant not only to weather but to all the vigorous struggling of fledglings, and to the constant visits of the parents who, bringing food, always perch on the rim to present it. This nest is another example of the birds' complete mastery of the building-craft necessary for their own requirements.

The hen alone broods, the cock singing when he is not searching for food which he brings her assiduously. After the eggs are hatched, about the fifth day, both parents work hard to satisfy the wants of their family. Oliver Pike gives a moving picture of the hen's devotion:

> On three occasions I have seen the female return to the nest in an exhausted condition. She has given the food she has brought to the young, then with spread wings, drooping head, beak open, she has slowly subsided until she almost fell off the nest. Her eyes closed, her head fell over the side and I thought she was on the point of dying but she pulled herself together and after a rest of about five minutes, stood up on the approach of her mate and flew off to continue her work.

I was interested this year in two nests of the whitethroat; one I examined when the young birds had flown. I was surprised to find that it possessed no lining of horsehair nor any packing of down. The other, though down had been stuffed into the interstices, was not so well built and I felt pretty sure this was a cock's nest.

I have known a magpie clear out a nest full of young whitethroats, much to the distress of the parents and strangely enough also of a willow-warbler. I was surprised to see all three birds hovering over the empty nest in great agitation; it was interesting to me that a bird of another species should come round almost like a human neighbour, in order to sympathize and share in the lamentation.

13

NO FIXED ABODE

Robin; house-sparrow; blue tit; great tit; spotted flycatcher;
pied flycatcher

ALL six birds that I have placed under this heading seem to me impossible to label as favouring any particular site; they like variety and their fancy is very free. Like Emerson, they 'dare to change'.

ROBIN

The robin is perhaps of all birds the one most loved by man and it would seem he realizes this, for in return he appears to have no fear of the human biped. I should say he is one of the very few winged creatures safe from slaughter; I doubt whether any poulterer would dare to display Robin as desirable for the pot and bold indeed would be the hotel-keeper who would put him on the menu. The weight of most song-birds is so negligible that it seems absurd, from a material point of view, that they should ever be considered for food. The robin for instance rarely scales more than three-quarters of an ounce though he is five and a half inches long.

These redbreasts are particularly individual in their likes and dislikes, the site they choose is unexpected and the manner in which they adapt their nest to the site is ingenious. No one can predict exactly where the robin may build or say that any place is precluded from his versatile ideas for desirable residence.

> Most of all to haunts of men
> Familiar, though to savage glen
> And woodland wild he oft may roam
> Secluded, oft his wintry home:
> No less the redbreast makes his bower
> For nestlings in the vernal hour
> In thatch or root of aged tree,
> Moss-grown, or arching cavity

> Of bank or garden's refuse heap:
> Or where the broad-leaved tendrils creep
> Of ivy, and the arbour spread
> O'er trellised porch or cottage shed.[1]

They are said never to build higher than three feet from the ground. Sergeant Joyce Kilmer has often been criticized for writing: 'A tree that may in summer wear, a nest of robins in her hair', but it should be remembered that he was thinking of the American robin, a very different bird from ours; yet I have found the nest of our native robin in a macrocarpa-arch nearly eight feet high. This may have been peculiar to a special pair and their descendants, for there has been a nest in this same place for several years.

Some people say robins are the quickest builders. The dry leaves, moss, and grasses they require are generally at hand and thus much time usually spent in seeking the desired material is saved, but the whole is always carefully felted together and neatly lined with hair or something similar, such as a few feathers. My neighbour tells me he once saw robins build a nest in five hours; they must have been a speed-ace couple. They are expeditious birds, some may think foolhardy. I have known them to build even during the second week in January, though this is exceptional as they generally nest in early February.

It is very difficult to distinguish the cock robin from the hen as they both have the same colouring, though the breast of the hen is not quite so bright. As there are many more cock robins than hens, perhaps that is why it is she who is selective in the mating season. Judging by the competitive singing of the many suitors, I imagine capacity for song may be regarded as one of the qualifying assets.

There is no doubt that robins have a very special urge to express themselves in song for even in winter they are vocal, though there is no doubt that they suffer from the cold and avail themselves of any opportunity for shelter. My father always had a brick removed from the walls of his barns in bitter weather so that the birds could go in when they wished; but I have seen a hen patiently suffer terrible storms rather than leave her nest when brooding. For three days I carefully watched a sitting hen in my garden and I am positive she never moved from her nest for either relaxa-

---

[1] Bishop Mant.

tion or food and during this period there was a continual downpour of rain accompanied by a wild west wind. I have heard that a hen will endure even longer periods at the nest without respite.

There is a widespread belief that young robins kill the old ones but I do not think this is invariably true, though they certainly give them a thin time, wresting from father his estate when he still wishes to hold on to it. This must be a bitter thing for cock robin senior because he is exceedingly jealous of his chosen territory, though this proverbial tenacity of a chosen site is sometimes over-ruled by an attachment to a human household. An instance of this was given by Mr Watson Williams, B.Sc., who lived at Saughall near Chester. A robin was a constant visitor there, following Mr Williams about in both house and garden and even seeming to understand most of what he said. Circumstances made it necessary for the family to move to Birkdale, Southport, and the robin appeared to sense the approaching change of residence in the same way as a cat or dog will do. He became obviously anxious and restless, following the various members of the household from room to room, refusing to be driven away. When the van containing the furniture arrived at the new address and the door was opened the robin flew out. This determined and faithful stowaway then settled down and resumed his old habits of coming round for food and paying visits to his chosen humans at the new abode as if nothing had happened.

Since we find the robin so friendly, it seems strange that he should be so unsociable with his own kind, with whom he never consorts except in adversity, such as bad weather or shortage of food, when there is a temporary truce.

Many countries have robins or rather birds who have been given this name by settlers. Magpie-robins give delight and nostalgic memories to Britishers who happen to be in the tropics. Their song is equally refreshing and they have the same habit of haunting the dwellings of man and very many of the other characteristics of the English robin, though they do not possess the same plumage, being for the most part bluey-grey. The American robin also has a sweet song, something like the blackbird's, and he is equally tame and ready to build near houses. India and China know him and it would seem the name of the bird we think of as the friend of man has been generally adopted in both hemispheres.

HOUSE-SPARROW

House-sparrows certainly have no fixed abode; they take up their residence in both rural and urban districts; few places come amiss to them. They will build in a lead spout, wooden chute, chimney, loft, the eaves of a cottage, or hole in a tree. To-day woods and thickets are cut down relentlessly and there is a consequent reduction in the number of birds who depend for their lives on this natural shelter. But sparrows do not mind, any place seems to serve their need; they accommodate themselves anywhere. Nothing daunts them. If their nest is cleared away, another is built and if this is demolished, another and yet another. They are tirelessly persistent; even when ousted six, seven, or eight times they will still continue building. The one thing that does upset them is the prying eye and any interference when brooding; in such circumstances I have known them desert and even destroy their eggs.

The nest is usually an untidy mass of bits and pieces, hair, feathers, paper, cloth, wool, anything indeed which comes within sight of their bright acquisitive eyes. But often they will prefer to take possession of another bird's nest, even ejecting the rightful owners. I was told of a certain housemartin who felt this injustice so acutely that he walled up the intruder. A terrible revenge indeed!

Their food is as varied as their building sites; sometimes they favour my primroses and crocuses in the spring, particularly the yellow ones; this may be because they dislike the colour and wish to destroy it; on the other hand they may have a special liking for it. They constantly monopolize the food on my bird-table, driving other song-birds away; this always seems inexplicable to me. I have often wondered what quality they possess which induces this attitude to their feathered fellows. Are they avoided, tolerated, or despised?

All must admit that sparrows have good qualities. They are devoted mates, sharing the nest-building and incubating of the eggs, also the tireless feeding of the young. They give the lie to the idea that birds always kick out of the nest the weakling and injured. A watcher I know was amazed to find that after the young birds had flown from a nest in his garden the parents still visited it continually. He found one of the young ones was held prisoner, having twisted round his leg a piece of worsted which had formed part of the nest; the parent birds would not allow any human near enough to help but they assiduously fed the unfortunate nestling every day, at the same time making continuous attempts to liberate him, which at long last they succeeded in doing.

Another instance of their persistent care came to my notice. Three young sparrows were entangled in chewing-gum and black cotton, a deplorable method of trapping employed by some gardeners. The little birds were unable to move and were fed by their mother, who maintained a steady air-lift of food to them until the owner was moved to free the unfortunate victims.

Nevertheless there can be no doubt that they delight in endless quarrels, twittering and chirping, tumbling over each other, rolling in the dust, more joining in as the quarrel continues, until all suddenly ceases, with apparently nothing settled one way or the other.

I should say the sparrow has, like the robin, a distinct fondness for human habitation; wherever man lives they are found, at all seasons, in both country and town. I think we are fortunate that our cities still have these small, pert, noisy scavengers as there is something about them which is endearing. I like their cockney cheeriness, independence, and persistent courage. They are now more rarely seen in our streets for the obvious reason of increasing traffic and there is less for them to eat with the disappearance of the horse and his nose-bag, but every park, back-garden, railway-siding, or piece of waste ground is the sparrows' happy hunting-ground.

In a London office that I know there is always a tray of odds and ends on the desk, including string. It seems that the office staff had become interested in a pair of sparrows who continually flew in through the open window, taking hold of a piece of string and pecking at the end until they had fluffed it out and made it sufficiently pliable for nesting material. One of the clerks who was particularly fond of birds, thinking to help them, frayed some bits of string to save them trouble, but the birds ignored these and continued to make their own selection and to prepare it to their satisfaction.

I have been interested in sparrows that roosted persistently in a very fine holly-tree standing in the garden of a famous Sussex artist. Men had been instructed to cut the overhanging branches of certain trees and to the utter dismay of the artist they unfortunately included the holly-tree, cutting it down to a stump. That same evening when he went into his bedroom he found, to his surprise, that six sparrows had come in through the open window to roost and were comfortably settled on the top of the wardrobe. This has now become their permanent roosting place instead of the holly-tree; early in the morning they take their departure.

I have always been intrigued that the correct name for a sparrow's roost is 'chapel'. He is certainly no religious bigot, finding his chapel either on a tree, the ledge of a building, or upon occasions a wardrobe door or a bedrail. I was once favoured by a tame sparrow who roosted every night on my bed-rail; at about seven in the morning he would slip out of the window and was gone all day, invariably returning at nightfall and appearing quite undisturbed by my presence and bedside-lamp.

Sparrows seem to multiply more than any other birds for they have several broods a year, laying five or six eggs each time; therefore it is easy to visualize how very many descendants they must have. They are supposed to consume food amounting to their own weight in a day and are certainly responsible for destroying an enormous amount of weed-seeds, caterpillars, and grubs, which well repays their toll of corn; indeed without them the crops would suffer a greater loss by insect-pests and weeds. I have watched large flocks accused of stealing grain really regaling themselves upon these weeds; surely the service they render the farmer is worth a dole. Sparrows and other small birds were at one time exterminated in parts of France, even as the rooks, but they had to be re-imported, regardless of cost, because of the destruction wrought by insects.

My father always said that if it were not for the labours of the sparrows in the garden all the year round, feeding their brood so exclusively on insects and destructive 'creepy-crawlies', he would never have had such good fruit. I have seen both birds bring two or three caterpillars to the nest at a time and they certainly feed their young quite thirty times an hour. This means that three hundred and sixty insects are probably destroyed by one bird, or seven hundred and twenty by the pair in a day. How much fruit and flowers would those seven hundred and twenty caterpillars have eaten up if they had been permitted to remain alive? In these days of poisonous insecticides the position is changed; now destruction on a large scale is the rule and this, in my opinion, will eventually destroy not only insects and birds, but man.

It is perhaps remarkable that the sparrow is the one bird mentioned in the New Testament in connection with God's regard for His creatures: 'Are not five sparrows sold for two farthings, and not one of them is forgotten before God?' Much controversy has been carried on as to whether the word should be translated as sparrow or some other bird, but sparrow it has been since we have had our Bible and presumably so it will continue.

BLUE TIT

Tits are surely among the most lovable of birds; there are few people who do not find delight in watching them. Blue tits patronize nesting boxes and because of this the amateur watcher is able to observe very easily the coming and going necessitated by building and feeding, provided always that he or she has a little patience. These little birds, with their engaging 'school-boy' caps, nest in many odd places, preferring a hole in a tree or wall. I have been particularly engaged by tits building for five years in an empty milk bottle which had been somehow overlooked in my garden and was lying sideways in a bush. The mouth was only just large enough for the tits to squeeze in and out and it was not until three years ago that I saw the exit and flight of the babies. To my amazement the parents, perching on the edge of the bottle, pulled them each out in turn very carefully and slowly with the aid of their beaks.

I have found that the blue tit is very particular and selective. Many holes and crevices are examined before a final decision is made, and when the cock at last finds one that is to his satisfaction he still has to induce the hen to agree with his choice. I have occupied more time than perhaps I should in watching this interesting and amusing sequence. The cock will twitter and use many alluring bodily twists and turns; then he flies off, returning with a little feather, which I believe he plucks from his own body, and places it in the chosen hole. After this suggestive offering he again bows and curvets to his lady love; if she still shows no interest he obviously becomes annoyed and tries to force her into the hole; even this tactic often fails and the little hen keeps him on tenterhooks in order to enjoy as prolonged a courtship as possible. The cock sometimes appears to feel that all his efforts are in vain, for I have seen him sitting on a bough adjacent to the proposed home site, utterly dejected. But then something psychological happens, exactly what or when the human cannot say, but suddenly the pair will be industriously building together their desirable bijou residence of moss, wool, and feathers. Although so small, it will successfully hold nine eggs. These are most carefully guarded and covered when the parent of necessity leaves the nest. Later, ten birds including the mother, and at night eleven (because father comes home) are accommodated in the little residence. This would certainly appear to be congested quarters but the tits are evidently well satisfied.

I have noticed that before the arduous duties of parenthood start the hen usually goes to roost first, but the cock nearly always rouses her, no doubt feeling that she must have recreation, and they may be seen indulging in hops and jumps before they finally retire for the night, when, healthily wearied, they are soon roosting together. She is rather more unselfish than her mate once the nest is built, for though both birds seem to spend most of the day bringing food to the hungry family I have seen the little cock with his beak full, perching for a time on a twig adjacent to the nest, evidently wrestling with temptation—to which he sometimes succumbs —at last swallowing the food he has presumably collected for the family.

I fancy that few people have much idea of the usual day's work of a pair of blue tits when feeding their young. Once when convalescing from an illness I was able to note meticulously the activities of a pair who were feeding their fledglings; during the day they made seven hundred and forty visits with food, which means that with an average of two caterpillars apiece the destruction of fourteen hundred and eighty of these pests was effected. One has only to consider these figures day after day during the period that the young birds must be fed to realize how useful the blue tit is to man. It may be of some interest to note the three peak periods in the feeding of the pair that I was watching: approximately 6 a.m. to 8 a.m.; 10 a.m. to 12 noon; 5 p.m. to 7 p.m. One presumes the parents had to take some time off to obtain their own food and for a little rest, but they were still feeding the nestlings at 8.45 p.m.

The young birds are not allowed out by the mother until they can fly; it is a wonderful sight to see the tiny birds looking rather like bumble-bees, thrilled with their freedom and the anticipation of flight, poising on the slenderest flower-stalks, or waiting in a circle on my bird-bath, for one of the first things they appear to desire is a bath. I presume this procedure is much the same for all tits.

John Markham

Hen Harrier. Female bringing nesting material. She continued adding
to the nest until the young were half grown

John Mar

Reed Warbler at nest with young

GREAT TIT OR OX-EYE

The great tit, *ox-eye* or *sit-ye-down* as it is sometimes called (possibly because its notes can be said to resemble these words), builds a foundation for the nest with moss and grass, the interior being composed of hair or down. He builds in most unusual places and on occasions will take over the old nest of other birds. I have known a great tit use the nest of a nuthatch, taking up his residence immediately the owner had vacated it so that he benefited by the work of the old tenant. During my periods of watching this bird I noticed that the cock great tit woke first and then called the hen. She roused herself but often fell asleep again; he sometimes had to call her many times before she finally woke.

SPOTTED FLYCATCHER

The spotted flycatcher has several names all of which have significance but the least applicable of all seems that of *spotted*, as certainly the plumage of the more mature birds is streaked rather than speckled. It is the young ones who are spotted and it is suggested that they retain something of their ancestral decoration. But the surname, if one may so describe it, is well chosen for they are certainly remarkable fly-catchers.

I find them amazingly interesting to watch as they twist and turn in the air; their quick movements no doubt confuse the flies which cannot be certain from one second to another whether the birds are coming or going.

They are one of the last arrivals in the spring and are fond of building near man, never going far from their nest once they have chosen the site. They build in a variety of places, though the more conventional of the species are content with walls, fruit trees, and tree-trunks. Sometimes they do not hesitate to occupy the disused nest of a blackbird or thrush, which they will redecorate to suit their own requirements and taste, lining it anew with hair and cobwebs. They share all duties of parenthood, cock and hen taking it in turn to brood the eggs, always sitting very close on the nest.

The only flycatchers I was able to watch for any length of time built in the crevice of an old wall in my garden. At first they were not at all sure whether the site was desirable or not, flitting about inspecting other possible positions and consulting together before the final choice was made. They shared all duties and were obviously devoted, often perching side

I

by side on the wall. I never heard them voice more than a few notes and these sounded to me like the squeak caused by the turning of a rusty wheel. They were so very timid that I soon felt the nest would never be completed, certainly they would fail to rear a family if disturbed, so I put up a notice forbidding anyone to go along the path which led past their nesting place and forced myself to watch them only through binoculars.

Insects were caught on the wing in the manner of the swallow and swift, the cock carrying several in his beak at a time. For this he had my gratitude; I do not like flies. I have read that a pair will feed their family five hundred and thirty-seven times in a day, beginning at about a quarter to four in the morning and ending just after nine in the evening. I was not able to spare the time to watch persistently enough to make a careful record, but I saw enough to appreciate their unceasing search for food. I only once saw the little cock asleep, roosting on the stump of an old tree near the nest; I watched him wake, stretch, preen himself, and then again begin the inevitable dash after flies.

I shall never forget my delight when one morning I came out of my door to find six young flycatchers sitting on my clothes line with the parents feeding them. Needless to say the line was left undisturbed for their benefit and I saw them repeatedly swinging upon it until they were old enough to seek the branches of an adjacent oak tree, where they were soon occupied in catching their own food.

In the year 1956 I had another great surprise with a flycatcher. Maybe it was the same hen which had nested with me the year before, but on this occasion, strangely enough, I never saw the cock. This nest was built low in a rose tree growing up the south wall of my cottage: to my surprise when the little hen had finished building, I watched her pluck a rose and stick it in the side of the nest. I thought this quite remarkable as it obviously had nothing to do with the formation of the nest and therefore must surely have been solely for a pleasurable decoration. After she had laid her eggs there was a catastrophe, not caused by the grey squirrel which frequents my garden, nor by the chattering, thieving magpies that menace the small birds, nor by any one of my neighbour's three cats, but by a storm which raged for two days and a night, tearing down the rose tree with the little nest and its eggs. Miraculously, however, both nest and contents were preserved intact, wedged between the fork of the rose, with the hen still sitting. Very carefully I lifted the rose tree from the ground; only then did she fly off. I knew I must not leave the tree lying there as then the nest would certainly not survive natural enemies, but I dared not do much tying-up of the rose and only temporarily fixed it. I felt sure that the eggs must be deserted, but my pleasure was great at finding the flycatcher still sitting next morning and five valuable little nestlings all hatched out. I mention this incident because it seemed to me a wonderful example of undaunted devotion on the part of the hen bird.

An extraordinary episode of feeding on the part of flycatchers occurred in an old plum tree where they had built a nest facing west. In the same tree robins had built, but facing north. The flycatcher laid five eggs and was extremely nervous; the robin was not in the least fearful of man and sat unperturbed; these eggs hatched first. Surprisingly, the cock flycatcher proceeded to feed these young ones as if they were his own. The cock robin evidently approved of this helpful neighbour but the hen disapproved and fought the flycatcher; nevertheless, he continued to feed the young robins even to the neglect of his own brood, which were consequently underfed, and only one survived. It was obvious that the cock's instinct to feed the young matured before his own brood appeared; this incident seemed very strange to me.

PIED FLYCATCHER

The pied is a rarer flycatcher and I have been able to observe him only when climbing in the Lake country. I noticed the song first, which had some resemblance to that of the robin, but I found he by no means always voiced his little warble, rather giving three short notes, then descending the scale and making a thin little sound something like that of an old spinet. The pair I saw was near one of the many mountain-streams and the two birds were quite different, the plumage of the male being black and white and that of the female olive-brown, with a whitish throat and breast; perhaps this is one of the kinder gestures of nature as the bird remains inconspicuous among the leaves. I found the nest with some difficulty; it appeared to be almost carelessly made with grasses and roots but it was lined neatly with hair and a few feathers.

14

HOLE AND CORNER

*Starling; wryneck; snow-bunting; stock dove; collared dove;
jackdaw; tree-creeper; hoopoe; redstart; barn owl; little owl;
tawny owl*

STARLING

THE chosen nesting site of starlings is usually a hole in a tree or masonry; they also seek the sanctuary of the church, the danger of the cliff, or the questionable desirability of the drain-pipe. Adventurous by nature, they sometimes have the unfortunate habit of building in a chimney.

The nest is to all appearances a rough construction, but evidently serviceable, and whatever the human may think of it the birds themselves find it satisfactory. As a rule it is built by the cock and composed of straw, grass, roots, or twigs, the hen supplying the lining of feathers, wool, or moss. Both birds are fastidious in keeping it scrupulously clean, even carrying the shells or half-shells of the hatched chicks some distance from the nest in the same manner as the woodpecker. Some say this is done solely to prevent detection of the site.

Among the many wonderful examples of good parenthood, starlings stand high. Both cock and hen are untiring in feeding their voracious and demanding chicks, by flying incessantly to the nest, their beaks crammed with insects. The young continue to impose on the parents when they are perfectly able to fend for themselves, pursuing them and continuously crying for more food.

I once picked up a helpless fledgling, calling loudly for food, from the gutter of a busy street. I took him home and rather to my surprise he thrived with me. At first I did not recognize him, with his dullish grey-brown colouring, as a young starling, but when he grew older his feathers gradually became lustrous with the iridescent sheen which is so beautiful and typical of the adult bird. I once heard the starling spoken of as the 'coster-monger bird', which I thought an amusing description of his somewhat ornate, bespangled plumage.

Except during the nesting season these birds are distinctly communal in their habits, being rarely seen alone. They frequently gather in large flocks and when they alight I have known them to cause very considerable destruction to plantations, often breaking down the younger and more tender branches. In the country I have noticed the shelter of ivy is favoured for roosting. It is interesting to watch them congregate at dusk when they will dart and whirl, shriek and swirl, and very like children become inordinately active at the wrong time, putting off going to bed as long as possible. However, at an apparently given signal, which they know they must obey, their activities suddenly cease, but before they actually settle for the night they indulge in an evening gossip, all evidently having a beakful of news to communicate. I have heard them voicing their late-night-final at a distance of even a mile; this chattering is invariably followed by a sudden, surprising silence; they have gone to roost.

In towns the ledges of buildings are favoured; I should say thousands find their night's lodging in Trafalgar Square, where even the noise of traffic cannot drown their clamorous arguments. As they claim their respective perches they will press close together, heads facing downwards, this position probably being adopted as a defence against frost and rough weather. I am told it was during the winter of 1894 that they first found St James's Park so desirable a territory; since then they have moved to many other places throughout the central area of London, superseding even the pigeons.

An hour before sunrise they rouse and again resume their chatter which the necessity for rest disturbed; when these discussions have sufficed for the time being, they rise together, almost as one body and, after circling, move on to their various activities.

Man often complains about these vast flocks but it should be remembered that starlings are useful, for in addition to quantities of wire-worms from garden and field, twenty larvae of the daddy-long-legs can be caught and consumed by one starling in half an hour, and I have watched them at work, perched on the backs of sheep, feeding on the liver-fluke which is so tiresome a parasite.

If provoked, starlings can be very fierce. I have seen a hawk, while attacking one of their number, beaten up with such vigour that he was compelled to relinquish his prey. Not only are they successful in defending themselves against a hawk, but it has been recorded that a man in Dorset who had been molesting starlings was assailed by a whole flock simultaneously and when they dispersed he was found to have been actually pecked to death.

On the other hand they can be friendly and companionable to man; several people who have succoured injured starlings have found this to be the case. Two starlings somehow became imprisoned by a fall of masonry in a school wall near my home: their frightened and importunate cries drew the attention of children, but by this time the mother bird had evidently given up all hope of being able to set them free; indeed one fledgling had already succumbed, having starved too long. The other survived and thereafter lived in a large cage and proved most entertaining to the family who adopted him. They told me his diet consisted of rusks, bread-and-milk, shredded wheat, caterpillars, plus a drink of water from a dropper; meal-worms also were much appreciated. The cage was cleaned every day but almost immediately this was done he usually elected to bathe, and as starlings' ablutions are very vigorous, cage-cleaning became quite an arduous occupation. When he had attained full plumage he was set free in the conservatory where he strutted over the brick floor with his curious jerky gait, gobbling up the ants with which it was infested. A useful guest indeed and full of entertainment, soon imitating the voices of other birds, even accompanying the daughter of the house when she went shopping, and generally being a merry, sociable, and fearless companion. He lived for eight years, preferring his domestic surroundings to the rather more precarious existence afforded by either street or open country. One morning, for no particular reason that could be discovered, he was found dead, perhaps having come to his appointed hour. The family told me his death had left an unbelievable gap in their lives.

Starlings have many qualities that must interest watchers; they are alert, ceaselessly energetic, gay, and mischievous. Each moment of life appears to be of supreme importance. In their tireless quest for food, they search carefully every available inch of ground. They are also accomplished mimics, often reproducing the notes of many birds; I have heard them voice those of the goldfinch, blackbird, thrush, and peewit.

To discover if the females could recognize their own young, Dr Robert

Carrick, the well-known ornithologist, carefully observed two nests in his garden. While the birds were procuring food he exchanged the fledglings from one nest to the other. In each case, on returning to their respective nests, the hens appeared bewildered but did not enter the nests; then, after some hesitation, each flew to the one which contained her own young, who were fed and cared for and both families successfully reared. Some ornithologists probably regard this experiment as very interesting; my own feeling is that we should not disturb and distress the birds to satisfy a curiosity which avails us little. The birds voice their protest—they can do little else—but some watchers regard this as merely entertaining and pay no heed, continuing with their investigations. I am always a little ashamed that we, who appreciate our own privacy, should allow so little to the feathered creatures.

WRYNECK

Wrynecks, arriving just before the cuckoo, during the first week in April, may thus earn the name sometimes used by country people—*cuckoo's mate* or *cuckoo's messenger*. They have a rather weird, shrill, cry sounding very like *peel-peel-peel* and this is probably responsible for yet another of their names, *peel-bird*.

They are difficult birds to watch, being both shy and elusive; their plumage is unobtrusive. It has a wonderful intricate pattern of pale brown, buff, and white with dark streaks, and a striking erectile crown. They have two toes in front and two behind, like the woodpecker, and in company with that more colourful bird they feed on ants, having the same extensile tongue coated with a sticky mucus. The rapidity with which this is thrust forward and backward is almost incredible.

They choose for their nesting site a cavity in a wall, bank, or tree, and as far as I know never excavate for themselves, neither do they use any nesting material. Once they have chosen a particular site they are very faithful to it and will return season after season if undisturbed. Should the nesting hole be visited during incubation the wryneck twists her neck in that remarkable manner which is responsible for the name; at the same time she ruffles up her feathers and hisses in fierce protest. There is little doubt that this hissing causes the belief that the hole is occupied by a snake and probably accounts for the name *snake-bird* which I have sometimes heard used. Neither fear nor threat of danger will ever induce the hen to desert her eggs, but if one should be taken she will lay another to replace the loss; she produces prolifically, laying eight to twelve of her white eggs in one clutch.

It is strange that the wryneck is disappearing and becoming one of our rarest British birds. There seems no apparent explanation, as modern mechanized methods of agriculture do not interfere with his existence, neither, as far as I know, does the disappearance of hedgerows and verges.

I have been able to observe them at all closely only since I had a cottage in Sussex. I was delighted when a pair built in my old wall and I was able to watch some of the varying contortions of which they are capable. Their twists, turns, and writhings I found fantastic, and probably the reason why the fathers of scientific ornithology called the birds *twisters*. I count the day memorable when I enjoy the sight and sound of this bird with such peculiar characteristics.

SNOW-BUNTING

The snow-bunting's plumage changes with the season and that is perhaps why he is sometimes called *tawny bunting*, for in autumn the upper parts become generally chestnut and the under parts a warm brown. In summer the tawny colouring disappears, the head, breast, and face are white, only the back, middle tail quills, and part of the wing being mostly black; the hen has less white than the male.

The little cock does not help with the brooding of the eggs, but he works hard with the feeding and cheers his wife with song, which helped me to locate the only nest I have ever found. This discovery was made when climbing in the Grampians and I remained watching the pair instead of achieving the climb I had set out to make. The nest was cosily placed in a cranny of rock and built of grass-stalks and moss, lined softly with hair, wool, and feathers. I am told that it is always tucked out of sight in some such place, under a boulder or among stones in screes.

It was obvious the nest I saw was not quite completed, as both birds were running rapidly to and fro over the ground, probably searching for food; occasionally they would pause as if to rest and then it was I noticed their long straight hind claws, more suitable for resting than perching; this seems to be another provision of nature, as trees are very unusual in the localities where these birds are found. When at last I moved, they rose, twisting and turning in the air until assured I was leaving their habitat.

I have heard the snow-bunting sometimes spoken of as *robin of the dreary wilds*. He certainly has the same friendly call as the robin, and the same engaging confidence unless deliberately disturbed; this may be because he has not learnt to fear man. Some watchers say his notes somewhat resemble the trilling or purring of the dunlin; I find them suggestive rather of the linnet's song.

Though these birds are rare with us, an explorer friend of mine told me that thousands may be seen in the arctic regions, from which they migrate only when their food is covered by a great depth of snow. Linnaeus described the birds as the only living creatures seen two thousand feet above the line of perpetual snow in Lapland.

STOCK DOVE

Stock doves are so called because of their habit of nesting in stocks and holes of old timber; they also favour a cliff or rock and occasionally a church tower. Sometimes they will adopt the old nests of other birds and animal burrows.

These doves are smaller than wood pigeons and lack the white on neck and wings. Many regard the plumage as dull, but I find the metallic green on the side of the neck and the warm reddish tinge on the breast feathers particularly attractive, greatly enhancing the slatey-grey plumage.

Like other doves they are affectionate, going about in pairs, never in flocks. Both male and female share in the brooding, yet in spite of their obvious devotion during most of their lives, the male bird, even as the rock-dove, has the strange habit of driving the hen before she lays. He keeps her continually on the move, never letting her settle or rest for a minute except on the nest; perhaps he has a good reason, for she must be more than content when allowed to settle down in peace and undertake her arduous duties of motherhood.

COLLARED DOVE

The collared dove is a close relation of the turtledove. A male was seen and heard in Lincolnshire in August 1952, being first observed when found feeding with the fowls near some labourers' cottages and recognized by a country postman who is a keen amateur ornithologist. Later he was identified by more experienced watchers; a record was taken of his notes which were broadcast in September of the same year. Unfortunately no female came to him, which was not only deplored by ornithologists but must have been sad indeed for the dove himself. I had the good fortune to see this bird. He was about the same size as a stock dove, with beautiful plumage, soft and tender, reminding me of a quiet evening sky with his lovely blush-pink breast. I saw him later feeding quite contentedly with the chickens, but he would not allow the near approach of any human.

JACKDAW

These interesting birds choose a variety of sites, but I would say they prefer a hole or corner for their building. I have seen one of their dome-shaped nests in a holly tree, but usually they choose holes in trees, cliffs, ruins, and church towers.

> There is a bird who by his coat
> And by the hoarseness of his note,
> Might be supposed a crow—
> A great frequenter of the church,
> Where, bishop-like, he finds a perch
> And dormitory too.[1]

There are many records of jackdaws favouring belfries; in the early eighteenth century they chose to build at King's College, Cambridge, and have so continued until the present day. A great nest was recently found in the belfry of Oxenden Church in the Cotswolds, eight feet high and not much less in diameter, a huge network of sticks. Why these birds should expend so much seemingly unnecessary labour on their building remains unknown to the human but they probably have good reason. A friend of mine kept the household for a month or two in kindling-wood gathered from the jackdaw's surplus collection which had fallen down a chimney.

In company with all bird-watchers I have been constantly surprised by some of the places chosen for building sites. I have often wondered why jackdaws should choose a chimney unless from a certain liking for warmth; but do they realize the risk they run by this choice, for they are usually extremely careful to select a chimney that is not actually in use? I noticed

[1] *The Jackdaw of Rheims: Ingoldsby Legends.*

that where all the smoke from the fires of two houses was drawn into a centre stack that had four to six chimney-pots, birds had chosen one from which smoke never issued.

When I was last at Stonehenge I saw that a pair had built in a crevice of one of the great stones. The nest appeared to be almost carelessly formed of sticks piled in a conglomerate heap but with a comfortable lining of wool, hair, bits of fur, and other scraps of soft material. If any object is dropped in transmission it is never picked up again. They are very acquisitive birds and secrete all sorts of surprising things in their nests. Not long ago when I was in Cambridge I heard of a good example of this habit, a nest having been found in the Public Gardens containing eighteen dozen labels used for marking plants.

Jackdaws are devoted mates, and before they begin nesting may often be seen sitting together hour after hour apparently supremely content and happy in each other's company. They are monogamous, although they gather in flocks and spend much of their life in community. They are acknowledged to be exceedingly clever birds and imitative, developing early; directly their feathers appear they will start preening and exercising.

Boys are regrettably thoughtless, sometimes even perhaps actively cruel, as regards birds' nests and eggs, but there are exceptions. Only last spring I was called up on the telephone by a boy who had picked up a young jackdaw which had fallen twenty feet from his nest in the guttering of a roof on to the pavement of a busy street in Worthing. The bird was carried safely indoors, where he received first-aid and made a surprising recovery, very soon making himself quite at home. When I saw him he was perched on the foot of the baby's cot, which I was told was his favourite roosting-place. Then I watched him playing hide-and-seek with the children and even taking his food from the same dish as the cat or dog, whichever he favoured at the moment. He was still there when I paid the family a visit some months later.

TREE-CREEPER

The tree-creeper will choose any convenient hollow for his home, crevices in buildings or behind the loose bark of a tree. The nest is cup-shaped and formed with strips of bark, birch, or willow, such as I have seen presented by the cock during his courtship; it is interlaced into a framework wherein are laid dry grass and moss. In watching these birds, I noticed they seem to pause before putting in the lining, which evidently requires much consideration. When this important matter is settled, the hen sets to work unceasingly, seeking the suitable material—feathers, wool, or any soft scraps—on which to lay her eggs.

There is a lovely portion of ground near Washington in Sussex, now mercifully in the hands of the National Trust, where I have watched many of these birds among the beeches; and here I have seen five young ones cluster in a bunch clinging to a tree, all facing upwards, in which position they are fed.

Tree-creepers are some of the most entertaining little birds to watch, whether clinging to the tree which is both home and provision store, building a nest, or seeking food. They use their tails as a strut and always work up the bark of a tree several times so that nothing is missed. The family usually roosts in a crevice; they may even be seen having a catnap during the day, but it is a rare thing to find them actually settled in for the night, though on one memorable occasion I did see a pair tucked up cosily, fast asleep.

HOOPOE

I understand this striking bird invariably favours for nesting the hole-and-corner in a tree or among loose stones. In company with the gorgeously plumaged kingfisher he is among the very few birds whose nest is always filthy, for as a general rule the feathered creation is remarkably scrupulous in this respect.

When alarmed or disturbed the hoopoe emits a fluid which is disagreeably pungent. His oil-glands also exude an offensive odour which may be of protective service, for I am convinced that every part of the body is marvellously contrived for some particular purpose.

Now, alas! the hoopoe is a very rare sight, but once I saw this beautiful bird on a lower slope of the Sussex Downs just above Findon. I shall never forget the breath-taking thrill this gave me; I froze to the point of cramp in order to enjoy every minute of the unusual experience, gazing with admiration at his lovely cinnamon-pink plumage, barred across the wings, back, and tail with black and white. I watched him raise and lower his fan-shaped crest, tipped with black, which gives him so martial an appearance, utterly at variance with his nature for he is obviously very timid. I heard his unusual note 'hoo-poo-pooo' which is doubtless responsible for his name. I have been told he has other cries, including a curious mewing, but this I did not hear.

Though I sought the same locality for several days after, hoping for another glimpse of him, to my great distress I was told that he had been shot and eventually found his way to a case in the local bird-museum. Alas for beauty and rarity, qualities which so often attract the acquisitive eye and lead to capture and slaughter!

To my great delight the hoopoe has been seen again this year at Offington, near Worthing, in a garden which leads on to the golf links. He was first thought to be a jay; then, alighting on the lawn, he began to feed on worms and my friends were able to identify him. I hope very much he may be fortunate enough to escape the museum-case.

REDSTART

Redstarts usually build in some fancied hole or corner, in trees or any odd place, the nest being formed of moss and roots, lined with hair, wool, and feathers. As the birds sometimes take over old nests of the swallow or woodpecker, they may also be called intruders; when they in turn suffer from an unwanted marauder they utilize their gift of ventriloquism in order to distract the invader.

They are very restless birds and continually fan their beautiful chestnut tails, almost as if aware of this special beauty and anxious to display it; the cock invariably uses his tail to advantage during courtship. When the hen is roosting the cock will sing to her; perhaps that is why I have heard his voice most frequently at dusk. This singing to his chosen mate may be to cheer her up, a sort of welcome nightcap or a signal that all is well and that she can sleep without fear.

BARN OWL

The barn owls' nesting material is of the scantiest, a few odd feathers and disgorged pellets. They mainly favour old buildings, barns, church towers, or rocks. They are sometimes called the *screech* or *white* owl, and they certainly do screech as they fly; they also snore and hiss. But I have always thought it strange that they should be called white for only the under parts of the plumage are actually white. The white feathers are, however, clearly seen when the birds are in flight and then they do give the appearance of being white, especially in the dusk. The quaint face is orange-buff with grey, white, and brown markings; it is heart-shaped when the bird is awake but becomes elongated during sleep and round after death.

I have always thought it interesting that the barn owl has one ear apparently longer than the other and have sought the explanation of this. It is said that they have a flap of skin which can be raised and lowered, a kind of ear trumpet, to increase the capacity for receiving sound. The ear itself is entirely hidden by a ring of downy feathers curving inwards and closely set together, which no doubt carries the most minute sounds to the highly-developed brain.

When I was working on a farm in the north, I shared quarters with a family of owls in an adjacent barn, as I wanted to watch these interesting birds with their young. One night when the parents were absent I peeped at the four chicks and noticed the distinct difference in size. The eggs had evidently been laid in pairs and that usually means there has been about a week's interval between the layings. I was able to take one chick in my hand; I think it could have been hatched only about five days for the eyes were not yet open; it had a pinched little face and prominent bill. I had only just time to put it back in the nest before the mother appeared; she knew very well that a chick had been lifted and, seeing how perturbed she was, I thought it wiser to hide myself under the hay.

After a time I saw the father return, obviously for a consultation. Finding all was well with the chicks, there was a little conversation, a puffing out of feathers and stretching of head and neck, after which the pair pressed close together, caressing each other's faces by rubbing cheeks and clicking their bills in evident affection. Finally, with a noise something between a snore and a wheeze, they settled down.

I received two or three nasty wounds in the hand during the time I spent in the barn, for these birds do not welcome curiosity. They were certainly very much aware of my intrusion but though finding it boded them no immediate ill, they were still not completely satisfied as to my intentions and would follow me up the fell-side track when I went for moonlight walks. I watched them flying like white-winged ghosts, dipping behind the trees, skimming over the stubble, making no sound, their down-fringed wings fanning the air, until they gave themselves up to the task of seeking necessary food. When capturing their prey, they would lift up their voices triumphantly.

Some years ago I rented an old house in Buckinghamshire where barn owls had nested for years in a pigeon cot fastened to the house and I was very interested to observe that the eggs were laid at intervals. The hen brooded only the first clutch, when she appeared to do all the sitting and was fed by the male; after the first eggs were hatched, the heat of these young ones hatched out the others. When the weather was cold the old birds lent a hand, otherwise they left practically all the work of the last eggs to the elder chicks. There was a cornfield adjacent and just before dark I used to see the parents suddenly swoop over the corn, evidently to pick up mice who climb up to the ear. I watched this take place until it was quite dark, a mouse being brought to the nest every ten or fifteen minutes.

The white owl is sometimes called *cherubim* because it has a habit of sheltering in churches on ledges or small apertures in the tower. Tennyson was quite right in saying they even favour a belfry:

> Alone and warming his five wits,
> The white owl in the belfry sits.

I remember a pair of owls who made their home in the church tower of Washington—the little downland village at the foot of Chanctonbury. Their ancestors had found sanctuary there for many generations. The particular pair I knew were sadly disturbed by workmen who were executing necessary repairs to the old tower. One of the men employed by the London firm engaged on the restoration managed to secure the female, which he took home with him as a curiosity. This separation of the pair caused the forlorn male inconsolable grief. Every night his lamentations were loud and unceasing and roused the whole village, until finally the parishioners felt some action to be necessary to restore their own peace of mind and body. It was agreed that either the mate must be returned or the bird that was left destroyed. This latter course was regarded as a regrettable solution, as the villagers had a fondness for these birds of the night, who had lived among them for so long.

The two churchwardens therefore actually journeyed to London and sought out the workman who had taken the owl. The bird was found more dead than alive, but nevertheless she was brought back and the reunion was described by the sexton as very affecting and pathetic. After the first chitterings and owl caresses were over, each day brought an improvement, not only in their spirits but also in their health and it was not long before they had contentedly resumed life in the old quarters and peace once more reigned in the village.

Even in brass the owl has managed to find his way into church. There is a lectern at Bigbury in Devon in the form of an owl, chosen presumably for the wisdom with which he is credited.

All owls are to me mysterious and I can understand the fact that many superstitions have existed concerning them. They were supposed to possess magical powers, some of value, some embarrassing: it was thought that the heart, if carried into battle, inspired valour and averted danger but if laid on the left breast of a sleeping woman, caused her to divulge her secrets.

LITTLE OWL

This bird is the smallest of the owls and has a somewhat glowering aspect. He came originally from Italy and ornithologists agree that he was brought to this country by Lord Lilford in the nineteenth century. I have myself seen him only in the north and then noticed that he appeared to prefer the day, often sunning himself on an old post or a bit of dead wood. I remember that this was the bird the Greeks honoured by having his image stamped on their silver coins: no doubt the little owl, if consulted, would prefer safer obscurity.

His nesting material is negligible and he seeks a site in trees or holes in buildings and has even been known to choose a shelter among piles of wood. Only one brood is raised each year, the female incubating for twentyeight days.

When the parents arrive at the nest to feed their young it is interesting to watch them alight. Their tails act as brakes, the wings are thrust forward, and as they feed they hang on to the bark of the tree or crannies in the building with their talons, their wings extended and constantly flapping. Both parents and young shut their eyes during this process, presumably to prevent damage to the eyes by beaks. It is curious that the food

Barn Owl at nest with young in a derelict windmill

Tawny and I

brought to the nest seems to change as the night darkens. After dusk they first eat moths, but later the young are fed with earthworms and field-mice. The chicks snuffle and wheeze like young asthmatics.

TAWNY OWL

The tawny owl, also called *brown* or *wood* owl, builds in the hole of a tree, a rock near the ground, even in cliffs, though he frequently chooses an old nest of rooks, crows, or magpies.

These are the only owls who voice the well-known *tu-whit*, to which the mate replies, *tu-whoo* or *hoo-o-hoo-hoo-o*, an unhurried cry, so well expressed by Teresa Hooley in one of her poems as 'a haunting, windy cry'. It is not always realized that the cock and hen have several different notes, some very intimate and low: when the male calls imperatively to the female, it evidently stimulates and thrills her, for no other interest or occupation will prevent her from responding. When the pair fly together on hunting expeditions they often give voice: this is just an expression of an exuberant spirit and pleasure in each other's company, or perhaps the excitement of the hunt.

I had a tawny owl as companion for a year while he was recovering from an injury. This gave me great opportunities to observe my favourite owl at rather special advantage. When I was forced to leave my country cottage he came with me to London. I had a stout branch fixed across the bay window in my flat, where he loved to perch. The hour of midnight he particularly favoured for seeking his food and when I opened the window, off he would go and I could hear him in the little square below. His cry was a welcome change from the wailing of the sirens, to which he gave no heed.

He seemed to sense the admiration I felt for him and in return permitted my rather curious inspection. He would perch on my hand and we looked at each other long and searchingly, while he let me part his soft feathers and rub his ears. He permitted me to stroke his lovely greyish plumage, streaked, mottled, and barred with brown; and I was able to observe the downy surface of his feathers, the fringed leading edge of the wings which ensured his silent undulating flight, his cushioned feet for grasping, and his reversible fourth toe.

I had never before been able to examine a bird of the night in so intimate a fashion and without fear of consequence. I had always heard much

K

about the owl's remarkable eyes, larger and more wonderful than any human's, and I have never ceased to wonder at their amazing telescopic faculty which enables them to focus near and far and to employ both lenses independently. As Tawny's black eyes gazed into mine, I saw they had a feathered fringe and I was able to observe his ability to protect his eyes from the light by drawing over them the blue-white film—his third eyelid, which he used as a sun-blind. In spite of his amazing sight, an owl's eyes are set in front of the head like a human's, whereas it would appear that most birds can look sideways and in front at the same time.

Farmers are certainly never more foolish than when they shoot owls; they do this because they see the bird flying over their chicken-houses and think their poultry is menaced, whereas the owl is actually seeking for rats and mice. One ornithologist records that when 700 pellets from the crop of an owl which had been shot were examined, they contained the remains of 16 bats, 3 rats, 239 mice, 93 voles, and 1,500 shrews. This means that these birds are ridding man of the creatures he regards as pests; yet he rarely appreciates this valuable service.

15

COMMUNITY BUILDERS

I. LAND STICKLAYERS

Heron; crane; snipe; bittern; rook

THERE is no doubt that many birds are fond of community existence, save in the breeding season, and will feed, roost, and face the hazards of life together the greater part of the year. In addition to the multitudes of gulls and diversity of wild fowl that I have seen nesting in communities in various parts of the British Isles, I have recently had an astonishing view of birds roosting in community near London. Though the city has afforded me the amazing sight of starlings and pigeons in their thousands in Trafalgar Square and other of its great places, I had never actually seen the roosting site of gulls and wild fowl which spend their lives in and around the Home Counties.

I had often watched flocks of birds flying in one direction about 3.15 p.m. towards an unknown destination and had been told that they were probably making for the three great reservoirs near Staines, Middlesex, and that approximately one hundred thousand of these gulls and wild fowl gather there every evening. Through the kindliness of the Metropolitan Water Board I was given the privilege of seeing this amazing spectacle at the Queen Mary Reservoir, which is four and a quarter miles round.

My visit was on a bitterly cold afternoon at the end of January but it was one of those rare days on which we enjoyed sunshine and as the sun was setting over the vast expanse of water I watched the birds arrive. I shall never forget the red ball of the sun sinking lower and lower in the sky appearing to shed its life blood over the still waters, staining for a few moments even the plumage of the great companies of feathered life congregating to roost.

Before using my glasses I thought the great patches I saw could not possibly be birds but my glasses showed them as thousands of herring gulls, great and lesser black-backed, black-headed, and common gulls; and there were wild fowl in great variety, mallards, widgeons, shovellers, golden eyes, teals, pintails, tufted ducks, pochards, hundreds of coots, and at least two hundred great-crested grebes. In addition I saw about four goosanders and even a red-breasted merganser, a rare sight on inland waters.

Suddenly one or other of this great living mass of birds would rise, agitation appearing to prevail for no apparent reason; they seemed to be as a cloud rising from the water, only to sink back again to an amazing immobility in exactly the same area as before. These patches of winged life were inexplicably localized and I wondered why each spot was chosen and was left wondering, as with so many things about birds, which perhaps adds to their attraction for curious man.

Even as the sun was lost to sight I remembered my age and that it was cold. It seemed almost impossible that in a few minutes I was outside the gates, back from the community of birds to the equally crowded community of men.

Bird builders in this category apparently take their orders from a chosen leader, for suddenly at some given signal of which we are ignorant the whole flock rises, wheels, and circles, proceeding to the appointed business or destination.

Rooks and crows are proverbial for their habit of community life, and starlings assemble in companies; fieldfares and redwings gather in cold weather to consume the available berries; linnets and finches are often seen in parties; and as goldfinches collect in little groups one hears their musical tinkling when they settle or take off from their favourite thistleheads.

Few have not been thrilled by watching the arrival of the wild fowl, geese, and swans. Flocks of birds pass over my cottage when a blizzard is approaching; there is no question but that they are aware when bad weather is on the way. On the whole birds seem to prefer facing the hazards of migration in company.

Many birds are community builders, though their type of home differs. Herons, cranes, and rooks are sticklayers; common terns favour a mattress of a sort; great skuas a shakedown on the shingle or earth; guillemots and razorbills favour hard beds.

HERON

I have always been rather bewildered by the passage in Kingsley's *Westward Ho!*: 'Lines of tall herons stood dimly in the growing gloom, like white fantastic ghosts . . .' They may take up their static attitude in company but I have never seen them; rather I think of the heron as a solitary bird save in the breeding season. I like Wordsworth's description:

> The moping heron, motionless and stiff
> That on a stone, an apparent sentinel, as if
> To guard the water-lily.

I remember on one occasion in Westmorland when I was taking a long walk I passed a heron, and returning some hours later found him still at the same place in exactly the same attitude, his head sunk on his shoulders, standing in icy cold water. Yet I was aware that this was not because he was bored or weary, but rather because he was a patient and successful fisherman. I have often been amazed at his capacity for utter stillness; surely no one would credit that anything so motionless could be a living menace.

Herons abandon solitude in the breeding season, when they become community-birds building, in company with others of their kind, nearly always on topmost branches. I have known them to build in reeds, but this is very rare. They will sometimes steal from a neighbour's nest if the occupier is not on guard, but if the rightful owner should return, the marauder invariably adopts a very innocent attitude suggesting that he never entertained any dishonest intention.

A friend of mine has a heronry and I have many pleasurable opportunities of watching this bird. I have always thought it remarkable how easily he moves among the twigs and branches, sometimes even clinging upside-down to a branch. His wings serve him well; before taking flight he will cross them over his breast, then spread them again to get a greater impetus before taking off and up. He seems surprisingly able to fly at top speed from any standing site. When in settled flight his legs are extended and his head is drawn back, whereas the majority of birds stretch their necks. The heron soars almost as high as the eagle and perhaps this is his greatest protection. When flying he often utters a harsh cry of *frank, frank* which is no doubt why some country folk call him *Frankie*. The many sounds that come from his beak are entertaining, and he is something of a ventriloquist, as the notes he utters often seem to proceed not from the bird responsible but from some other which the hearer cannot locate.

Most people think of the heron as a large bird, but his body is not so very big, weighing only about three and a half pounds. He is, however, the tallest of British birds, three feet from beak to tail and four and a half feet from one wing-tip to the other; he is the only long-legged bird that builds in trees.

He is one of the fortunate birds blessed with a tiny comb which enables him to clear the slime and fish-scales from his slate-coloured feathers; during the long process of preening he continually dips his bill into the powder which nature has given him in generous supply.[1]

---

[1] THE TOILET OF BIRDS. vide *Ornithology and Other Oddities,* Finn.

'There is, in the first place, the pomatum-pot formed by the oil-gland, almost the only skin-gland, by the way, which birds possess. This is a heart-shaped mass situated on the upper surface of the root of the tail, and ending in a small pimple, often tufted with feathers, and exuding a buttery secretion with which the bird anoints his plumage. . . Everyone must have seen the duck assiduously oiling its hair by rubbing its head on the root of its tail. . . It is absent, or poorly developed, in pigeons and nightjars.

'Nature has been even more sparing in her distribution of another appurtenance of the bird's toilet table—the powder puff, whence the delicate powder which forms a bloom on the plumage of some species is derived. This powder emanates from certain peculiar feathers which disintegrate or rot as they grow, thus producing the powder. . . They may be . . . collected into large patches in definite regions, as on the breast and back of the herons, where they are very conspicuous when the feathers are parted so as to show them. Something of the kind must also exist in many other birds, where it does not seem to have been noticed, as in the pigeons, which are very powdery birds, as any one who has handled them much will testify. But books on birds usually mention these "powder-downs" as restricted to few groups, or to a few isolated members of large families; thus, among our hawks, the harriers have powder-patches, but no others. Powder appears to some extent to replace pomade in birds . . .

'But the greatest luxury of all would appear to be the comb, which is given here and there to the most incongruous birds in a way there is no accounting for. It is situated on the inner edge of the claw of the third toe—and it is with this third toe—the first being, I should remark, the hind toe—that birds always scratch themselves, for some occult reason. . . This serrated claw is found in herons and cormorants, in nightjars and grebes and in a few more isolated cases. In the nightjar it is most perfect and it has been suggested that in their case it is a moustache-comb; but that explanation breaks down, because some of this family, such as the American nighthawk (*Chordeiles popetue*) have no moustache to comb, unlike our bird with its long, straggling bristles round the mouth. The heron's comb is a very good one, coming next to that of the nightjars. The barn owl and its kin, also, are exceptional among the owls in possessing this curious implement, and in their case there seems no possible reason why they alone of their family should be thus gifted.'

He is a patient wooer and though the offering of twigs, which is his obvious proposal, is often at first ignored, he persistently returns with them until, if he proves fortunate, his chosen mate accepts one and returns it with equal ceremony. This exchange means that mating will follow and nest-building begin.

Herons take considerable time before they are completely satisfied with their nest and seem to be continually altering it in some small particular. If any sticks are dropped in the course of building, they are never picked up again; this I have noticed is the case with many sticklayers. The nest when finished, although of immense construction, has the deceptive appearance of being jerry-built, but it withstands wind and rough weather, though sometimes in a storm the eggs may be blown out of it.

The bird lays her second clutch and hatches it while the first young are in the nest. I was interested to find that both male and female continue to observe a ceremonial exchange of courtesies when they take their turn with the brooding of eggs. The hen will rise and stand with crest raised, giving loud calls for her mate's assistance. He then returns and the birds face each other, raise their wings and puff out their breast feathers; the male bows, snapping his bill, as he did during courtship, before taking his turn. Both birds brood with their legs under them; if they are disturbed they will silently leave the nest and watch near by until one or the other gives the all-clear signal.

In 1942 fifty-six heron's nests were counted in Richmond Park, but when I was there recently I could find only one. Herons usually choose spruce, pine, oak, elm, beech, or Spanish chestnut for their nests, but in the heronry at Halkham I was told fifty-two nests had been counted in the ilex trees which are about fifty feet high. A friend told me that at one time there were actually twenty-five nests in one tree in his heronry and these were added to each year; I should think this was a record.

Formerly there must have been many heronries in England; all place names beginning with hern or heron were haunts of this bird. They can boast of an ancient ancestry, fossils having been found that prove their existence millions of years ago.

Man seems to have been fairly considerate to this long-legged, grey fisherman. Henry VIII's particular Company of Archers was granted the special privilege of shooting all birds except the pheasant and heron.

Both were then safe (save from hawking and the longbow) under penalty
of a heavy fine for the theft of a young bird from the nest.

CRANE

To-day we have but occasional crane visitors to Britain, though they
certainly nested here in the sixteenth century, and even as late as the
seventeenth large flocks were seen in Lincolnshire and Cambridgeshire.
I have seen these birds only in the Shetland Isles when I noticed in the
nesting season they were independent, choosing their own nesting sites
in the desirable bog or marsh and living their individual lives with their
chosen mates; but in the migrating season they are certainly community-
birds. The word 'congress' is derived from the Latin *congressus*, 'gather
together like cranes'.

They have evidently a great respect for discipline, and the exact time
for departure is a matter for consultation. A leader is appointed, probably
according to merit and capacity, such as vigorous flight, keen sight, and a
special gift for ways and means. The safety and welfare of the whole flock
depends upon him and naturally the subject is given consideration; with
careful watching it is possible to hear and see such a selection made. The
flock, when migrating, forms into two lines meeting at an angle and they
fly in meticulous order.

SNIPE

The habits of snipe are secret, and when alarmed they crouch amid the
coarse grass in the marshy districts that they favour. Their camouflage is
so perfect that it is almost possible to tread on a bird before he takes flight
—always against the wind.

In courtship both sexes appear equally ardent: the female does not
attempt to hide her feelings of attraction or exhibit any reluctance. Both
birds take their share in the musical wooing, but it is the male who provides the greater thrill to the watcher, orally and visually. His flight is remarkable: ascending at a rapid rate, falling like a parachute, mounting
again, then descending in one clear swoop through the air. During this
descent, when he dives head first, the wind in his tail feathers, the peculiar
drumming sound is heard which some have likened to the bleating of a
goat. This is achieved by both male and female and has been the subject of

much controversy among ornithologists. There are many who contend it is produced by the bird's tail feathers gyrating at a particular angle during his spectacular dive to earth, but the bird does make this strange sound while standing on the ground, when a definite movement may be seen in the throat. So it would seem that as yet the manner in which the drumming is produced remains an unsolved mystery. At one period of my life I worked for a considerable time assisting on a turkey-farm and it interested me that turkeys made something of the same sound with their wings.

There are few watchers who are not intrigued by the drumming, and the exceeding vigilance of snipe when the young are hatched is of equal interest. If they stray too far from the female's ever-watchful eye, she calls them back to her in much the same manner as does a partridge hen. No bird is more sensitive to danger, and when alarmed she will utter a sharp cry of two notes in succession, then rise in zigzag flight which doubtless she feels will baffle the intruder.

BITTERN

There is something mysterious about the bittern which is perhaps accentuated by his lonely habitat. He is, alas! now rare, owing principally to the depredations of collectors and the reclamation of marshlands.

Though I have heard him in our eastern counties I have been able to observe him at close quarters only in Ireland. I had always imagined him as a larger bird but he is actually smaller than the heron. In particular I was struck by his erectile ruff, long green legs, spear-like beak, and what I would describe as a bearded breast.

When alarmed he will at first remain quite motionless, probably realizing that this serves to protect him, and indeed the markings on his plumage make a perfect camouflage; then he will thrust forward the fore-part of his neck and throat towards the threatened danger, but by reason of his protective colouring he still remains practically part of his surroundings.

Though the sexes are alike in plumage, it is only the male who makes the unique, booming love-cry which is usually heard at night. He grunts, gives two or three gasps as if taking in breath, then utters the boom while his whole body vibrates, the head and neck being raised skywards. Sometimes the bird will boom as many as three or five times, always an uneven number. It is strange that this does not seem any louder when heard in close proximity to the bird than from a distance of over a mile.

Although he spends his life in muddy, marshy places he obviously dislikes his feathers getting soiled, for he is a dandy and his elaborate toilet takes the best part of two hours. He first powders and combs his plumage with the serrated edge of his middle toe, then erecting his feathers he dips his beak into his oil supply, and this meticulous process always ends with an assiduous preening.

The booming of the bittern, even as the drumming of the snipe, is a bird-sound that never fails to thrill and for the time at least conveys the harassed spirit to less confined places where solitude reigns over the stretches of the wild and lonely marsh.

ROOK

Those who give any time to studying birds must find the rook both interesting and provocative. They will be left wondering how a rook knows when a certain tree in a rookery is unsafe, though apparently sound, for when he deserts a tree it will almost invariably fall, proving that often this bird knows more than man about trees.

There is a belief in some parts of the country that if rooks desert a rookery for no apparent reason, which they will do sometimes even in the middle of a breeding season, this foretells death to the heir or the downfall of the family. There are certainly many instances of disaster coming to great houses where rooks have deserted.

I once observed rooks occupied in what I imagine was a meeting arranged to decide on a site for a rookery. One bird flew to a group of trees rather in advance of the flock; he was carrying a large twig about eighteen inches long, which might well have been a badge of office and the bird a sort of Prime Minister of the assembly. He took up position on a tree, placing the twig on the branch by his side; then followed discussion which continued for about half an hour, when it was evidently decided that the site was not suitable, for the leader again took up his badge of office, the meeting broke up, and they all departed, presumably to try another more favourable site.

There can be little doubt that the rook community is highly organized and that special birds are assigned to determine whether a tree is fit for occupation. It would seem that if any bird builds without the formal consent of the assembly, he is ostracized and punished, being banished to a tree far from the rookery, though this punishment has a time limit. When the young are hatched the culprit is allowed to return with all rights and privileges restored. They certainly have degrees of punishment, which evidently vary according to what the birds consider the degree of guilt, up to the death penalty. I have seen something that corresponds to our criminal court. Several rooks, who were apparently chosen to decide matters, assembled first. There was a consultation and much cawing, then a quantity of rooks gathered and one unfortunate bird was pushed into the middle of the circle, when more cawing took place. This was followed by dead silence, then suddenly the rooks charged and the bird in the centre was killed. When the gathering dispersed I found no sign of the body: it had been removed.

A friend of mine who lives in Dorset wrote to me of an incident concerning rooks that I think sufficiently interesting to record. The avenue leading to his home was favoured by these birds and one morning in June he was awakened by an unusually loud cawing; upon looking out he saw a circle round a couple who were wrangling over an outsize worm, each trying to wrest it from the other. The clamour increased as one rook after another arrived quickly on the scene and joined the circle; only the two in the centre were silent, fully occupied with the contest. As the pair struggled together, fluttering backwards and forwards till the worm had almost disintegrated, the onlookers' comments rose in crescendo. Then a greyheaded old rook who, unlike the others, had stood quietly on one side of the ring watching the proceedings for several minutes, took a couple of steps forward and uttered a loud resonant 'caw'. There was instant silence. Then the old rook cawed twice again, upon which one of the combatants immediately dropped the worm and the other picked it up and flew off with it unmolested; whereupon the whole gathering dispersed. It would appear that the old bird was accounted of supreme authority and that his judgment was sufficient to settle the dispute.

Although modern ornithologists often discard the findings of past birdwatchers, with perhaps even more careful observation they sometimes return to the original deduction. There can surely be little doubt that rooks do appoint a sentry for many reasons best known to themselves, and it has been recorded that when food is put down he will somehow communicate this fact to the flock. When the rooks have eaten sufficient they will then sometimes bury the remainder, and the following day dig this up and eat it before touching fresh food. Their powerful beaks are most useful in digging into the earth for the insect grubs, and their throat pouch will hold the surplus food for later feeding.

Rooks certainly become attached to certain localities or groups of trees. Many old rookeries which seemed a part of England are disappearing. Those that existed at Gray's Inn, Connaught Square, Kensington Road, and Hyde Park have already gone, but these sites still have attraction for the rooks and occasionally a pair can be seen returning to the old site looking disconsolately around.

A rook's nest is a fairly substantial structure of sticks with an inner foundation of mud lined with grass, moss, and roots, occasionally hair or wool. The birds will remain on the nest if a tree is cut or blown down, refusing to desert their brood, though this would mean safety for themselves.

The young leave the nest before they can fly and perch near it on the topmost branches; when escaping the gun they keep close to their parents even when able to seek their own food. A rook will travel a great distance for his varied diet; I do not think many people realize that upon occasion he even fishes; only this year I saw one flying home with a fish in his beak.

Rooks are loyal mates, faithful to their own nest which they repair year after year. They are also very conservative. In the vane of the Exchange at Newcastle-upon-Tyne a nest was constructed annually for ten consecutive years and was whirled round with every change of wind; it could not have been a comfortable site to say the least of it, but with a rook what was chosen by his forbears is good enough for him.

The male will assiduously feed the female; probably this is to enable her to stay with the eggs or the chicks, for the nest is placed high and exposed to wind and weather and it must be essential that neither eggs nor chicks should get cold. I have only once seen a rook ousted from a nest; this may have been because the parents felt the bird to be a disgraceful freak whom they did not wish to own, it being a pure albino without a speck of black on the plumage; even the legs were white.

Rooks are sociable birds; they breed, feed, play, and have their convocations in company. Virgil wrote:

> Soft then the voice of rooks from indrawn throat,
> Thrice, four times o'er repeated, and full oft
> On their high cradles, by some hidden joy
> Gladdened beyond their wont, in bustling throngs
> Among the leaves they riot; so sweet it is,
> When showers are spent, their own loved nests again
> And tender brood to visit.

One quarter of the year they are fearless of man, but shy and suspicious of him for the other three quarters, as well they may be. Like most creatures they respond to kindness and often too readily learn to trust. A neighbour of mine has a rook that was brought to her, badly injured, his wings having been cut for some unknown reason; so close, in fact, that the feathers grew twisted and the bird will never be able to fly. My friend has had this rook for ten years; he is not caged at all during the day and at night he roosts in the same aviary with two pigeons, who also had been brought to her injured. Perhaps it is adversity which has made the birds such good companions; we also have proof that it is not only birds but humans who find that hard times often form unusual friendships.

A certain Dr J. Watkins Pitchford writes of his pet rook: '. . . to me she [the rook] smiled, looking up into my eyes, never at my legs, hands or body, but eye to eye. When a bird smiles the eyelid is slightly raised and the crest also.' It may be that Dr Watkins Pitchford is right and that this is their manner of smiling. There is no doubt whatever that birds' expressions change, that is, one can tell whether they are pleased, angry, fearful, inquisitive, and so forth.

The wholesale slaughter of rooks is something about which I feel keenly, not only from the humanitarian point of view, but because it exhibits a folly which is little short of disastrous; their minute scrutiny of the earth for grubs probably exceeds any other bird's. The Ministry of Agriculture has publicly stated that the rook is the farmer's friend but, clinging to his ancient beliefs, he still looks upon the bird as a deadly enemy. It has been established that the amount of damage done to crops is not comparable with the good done in decimating harmful insects.

Man is often stupid, but never so stupid as when he attempts to interfere with the balance of nature. It is estimated that if all rooks were destroyed, seven thousand tons of pestilential insects would survive. Anyone with the slightest knowledge must realize the magnitude of the destruction which insects, with their prolific capacity for reproduction, effect. It should be considered that rooks feed nine months out of twelve almost exclusively on grubs, especially wire-worms; surely they may be allowed a few ears of corn in return for all their service. When the crops of rooks are examined, the insects and the quantity of grain noted, is it considered how much more quickly insects are digested than grain ? I often used to watch these birds following the plough after grubs, leaving the freshly sown seeds alone, and it is acknowledged they consume quantities of cockchafer grubs and other pests. In certain parts of France rooks were exterminated and farmers were compelled to reintroduce the birds at great cost, because of the terrific increase of insects, but once scared away it is difficult to get rooks to return.

Rook destruction appears neither just nor reasonable and certainly not what one hopes to find in the British attitude. To allow them to build nests and lay eggs and then inflict upon the parents the torture which the present methods entail is appalling. The massacre of young birds in May is to me a pitiable thing.

F. H. Perry, F.Z.S., writes:

I would rather lose half a loaf of bread than miss the sight of rooks 'bucketing' in a fresh spring sky, or miss hearing their caws competing with church bells on a Sunday morning. Sights and sounds like these make England what it is, an incomparable island. Let us not be made callous by human wars that foster death—but live and let live.

How thoroughly I agree with him!

2. SEA STICKLAYERS
Cormorant; shag

What intense delight there is in watching sea birds, and not necessarily rare specimens: the tide goes out and they are with us, the shore and mudflats yielding vast possibilities of interest. There are the godwits with their long bills and resplendent burnished-chestnut plumage; the grey plovers with their silvery white backs; dunlins, most confiding of birds; sanderlings, twinkling over the ooze, extraordinarily tame; the little terns, strong on the wing; great black-backed gulls in quantities, particularly in the late summer; the quaint, heraldic-like cormorants, standing immobile on posts; turnstones—birds really aptly named—with their trilling note, perhaps just over from their migration; the musical chatter of oyster-catchers, particularly in the late autumn; the twitter of the smaller waders; the dusky-winged black terns, so different in their apparently lazy flight from the other sea birds; skuas; kittiwakes; knots, who arrive in September still possessing their handsome summer plumage of brickish-red on head, neck, and under parts; the little shore larks—these I always look for in the late autumn—with their mottled yellow heads but whose voice I have never heard, though in Lapland I am told they have a musical call-note which gives them there the name of *bell bird*.

Probably everyone who is fond of observing sea birds will at some time or other visit the Farne Islands off the coast of Northumberland to watch the guillemots, kittiwakes, puffins, herring gulls, arctic terns, razorbills, and blackjacks; or will make the journey to Fair Isle, which is a port of call for migrants and a paradise for sea birds. Here puffins, gannets, eiders, and oyster-catchers breed and the great skua may sometimes be seen.

Once in Northumberland I went seven miles up a lighthouse-track in a thirty horse-power haulage tractor belonging to the lighthouse. I had to set my teeth and hang on, the noise was terrific and the bumps beyond description; the track had been repaired with rocks. I was given a plank to sit on but I soon slipped off that and gave myself up to the bumps on the floor. Yet how worth while it was! I could see all along the coastline far out to the north. The cliffs were magnificent, abounding with bird life; puffins up on the grass edges and far below guillemots, razorbills, fulmar petrels, kittiwakes in thousands, looking rather like clouds of moths in the distance. The sea and shore were alive as far as I could see. The puffins were curious and came quite close, solemnly observing the stranger; I found their ways vastly entertaining and left them with regret.

Homer was the first poet to sing of the sea and he loved to speak of the 'long-winged fowl that have their dwelling on the water'. Cries of sea birds are wild and often eerie; they fittingly accompany the favoured habitat. Everyone knows the scream of gulls, the cry of the blackthroated diver, which has been likened to that of a child in distress, and the lovely call of the eider duck which delights and thrills.

Some of the shores and cliffs on which the birds congregate seem almost like great bird clubs. I noticed long-legged gulls, little dunlins, oyster-catchers, sea-pies, and the rock-pipits flying over the sea. It struck me yet again how marvellous it is that all these sea birds should find their way unerringly to their own nest or desired landing place, no matter what the weather, even when the fog is so thick that a human cannot see his hand before his face.

Many community-building sea birds obviously understand that it is possible to live in close proximity with another species, retain their own individuality, and yet avoid war by the simple process of not interfering with each other. Gulls, guillemots, razorbills, and puffins often breed together without any dire consequences.

All sea birds are fascinating to watch, not only because of their beauty of shape and flight, but also for their varying characteristics. Each has a particular manner of wooing, of bringing up young, of relaxing, and taking food. It is the observation of these differences which is so engrossing to the bird-watcher, giving an infinity of pleasure and absorbing interest. It is deplorable that there should still be a flourishing trade in sea birds' eggs and an almost equal demand for their plumage.

CORMORANT

The name cormorant is a corruption of *corvus marinus* (sea-raven). These birds always look to me like dignified, sinister, heraldic, long-necked eagles, rather evil-looking; and I am not surprised that Milton wrote of Satan:

> Thrice up he flew, and on the tree of life,
> The middle tree and highest there that grew,
> Sat like a cormorant.

In company with many other sea birds, they build in colonies and usually favour rocks and cliffs, but unlike the shag they sometimes nest inland and may change their nesting place every two or three years. This may be because the cormorant is so indescribably dirty and smelly that the birds find moving to a clean site desirable. I once examined a cormorant's nest; it was an untidy conglomeration of seaweed, stalks, and sticks, altogether unsavoury.

Bird Rock in Merionethshire is an excellent place to watch cormorants

Heron at nest in oak, fifty-five feet above the ground

James G.

Young Cormorants in nest

nesting and also to listen to their various voicings, but one wants to be fairly active to enjoy this particular resort. It seems rather strange that from here they have no sight of the sea with which one usually associates them; it is six miles away. They certainly have difficulty in acquiring their food, for they have to travel probably as far as the mountain lakes.

These birds are good divers, they spring a few inches into the air and there is scarcely a splash when they disappear head first into the sea, swimming under water. Their food is fish, crustacea, and eels: the young cormorants tickle the parents' throat in order to induce them to bring up half-digested fish.

In China even at the present day fishermen train cormorants to fish from a boat or raft. I have seen ten to a dozen birds at a given signal plunge into the water and it is astonishing to see the size of the fish they bring back grasped in their bills. It was perplexing to me why they returned but I was told this is a matter of training. A piece of leather or a ring was put round the necks of the cormorants to prevent the catch being swallowed.

It has been suggested that hearing plays a great part in catching fish, for these birds can seek their food with equal success in muddy water. After prolonged diving it is necessary to dry their plumage which does not resist water so completely as that of other diving birds. This they do with outstretched wings, usually with the bill open, for long periods at a time; they look almost as if stricken with paralysis when lying with wings outstretched and motionless. I have watched them most continuously on the southern and western coasts of England and have always been struck by their extraordinary power of remaining absolutely immobile for hours until one almost feels them to be carved images and not living birds.

It has always interested me that the cormorant has a bill similar to, though not quite the same as, the parrot's. Near the base of the mandibles there is a transverse hinge which makes the bill flexible and capable of opening wide. The upper part of the beak has its sharp tip curving downward and over the under part, a hook formation which enables him to hold his prey.

I have always been fascinated watching cormorants: there is something about their superb uprising and flight that is breath-taking and their descent is equally spectacular. They roar past in corkscrew fashion to their particular nesting ledge, with the wind rasping their feathers. After their accustomed greeting they are still and silent. When the sun shines on their plumage one sees it is iridescent.

Another distinctive feature shared only with the gannet and pelican is that their external nostril is closed, though vestiges remain in the embryo. This atrophy may be due to the fact that these particular birds are not long enough under water to make use of this organ as do other divers who remain submerged for longer periods.

There can be little doubt that anglers are partly responsible for the decrease of cormorants in certain localities, an award being still offered for the heads of these birds: also the pollution of the sea by oil obviously affects their very existence.

SHAG OR GREEN CORMORANT

The green cormorant or shag is the only other cormorant found in Britain. He has only twelve tail feathers to the common cormorant's fourteen and is a smaller bird; he can be distinguished by his dark green iridescent head, neck, and under parts, also by the fact that he has no white patch on flank or chin. During the first six months of the year, in the breeding season, the mature shag has a noticeable crest, which is raised during any excitement or disturbance.

This bird sometimes breeds in company, sometimes in single pairs, favouring for his residence either cliffs, boulders on the shore, or the roofs of sea caves, and the nest is composed of seaweed, stalks, and sticks. The shag's worst enemy is man, but fortunately the situation of the nest makes it rather difficult for the robber.

To obtain the pre-digested food they need, young shags push their heads so far down the beak of the parent that they almost disappear. The shag always swims low in the water with bill pointing upwards, using his tail not as a rudder but for elevation, his webbed claws propelling him; his legs are flexed and extended both together instead of alternately, as with ducks.

These birds seem to be on very good terms with the fulmar-petrel and it has been reported by a watcher that a shag has actually been seen to guard a fulmar's young while the parents were away. Unlike the common cormorant, who is known to build inland upon occasion, the shag never frequents fresh water, and the two birds are seldom found building in the same area, though they often choose the same stretch of coast.

The worst thing that can happen to a land bird is to be caught by a puff of wind and carried out to sea. The worst thing that can befall a sea bird is to be blown ashore—like a ship that is stranded. Not long ago I saw a shag who had been blown inland during a fierce gale and had landed in the garden of a house in North London. He had injured himself severely on crashing, but he was taken to the Zoo, given every attention and saved. Growing tame during his convalescence, he became a great pet.

I have always thought it strange that man, once he becomes interested enough in a wounded animal or bird, will take an infinity of trouble to preserve life in the very creature he would normally destroy.

3. WEED MATTRESSES

Common gull; herring gull; black-headed gull; great black-backed gull; little gull; kittiwake; gannet; chough

GULLS

During the many months I spent off the east coast sailing, I was intrigued by the endless hours passed by gulls standing on the mud flats, apparently considering or ruminating, perhaps planning their expeditions or solving various problems.

My father's old skipper told me that when the gulls go fishing far out from the shore it is likely to be fair and calm but if they keep close to the rocks and gather in the bays, wind will in all probability rise and clouds form; when they come inland it is usually a sign of rough weather and just before a severe frost they always fly up the rivers and are even seen in our great cities. The flight of gulls is one of the wonders of wings; they are not in the least perturbed by the fury of a gale, their only acknowledgement of its force being to alter the tilt of their wings. They never seem to lose their easy flight save when they drop to the surface of the sea, when it becomes rather more laboured and considered.

Gulls are community birds; they build together, their nests, composed of weeds and sticks, being in close proximity. Some gulleries have existed for centuries, indeed the older the site the better satisfied the birds seem.

The size of their breeding quarters exceeds that of any other bird; though they build on rocks and rocky islands, they also favour the grassy shores of inland waters and moors, nesting on the ground with whatever materials are to hand without any attempt at concealment. They feed not only on the seashore, but follow the plough as it breaks up the stubble, finding food for themselves and doing good work for man.

I sympathize with those who find difficulty in differentiating between the various gulls; certainly the name does not help. The common gull is not common in the accepted sense, and the black-headed gull is brown-headed in summer and white-headed in winter. But there are certain broad differences such as the black mantles the greater and lesser black-backed wear all the year round; others have a grey and white mantle with black tips to their wings. I think winter the most difficult time, when the black-headed gull casts his hood and the common gull his spotted cap, and all alike are white-headed. The best way, I find, is to note the always individual legs, bills, and claws: for instance, the herring gull has a yellow bill with a red spot on the lower mandible and salmon-coloured legs; the black-headed deep-red legs and bill; the common gull has yellowish-green feet and bill.

Many gulls do not get their mature plumage until they are three or four years old; I think them most attractive as piebald little fledglings, covered with down. In comparison with many birds gulls have a long life, some of the larger ones living thirty or forty years.

Recently I saw a gull spinning slowly round and round in the shallow water of an estuary, her head submerged and wings beating spasmodically. I asked a fisherman to wade in and bring the half-drowned bird to the shore, thinking she was in difficulty and something might be done to help her. No injuries could be seen and her wings were free of oil, but she was thin and apparently very old. The man explained her condition to me by saying: 'No good a-trying to do anything, she be bent on drownin' 'erself. Seagulls does that when they be too old to look after theirselves. I've seen it afore.' Certainly when the bird was put back in the water her previous actions were repeated. She grasped a piece of seaweed and kept her head under and remained in that position, wings beating with diminishing force until with a last convulsive flutter they lay silent on the ripples and she was found to be dead. I never knew before that a gull will commit suicide; it seems they sometimes take this course to end a life which has become a burden.

A friend of mine told me of an amusing incident that took place on a golf course. A sea-gull picked up a ball and after carrying it fifty yards nearer the hole, dropped it. The bird then stood watching, as if an interested spectator of the consequences; after a pause he swooped on the other ball and carried that forward for much the same distance. This equalled matters and no doubt the hole was halved and the gull let off with a caution.

These birds certainly do the strangest things. One remarkable incident I watched concerned a small black cat which was creeping up behind gulls on the beach and springing at them, without ever effecting any damage, though doubtless irritating the birds very much. After repeated efforts she evidently grew tired and went to sleep on the sea wall. A gull approached warily, and picking her up by the scruff of the neck carried her out to sea, ducked her several times, and to my amazement returned her to exactly the same place where she had been lying, and then flew off. Can this incident be explained as instinct? I do not think so; it would seem that the bird actually wanted to teach the cat a lesson, which suggests reason!

HERRING GULL

The herring gull is the heaviest, weighing about four pounds. It builds a rather untidy nest of grass and seaweed but always carefully lined with fine grasses and will lay twenty to thirty eggs in a season. The favourite site is a grassy ledge on sea-washed cliffs which, being difficult of access, protect the eggs more or less from the collector.

To see this beautiful gull flying—or perhaps one should say gliding—in the teeth of a strong wind is a wonderful sight: he gives the appearance of having soft grey plumage, whereas in reality his head, breast, and lower parts are snowy white; only his wingtips are black and he is always distinguishable by bill and feet as I have already described.

I have often watched herring gulls following the herring fleet and returning with it, a vast, fluttering, wheeling cloud of silver wings, and I remain amazed at the manner in which they avoid casualties; I have never seen two birds collide.

BLACK-HEADED GULL

The black-headed is the smallest of the common gulls, and is some-times also called the brown-headed, red-legged, or laughing gull, the last name being earned by his peculiar cry. I have heard him called 'sea-crow', owing to the manner in which he follows the plough. His plumage appears pearly grey, but even in winter when the characteristic blackish-brown head becomes white, the conspicuous beak and legs of rich coral make him still easy to identify.

The nest is untidy and usually in marsh or bog: the birds trample down the leaves and sedges, forming a slight depression. It seems pretty certain that the male starts the building but whether he finishes it I am not sure: certain nesting material is added after the eggs are laid, sometimes even after the chicks are hatched. The eggs vary in colour; some are light bluish green, sparingly blotched with umber, while others are olive, buff, or brownish with spots of a darker colour; unfortunately for the gull these eggs are often collected and sold as plovers' eggs.

The female seems to spend a tremendous amount of time begging for food which the male has to provide; sometimes if her mate does not give all she requires, she transfers her pleading to some other more kindly male. She will continue this pleading for food during nest-making and the period of incubation, also after the eggs are hatched. I find it very interest-ing to watch these birds settling into the nest before brooding. They usu-ally begin by standing on the nest, lowering their beaks towards the eggs and gazing upon them steadfastly as if with pride; then they sometimes touch or even shift them with their beaks. These proceedings are accom-panied by something which rather suggests a dance, the first movement of which is slow. One leg is lifted and then the other, the body swaying rhythmically to and fro. Gradually the tempo becomes quicker, accelerat-ing as the movements of a concerto, *andante*, *agitato*, and *presto*: all the time the bird keeps her balance over the nest though each foot is stepping backwards and forwards continually. This formula appears to be a pre-lude to the settling of the breast into the nest. There comes a pause, the feathers of the bird's under parts are now ruffled as she slowly begins to lower herself breast forward on to the eggs, wriggling her body from side to side. Then the legs are drawn into the nest, but the forward movement does not yet cease; her whole body quivers before she finally settles. If, however, any of the three eggs do not lie exactly in their brooding positions against the soft warm flesh in the feathered bed, she will rise and repeat the settling process. This elaborate prelude varies with the character of the bird but I have watched it in this sequence many times and it never fails to intrigue me.

The three patches on the breast from which the feathers have moulted and into which the eggs exactly fit show the wonderful provision of nature for each need, as does the large brooding-patch of the pheasant and domestic hen, both of which birds have to brood a clutch.

The male also has an instinct for brooding and when he feels the time has come for his shift he will remove his mate either by persuasion or force. If the latter proves necessary he puts his claw on her back, squeezing her off the nest; when she returns to take her place again she is equally determined to remove him. It may be that the birds are aware of the necessity for vigilance and realize that neither of them must get overtired and that a certain time off duty is essential.

During the nesting season they often seek their food miles away from the brooding site; at other times I have watched them literally dancing for their dinner. When the tide goes out they will patter over the sand or mud which is thus stirred up; then they peck at the surface which may yield the food desired, though sometimes their energy appears to be fruitless. This activity may serve as relaxation and may give an added interest and excitement to life. I am quite sure birds require interest like every other living creature, otherwise they mope.

When the black-headed gulls go inland to brood, as they sometimes do, they forsake their usual diet of fish and small marine insects and find their food in the fields with the rooks, where they eat a vast quantity of grubs, worms, and young mice.

In the sixteenth and seventeenth centuries, these gulls were commonly supposed to be lapwings, perhaps because of the similarity of their cry; they were at one time called *puet*.

GREAT BLACK-BACKED GULL

He is one of the handsomest and largest of the gulls and is often called 'the parson', perhaps because of his black and white plumage. But his habits certainly do not conform with his clerical appearance. He is not a kindly fellow but rather a robber pirate, never gathering food for himself if it is possible to steal it, and not only does he take from sea birds but also the eggs of grouse and other game birds, quartering the ground like a hawk on his raids.

In flight the bird looks almost snow white, probably because only the back and upper sides are black; head, neck, and under parts being white. When on the wing he has something of the majestic flight of the golden eagle and though he gives the impression of being slow over a long course, he could, with his regular great wing-beats, exceed the speed of the dunlin.

He has a weird screaming cry, changing in character from a dismal sound to something that suggests chattering and laughing, altogether different from the cries of other gulls.

These birds favour marshes for their nest which is composed of stalks, seaweed, grasses, and a few feathers.

LITTLE GULL

I have only seen the little gull on the east coast in winter as these birds do not breed in the British Isles and the sight of them is less common. I noticed them at once because they were so much smaller than the other gulls, their length being no more than about ten to eleven inches. Their grey wings had no black tips but they had the red feet and red-brown bills of their larger cousin, the black-headed gull. Their heads were white, but I understand from a Russian acquaintance that these are black in the breeding season: he told me no one showed any particular interest in these birds in his country where they were frequently to be seen with terns, and he added that the nest was fashioned with any available water plants, rushes, and reeds. He had seen as many as six eggs in a nest though usually but two or three are laid. He could not tell me how long the female incubates and as far as I can gather this does not seem to be known.

I only wish I could have had longer to observe these attractive little gulls but, alas! time disallows much that one would like to do—even as the seasons rule the goings and comings of our migrant birds.

KITTIWAKE

Kittiwakes are community builders, nesting in colonies of many thousands. The site chosen is always as near the sea as safety will permit and the nest is skilfully built of moss and seaweed, plastered together and attached securely to the wild, precipitous cliff, a very necessary precaution as the nest is much larger than the ledge on which it is built. They always seem to choose those cliffs and islands where the sea is roughest and the wind most boisterous but I have noticed that they are wise enough to favour lower rock-ledges than the guillemots and razorbills.

Both male and female incubate and they must have a very strenuous time, for the young never leave their home until they are able to fly, when the parents again immediately seek the sea. These gentle little gulls are very affectionate towards their chicks and it interested me to watch the feeding process. When the young are hungry they tap the bill of the parent, who immediately brings up the fish she has half digested: this is held for a second or two where it can just be seen in the throat and reached by the chick but only two or three quick pecks are allowed before the food is swallowed again. After a minute or two the young bird will again tap, the fish is brought up for the second time, and the same procedure is followed until the chick's hunger is appeased. If disaster should overtake the brood, the parent birds will stand day after day at their empty nest, perhaps finding a certain solace in the vicinity of their home, until the time comes for migration.

The kittiwake is about the same size as the brown-headed gull, but his wings are more pointed and longer in proportion; they tell of far, swift flights out to sea, and his short legs reveal how seldom he comes to shore.

All gulls are beautiful, but perhaps kittiwakes are my favourites. It is impossible to do justice to the beauty of the birds' form or to the tenderness of their grey plumage which is soft and silky as plush. Their lives must be full of adventure and dangerous living, as their feathers often give evidence. These are close set, revealing how well suited the birds are to resist the tide of a wave that may overtake them. Their name suggests their cry which to me has something of the wildness of their favoured life and habitat.

When I was on a walking tour in Cornwall I saw large flocks, looking like wind-driven snow; no doubt the precipitous cliffs there are to their liking. I was surprised that they were not in the least disturbed by my near presence and I was able to approach close to their chicks; they looked like little balls of grey down.

An old fisherman with whom I made friends told me that they always enjoy a leisurely courtship and process of nest-building; they evidently wish to prolong their pleasures.

To watch these birds with their silvery white and grey plumage, feeding on newly turned rich brown earth, in company with rooks and starlings, is a sight worthy of remembrance.

GANNET

No one can mistake this powerful and elegant bird with his dazzling white plumage, biscuit-coloured head and neck, long, blue, sharp bill, and eyes that suggest mother-of-pearl. His magnificent pointed black-tipped wings have a stretch of nearly six feet, and it is always a pleasure to see his strong, steady, effortless flight. It has been noted by several ornithologists that these birds fly in companies of odd numbers. I have myself counted them many times and found this to be an invariable rule; why it should be so nobody seems to know, any more than we know how they make their great flights, even in dense fog. There is so much that remains a mystery and I hope will continue so to be, for when all things are explained life will be dull indeed.

There is a gannetry at Grassholm, Wales, where vast hordes of gannets nest together. I have watched them principally at Bass Rock; perhaps of all places this has given to me the most amazing and unforgettable sight of sea birds in multitudes; some say there are at least five thousand breeding pairs of gannets at the present day; it is almost impossible to walk over the ground on which they are nesting without treading on them. I find the history of this gannetry dates from 1447 and for hundreds of years the birds were regarded as a source of food and highly esteemed for the medicinal qualities of their grease, 'fr it helis many infirmeties, speciallie sik as cumis be gut [gout] and cater [catarrh]'. Their oil was used as a lubricant and their feathers for stuffing pillows and beds; feathers from at least two hundred and forty young gannets were required to make one bed, and several hundredweight were collected annually from the Bass Rock for this purpose.

Their favoured site is always a rocky coast and the nest is rounded by seaweed or turf, the birds often adding other decorations as their fancy dictates. Only one egg is laid each year and the incubation is shared. If disturbed while brooding the bird makes a strange noise which sounds to me like the swish of a scythe. When the female is sitting the male bird shows his affection in a rather rough way, often seizing and shaking the head of his mate, which strangely enough she seems to appreciate. The young birds take three years to mature and to acquire their beautiful plumage; they feed as do the cormorant and shag, by placing their heads well down the throat of the parent. Sometimes gannets will fly a great distance out to sea gathering food for their young (this may be for special delicacies). No one has yet been able to say how they find their fishing grounds and return to their individual nests among the massed community. I thought this accomplishment amazing and never tired of watching their arrival, when they give voice and a type of triumphal display, waving their wings, making deep bows, and clapping their beaks. They often seize each other's bills, seeming to wrestle to and fro, but I do not remember seeing any injury inflicted during the displays and greetings that I witnessed.

When taking off in the search for food the gannet utters a long-drawn sound, which may be just a natural expulsion of air, also possibly denoting pleasure. They fly silently over the sea and it is marvellous to see them dive for a fish which their keen eyes can spy from a great height; they drop upon the sea like an arrow, catching their prey as they rise from beneath it. I have never been able to understand the mentality of those who find amusement in fastening a fish to a board in order to watch the gannet make his wonderful dive and so break his neck, but the savage in man dies hard.

CHOUGH

It is regrettable that these birds are now so rarely seen in England, mainly due to the depredation effected by the habitual human egg collector and thieving jackdaw. The first time I really had the opportunity of observing them was while I was staying in the Isle of Man, when I found several nests in the crevices of the cliffs; they were of moss and sticks, chiefly stems of furze, and lined thickly with wool and hair. I spent much of my time in the island watching these handsome members of the crow tribe. Their flight is magnificent; after a few wing-beats they glide on outstretched pinions, which they manipulate superbly as they land on the nest to feed their importunate young, who incessantly and noisily demand food. They seem to me quite the most attractive of their tribe with their cherry-red legs, curved red beaks, and handsome iridescent black plumage.

After the egg collectors, their great enemies are jackdaws and peregrine falcons, though in some rare instances I have known peregrines nest amicably even on the same cliff as the chough.

4. HARD BEDS

Guillemot; black guillemot; razorbill;
fulmar-petrel

GUILLEMOT

I have seen these birds nesting in the Orkneys and in the Farne Islands in vast numbers; indeed they are the most numerous of all our sea birds, yet can claim as ancestor the great auk, which became extinct a century ago.

The common guillemot uses no nesting material. She lays her one egg on the open ledge, holding it in place between her legs. At first sight it would seem impossible that it should not be knocked off and destroyed should she have to leave it to obtain food, but the long, narrow shape prevents this, for when knocked it revolves. This egg is, I think, very beautiful, being blue-green blotched and lined with blue or black markings.

I have been told that in company with razorbills, guillemots never sleep unless they are about ten miles out at sea; probably they even resent being compelled to lay their one egg on land.

The mother bird does not care to uncover her egg even to permit the male to deliver the food he has secured, for it is exceedingly precious, and perilously placed and, as in the gulleries, nests are in close proximity. The female will refuse to desert her egg, remaining steadfastly guarding it, usually being knocked on the head while the egg is stolen and then she herself is sacrificed, the plumage having some value. I have heard guillemots prefixed by the adjective 'foolish' and they may be in not distrusting man as they should!

Only one fish is brought to the nest at a time and if this is dropped it is never picked up again. I have seen so large a fish delivered that the little guillemot literally stiffened as the food passed down its throat.

Many sea birds become the victims of oil pollution. It is not a rare thing to find guillemots and razorbills on the coast, their plumage covered with thick, heavy oil cast out from tankers at sea. This deplorable practice is prohibited within three miles of the British coast; unfortunately, however, in rough weather large oil-patches are often carried inside the proscribed area.

Those who have seen the pitiable spectacle of an oil-smeared diver or guillemot, rendered helpless, with feathers clogged and clotted with black oil, struggling between land and water until death at last overtakes him, must surely feel that some measures should be taken to remedy this unnecessary torture. Man, war-hardened to horrors inflicted by himself upon others of his kind, is affected little by the fact that sea birds suffer and perish miserably by the hundreds of thousands every year. No doubt if similar disaster overtook his game birds, he might be stirred to action out of consideration for his appetite. As it is, though sometimes sympathy and pity is expressed, no active measures are taken to prevent this needless suffering and the devastating toll of our defenceless fauna. The oil menace seems to me a slur on our civilization and if more people recognized it as such, international co-operation might be achieved to deal with it.

Those who mistakenly believe that the animal and bird creation was put on earth for man's use (though surely aware that it existed millions of years before man appeared) must realize that they fail lamentably to justify their own valuation. If man considers himself 'lord of creation' and is not wholly insensitive, he must surely feel some shame at the manner in which he exercises his stewardship. But shame is not enough; it is too often inactive. Wild life has much to contend with in order to exist, without the ever-increasing menace from the 'lord of creation'.

BLACK GUILLEMOT

The black guillemot lays two eggs, usually on a few chips and shells, in a rock fissure in the lower part of a cliff face or near boulders; though I have seen the bird sitting on her eggs in a hole or turf, but I think this is rare.

These *tysties*, as northerners call them, are handsome birds, black-plumaged in summer save for a patch of pure white on the wing, while the winter plumage is white, barred with black on back and head, the tail and wing-tips remaining blackish.

They seem to be the least sociable of the auk family and less silent both on water and in the air; they indulge in much billing, cooing, and sighing. In company with razorbills they may be seen bowing to each other, and this polite gesture is accompanied by grunts. Their activities are incessant and they certainly seem to indulge in exercises and games, going round and round one another, scuffling and plunging.

During their courtship on the sea they appear to have organized dances and will dip their bills and pivot round each other, uttering a swishing sound over and over again, now and then ending in a sigh. Sometimes the birds swim in pairs, side by side, uttering whining whistles while caressing one another's bills; then they line up, advancing and retiring. The young birds never take part in these water-sports which are continually practised by their elders, even after the arduous business of incubating and feeding; perhaps then they may be a form of relaxation.

When the birds gather in flocks on the sea they float continuously and then their note is very high-pitched, rather like the sound a bat gives but not so harsh.

RAZORBILL

Razorbills are rarely seen on land, the sea being their home. They do not build in quite such close proximity as guillemots and puffins. The solitary egg is usually laid on a ledge or crevice that has some sort of shelter, though the birds use no nesting material. As with the guillemot, the egg is so formed that it does not roll off the ledge, but as it is large and evidently difficult for the bird to cover she frequently has to use a wing as well as her breast for this purpose. It is very rarely that the egg is left unguarded, for the razorbill is a very solicitous mother.

Razorbills show great affection for each other when courting. I have often watched them on a ledge or rock, fondling with their bills; this caressing at times becomes so violent that the two almost appear to be fighting and one or the other often overbalances, but soon returns to continue the courtship. If one of the pair is shot the other seems to lose the power of moving from the spot; whether this is grief, or something of which we have no knowledge, I cannot say.

I have often watched them sitting or standing for long periods with open beaks and raised heads, yawning, or so it appears, then flapping their wings as if to rouse themselves. When they do voice, which is seldom, the sound is like a long, deep snore, a fitting sequence to the yawn.

FULMAR-PETREL

It is a wonderful sight in the spring to see fulmar-petrels nesting on St Kilda among the sea-pinks, more or less undisturbed. This island is said to harbour the largest community of these birds in Britain, and some say the biggest gannet colony in the world. It is to be hoped that one of the islands in the Hebrides will be preserved as a sanctuary of wild life. Fulmars also favour Foula in the Shetland Isles, where thousands breed together, and they may also be seen at Flamborough Head and even in the Isle of Wight.

Many naturalists were interested in the fact that the bird has been prospecting in Cornwall, Devon, and Dorset, but these petrels take a long time before they decide to make a nesting colony. James Fisher tells us that it is often 'about four years before they lay an egg at a place in which they have taken an interest; they will fly up and down the cliffs, alighting on a suitable nesting place, displaying to one another and sitting tight as if they were incubating an egg, during which time they do not breed at all.'

They are again community builders and lay their solitary egg on the ledge of a sea cliff where they nest; otherwise the whole of their life is spent at sea where they sleep and feed, rarely seeking their food in daylight.

Sometimes the birds will scratch out a hollow in the turf or sand but I have never seen any nesting material used. Both sexes take spells in the brooding, which lasts for a period of about six weeks. If anyone disturbs the female when she is sitting she will eject an oily liquid which has a very unpleasant odour. The baby is at first fed by a yellowish fluid which flows from the parents' mouths, but after about nine weeks it is left to fend alone, even as the storm-petrel, the parents again feeling the compelling call of the sea. Also I should think they become weary in well-doing after the six weeks' incubation and long period of feeding their chick.

Unfortunately for these birds the oil they possess was found useful by the inhabitants of St Kilda for various purposes, among them a cure for rheumatism. Both the egg and the flesh of the bird supplied the islanders with food and the oil and feathers helped to pay their rent. Often the birds were killed to plough into the ground for manure; it is estimated that about ten thousand of them were killed each year, either for oil or food or for some other material use. The savage practice of using the birds as candles, the wick being drawn through their oily bodies and set alight, has now ceased.

I have often watched the wonderful flight of fulmars, which I believe excels that of any other sea bird; with but few wing-beats they silently twist and turn, their great wing-power enabling them to manœuvre with more ease than other gulls, and they must assuredly be given the palm for gliding; R.A.F. pilots have studied their flight to advantage.

Many sea birds are difficult for a casual watcher to distinguish, but the fulmar can never be mistaken; he is easily recognized by the curious beak which appears fitted together like a jigsaw. But I find it is the eyes I think of in particular; they have an almost human expression. This may be because they appear to be deep set owing to the dark shading of the plumage in front of them, but these eyes have to me a singular and unique appeal.

5. SHAKEDOWNS

Common tern; roseate tern; great skua; arctic skua

COMMON TERN

I have seen some thousands of these birds nesting together in close proximity at Blakeney Point on the Norfolk coast, yet each pair will unfailingly recognize its own chick and 'scrape'. They are graceful birds with long, fine lines and are much slighter than any other gull.

The tern is very devoted to her chosen love and will mope if she loses him. I have seen her present suggestive courtship gifts such as grass-stalks or weed, suitable for nest-lining, which I think is unusual as it is generally the male who presents. Not until she is ready to sit does the female improve the chosen depression or hollow on the sand or shingle by giving it a rough lining with odd bits which evidently take her fancy. I have seen her mate move round her, displaying with drooping wings, when she is actually on the nest and as she always turns to face him this helps to improve and deepen its saucer-like depression.

ROSEATE TERN

The roseate tern's beauty unfortunately attracts the collector and those who commercialize plumage, and now he is an uncommon visitor to the

Herring Gull at nest

John Markl

Cuckoo being fed by hedge-sparrow

British Isles; I have seen them in any number off the Irish coast where I listened with pleasure to their piping note, so different from the harsher sound of either the common or the arctic tern. The nest was sketchy, as with most sea birds, and was in a natural hollow of the rocky ground; only one brood of this lovely bird is reared but the incubation is shared by both sexes. I found it a wonderful sight to watch the bird with wings outstretched and long white streamers of the tail flying, bringing food to the two chicks, who looked up expectantly from the patch of practically bare rock they knew as home. I was thrilled by the beauty of the bird's plumage; the soft blush-colour of the under parts, the mantle of light grey, the red legs and feet, the blackish bill tinged with red at the base, and the long white sharply-pointed forked tail, all being so infinitely attractive.

GREAT SKUA

These birds are very often known as *bonxies*; they spend the autumn, winter, and early spring at sea, coming inland to nest in early summer. I have seen them nesting only in the Shetlands and Orkneys; the material they use is very scanty—a few sticks put together on the shingle or in a hollow among heather on open moorland.

It is recorded that in 1878 (when a whale was seen at Foula) the birds started to nest there, and sixty years later ten thousand skuas were using this habitat; though they breed in colonies the nests are not near together. Both parents are very fierce in defence of their eggs and young, and will swoop down on any intruder, sometimes making a rapid dive from about sixty feet. I found it difficult to believe I should not be struck by them but fortunately they always sheered off in time.

The chicks are able to look after themselves at a very early stage and soon escape from the nest, when they quickly seek companions of their own age.

Skuas have the reprehensible habit of thriving on another's labour, taking little or no trouble over their nests and stealing the fish which other birds have gathered; they are persistent pirates, powerful and bold, waylaying their cousins the gulls when these are returning from a hearty meal. The skua's method is to chase the unfortunate gull or tern until, out of sheer fright, he will disgorge his recently swallowed dinner in order to lighten his weight and escape. Then, swift as lightning, the pirate descends

M

and catches the food before it reaches the sea; and he not only thieves an-other bird's dinner but also plunders his neighbour's eggs and young. When I was in Scotland watching the skuas I was disgusted at their method of obtaining food, but then the human method is no more com-mendable, so criticism becomes irrational.

ARCTIC SKUA

The arctic skuas are smaller than the great skua but they choose the same habitat, form much the same nest, and have the same reprehensible habits.

6. DARK HOUSES

Storm-petrel; Manx shearwater; puffin; rock-dove

STORM-PETREL

Storm-petrels are perhaps best known as *Mother Carey's chickens*, 'Mother Carey' being a corruption of *mater cara* (beloved mother). There is a prayer to the Virgin used by mariners when they are threatened by disaster, the opening words of which are 'Beloved Mother . . .' Another name for this petrel is *Little Peter* because of his habit of skimming so close to the sea that it seems as if he is almost walking on the water; he certainly seems able to stand on the crest of a wave, though apparently totally incapable of diving.

These birds are again community builders and their very sketchy nest is fashioned in some cavity on the cliff-side or under a stone; not only do they favour a dark site for their home but whenever on land they will hide behind boulders.

When at sea the birds, as far as I know them, are silent, though at the nest and when bringing food to their young they have various cries. The period of incubation is roughly six weeks but, even as the fulmar-petrel, when the chicks are six days old the parents go back to sea, leaving them to fend for themselves.

They are the smallest sea birds, weighing only about an ounce, and though they look fragile their flight is even more rapid than the swallow's and they ride the roughest seas quite unperturbed. They have been found two thousand miles from land. In my mind there is a kinship between this sea bird and the land storm-thrush; about the same size, they both apparently rejoice in rough weather.

Many sailors think that when storm-petrels are seen, gales and high seas may be expected. I have myself watched these birds come round a ship during a storm, but this is obviously to seek the shelter of leeside; the very facts that they sleep on the surface of the water and that their size and colouring render them almost invisible help to foster the belief. With the advent of dirty weather they rise in a cloud and thus are noted even by the most casual observer.

MANX SHEARWATER

These birds are remarkable in many ways; though they are usually silent during the hours of daylight, at night when walking over their nesting sites I have heard a sort of crooning and, as there is no visible sign of life, this unusual sound, coming from under the earth, is eerie. It is perhaps even more uncanny to hear the birds who have been out to sea coming back to their burrows voicing a blood-curdling cry which goes on until they meet their mates, when it ends in a sort of smothered gurgle that I find almost indescribable, something like a human's mirthless laugh. It is usually answered by the sitting bird. Fraser Darling describes this cry as 'unearthly, cracked, a half-choked scream—the sort of noise you might expect from a tormented, disembodied spirit.'

When there is a moon they rarely come inland; I have seen them in hundreds, assembling on the water, waiting for dark. At first I could not tell what this carpet on the sea could be, until suddenly the birds rose, peeling off the water in a long unbroken wave.

When they return from their fishing expeditions each bird immediately finds his own burrow, which is about three feet long. Here the single egg is laid and is incubated for about seven weeks. Even after it is hatched it is practically ten weeks before the young one is fit to leave the burrow. During these weeks the bird is diligently fed by both parents, the male bird often making fishing expeditions which I am told sometimes cover as much as twelve hundred miles, taking him three or four days to complete. Meanwhile the female must suffer considerably from hunger and anxiety: she must circumvent her enemy, the black-headed gull, so she sits close and quiet on her egg; I have even walked over the burrow without being aware of it. This jealous guarding of the precious egg is responsible for the fact that the bird can even be dug out before she will cease from brooding, particularly during the dangerous hours of daylight.

It was the Manx shearwater who first made me realize that those birds laying a white egg, which is therefore not so well camouflaged by their surroundings, invariably favour some concealed spot in which to lay their treasure. At the end of the long period of incubation and subsequent feeding of young, the parents gradually lessen their vigilant care and at last, probably feeling their duty is accomplished and driven by an overwhelming urge, they return to the sea. The young bird who has been well fed for so long waits expectantly for about a week, when hunger drives him out of the burrow. The young adventurer makes his way, presumably by instinct, to the cliff edge, falls over, dives, and thence onward will know the pleasure and struggle of life in the great waters.

These birds have a wonderful homing instinct: one bird's recorded flight was three thousand seven hundred miles by sea and nine hundred and thirty miles across land, the journey being accomplished in fourteen days.

They walk as little as possible and then clumsily with the help of their wings, in the same manner as the fulmar-petrel, rather as if propelling themselves with the help of an elbow. There is a certain place in Stockholm where the sandstone rock has been worn by their toes and beaks during hundreds of years of laborious climbing to the required taking-off site. They always try to take off from a height, on windless nights usually making their way to a cliff edge in order to become airborne; if they should be unlucky they may be found dead, because they cannot rise.

Their flight is wonderful to watch. Their wings appear not to flap but remain rigid for gliding and when they fold them it is only to sleep or feed.

PUFFIN

This quaint bird is sometimes called *sea parrot* or *bottlenose* but the name I like best is the one for which Linnaeus was responsible, *fratercula* (little brother). Puffins are also often aptly called *clowns of bird life*: their manner of peering from side to side and rather comical movements certainly merit such a description.

I know few birds more amusing to watch; the fact that they can walk in an upright position is one of their outstanding characteristics. This may be because their legs are placed rather farther back than with most birds and therefore they are able to walk upright with less difficulty.

To the bird's unusual posture may be added his remarkable appearance. The large horny beak with a red fleshy rosette on either side is perhaps the most striking feature; red and slate-blue in colour, it is divided by a yellow line. This beak enables him to carry as many as eight to ten fish at a time, always arranged head to tail. The fact that the birds moult part of their beaks during the winter marks them yet again as unique. When the feeding period is over they also shed the horny eyelids which so successfully shield the eyes while the chick is being fed in the dark burrow; nature has elected that these should be discarded as soon as protective eyelids are no longer necessary. Added to all these characteristics are the short orange legs and feet with the curious elongated and curved claw of the hind toe which contribute to the birds' singular appearance.

Their courtship ceremony appears not only of absorbing interest to the pair concerned but also to others of the community, who look on apparently full of curiosity. The two birds stand opposite each other woggling their heads from side to side and rapping each other's beaks. After a time this evidently exhausts the pair, for they puff out their blue-grey cheeks and their mouths are left agape.

They breed in large colonies, honeycombing with their burrows the ground or cliff face. These burrows they will themselves excavate, if need be, though they often prefer to take up their quarters in one already made, refurbishing it to suit their taste and frequently appearing to succeed in keeping on at least tolerant terms with the owners, when the entrance becomes communal. The pair stand upright in this doorway, billing and cooing together for considerable periods during the day. Both male and female take turns at incubating, contented and watchful: if any human should be foolish enough to insert a prying hand woe betide him, for then the tranquil expression on the quaint little face changes, becoming outraged, and the brooding bird will seize the offending finger with a fierce tenacity. Puffins are quite determined that the sanctity of their nests shall not be violated, except by their probably unwilling hosts who, as far as I could observe, were generously permitted the right of entry.

Puffins are not noisy birds, in fact they often open their beaks without uttering a sound; however, an uncanny snoring sometimes proceeds from the burrows when there is no sign of a bird. I like to think this corresponds to a mother's crooning over her baby, probably the time in her life when she is most content.

Young birds do not leave their home till they are fully fledged; there is no waiting about, for they take to the water eagerly and immediately recognize it as both store-house and friend. Many who watch the birds for six months in the year are curious to know what happens to them for the other six and it is generally assumed that after the breeding season they spend the rest of the year at sea; but this is their secret session and apparently not for publication.

I have watched puffins on the north Sutherland coast near Cape Wrath and it is a wonderful sight to see these curious birds among the pink thrift on an early summer's morning; but it is on Lundy Island[1] that I have had the opportunity of more particularly observing them. I was very interested in their accomplishments as divers; when under water they use only their wings, which then seem to serve them well enough but are not so suited for landing, as they are short and the birds are forced to rise in spirals even to reach the cliff top. In actual flight they hold their legs spread behind on either side of the short tail, these apparently acting as rudders.

Skoma is another great puffin metropolis. In the Faroes puffins are netted, killed, and stored for the winter by the islanders: it is said that about half a million birds are killed yearly.

Puffins very rarely come inland save to breed, yet one actually appeared through the open window of a house in Brook Street, London. This unusual visitor arrived in late autumn and was supposed by puzzled ornithologists to have been hatched late, thus failing to join the general exodus, being cut off by rough weather.

ROCK-DOVE

Although rock-doves are non-community builders, they do favour a dark house. I have watched them flying to and from their nest in a crevice or hollow in the roof of a sea cave. They also build in some niche among the rocks if they can find an aperture deep enough to suit them, giving their hard bed a mattress of seaweed, twigs, and grass.

[1] In old Norse the word *lundi* means puffin.

Among the many memories of sea birds that I treasure is the picture of these lovely doves on the grey rocks with the sheen on their blue-grey mantles and under parts, the metallic green and purple neck feathers, strongly barred wings, white rumps so conspicuous in flight, and their attractive little legs.

This dove is only found on rocky parts of our coasts, sometimes in the west of England and Wales, but I have watched them principally in Scotland and Ireland. Though wild, they brought my own home with its homing-pigeons very near to me as they are so similar in appearance.

All the other doves I think of gather in peaceful surroundings, soothing as the soft purring notes they utter, but the rock-dove seeks the wild places; the tempestuous sea does not affright him, he hears in its voice the welcome of home and his valiant little heart beats to the accompaniment of the waves he loves.

7. OUTSIZE BED

ALBATROSS

The albatross is the largest of the petrels. It is amazing to me that these great birds belong to the same family as the little storm-petrel which is only five and a half to six and a half inches long, whereas the wandering albatross has a wing-span of twelve feet. His name is very apt, for he certainly wanders; one of these birds ringed on Kerguelen Land in the South Indian Ocean (also appropriately named Desolation Island) was recaptured at Cape Horn, a journey half way round the world. As far as I can gather all species of albatross repair to remote islands for breeding, where they often nest in large colonies, especially on the islands in the Southern Ocean. I understand they do not build in burrows as other petrels, excepting the fulmar, but construct a mound of mud and grass with a hollow at the top for the egg. The nest is sometimes merely a depression on the ground, often encircled by a trench ranging in size from a few inches to three feet and is used year after year.

I have only seen the albatross flying over the Pacific; to most of us in the ship the sight was memorable and unusual. His flight has been described by many adjectives and all are true, for he is graceful, grand, and majestic, whether gliding over the waves or suddenly shooting aloft to descend again and alight on the surface of the sea. This lordly bird followed us for nearly four days gliding effortlessly on the wind while our ship was doing over ten knots and making a great commotion about it!

The habits of the albatross are very similar to those of the little storm-petrel, both apparently rejoicing in rough weather. It makes no difference to them that clouds are black and threatening, waves mountain high; they apparently delight in the wild solitude of the ocean and are seen far out seeking their food and probably finding a glory in the adventure life affords them, as they never come to land save in the breeding season.

Many still think that the albatross, who rarely touches the water, sleeps in the air, a belief which can be explained by the fact that during the gliding flight the enormous wings are apparently motionless.

The solitary egg is incubated for ten weeks. When hatched, owing to constant care and incessant feeding, the young bird becomes enormously fat. Then the invariable habit of the albatross is to depart, in response to an unconquerable urge for the open sea. The fight for life is strong enough to induce the abandoned offspring to struggle for itself and when the parent birds do return the youngster has become fully fledged, ready to fly. Even then they do not allow any clinging to comfortable security but drive the young bird off, as by this time nature has decreed that another egg should be laid.

At one time the albatross used to be called by sailors *Cape sheep*, no doubt because the birds were sometimes captured to make articles of clothing out of their skins, but they have been largely protected by the superstition so generally held that it is unlucky to shoot them. Coleridge used this belief as the principal theme in *The Ancient Mariner*. As the birds' fossilized bones have been found in Suffolk, the albatross may once have been a British bird.

16

INTRUDERS

Cuckoo; wheatear; stonechat; coal tit; turnstone; peregrine falcon; kestrel; long-eared owl

CUCKOO

THIS intruder-in-chief is apparently without a conscience and never varies in his parasitic habits. There are many other birds such as the peregrine falcon, kestrel, sparrow-hawk, puffin, wheatear, coal tit, and turnstone who also intrude or take advantage of the nests or homes of other birds, even other creatures, but no other so far as I am aware inflicts the rearing of its young upon foster parents.

A friend of mine in British Columbia sent me a verse which I think amusing:

> The cuckoo shows considerable ability
> In evading maternal responsibility
> Although by doing so she renounces
> Her claim to family allowances.

I have heard it stated by a naturalist that the cuckoo does occasionally hatch her own eggs, a female having been seen with a breast destitute of feathers and with young ones following her, but this must have been a very exceptional case. The cuckoo has been known to place her eggs in the nests of not less than sixty different species of bird. Those of the black-bird and thrush are sometimes chosen but the birds most frequently victimized by this arch-intruder are the smaller varieties: reed-warbler, willow-warbler, hedge-sparrow, robin, yellowhammer, chiff-chaff, linnet, woodlark, nightingale, wren, pied wagtail, meadow-pipit, and tree-pipit. I have seen tree-pipits perch on the young cuckoo's head in order to feed him; these little birds are even called by the Welsh people *cuckoo's servants*. The spotted flycatcher is believed to be one of the very few birds to recognize a cuckoo's egg and to get rid of it, but even she does not always succeed.

Cuckoos have feet like parrots, two claws in front and two behind; this may in some degree explain how the bird carries her egg, for carried it must have been when deposited in dome-shaped nests such as those of the wren, willow-warbler, titmouse, and chiff-chaff, where it cannot be laid. Some nests could not possibly bear the weight of a cuckoo, and she must of necessity deposit the egg carefully with her claws. It is probably laid on the bare ground, or on a wide branch; then, flying to the selected nest, she takes out one of the eggs and replaces it with her own. She invariably chooses a moment during the owner's absence. She is never at the nest more than a few seconds, flying off with the stolen egg which she eats.

Surprisingly, the nests chosen by the cuckoo differ in structure and temperature: one being lightly built, with the breezes blowing through it, and it would seem offering but little shelter; another, such as the nest of the wren, is built carefully and lined with wool and feathers, even covered at the top and arched over, with not a breeze piercing it. Again, the yellow wagtail lives in damp places, often among rushes or even in a hole scraped in the moist earth and lined with blades of grass; yet in all these various nests the young cuckoo thrives.

Though none can admire the cuckoo's habits all must feel a certain admiration for the cleverness with which she never fails to choose the insectivorous bird, for the young cuckoo cannot eat seeds; also for the perfect timing with which she lays her eggs during the five days when the foster mother-elect is laying her clutch. If the cuckoo's egg is destroyed by some accident she lays another, depositing it in the same nest.

This bird, whose habits interest and puzzle so many ornithologists, is continually presenting some new problem to the watcher; I find it most intriguing that whatever may be the type of bird in whose nest the cuckoo chooses to deposit her first egg, that same species only will continue to be the one victimized for the rest of the season. On an average twelve to fifteen eggs are laid, though twenty-five have been known, one having been produced every alternate day. The cuckoo has all her work cut out seeking the required nests, but when her eggs are laid and placed successfully she leaves the country.

Sometimes more than one cuckoo's egg is found in a nest but these are certainly from different hens; it is very rare indeed that one hen will deposit two eggs in the same nest;[1] she apparently knows in some mysterious way that not more than one of her offspring can be effectively tended by these small birds. Another perplexing thing about the cuckoo is that she appears to have the capacity of laying an egg—though of a different size—with much the same markings as those in the chosen nest. I have heard this explained by the fact that she may favour the species of bird by which she herself was reared. I have also heard a theory that the cuckoo sometimes actually mates with the female of another species. This is thought by some to be a possible explanation not only of the egg being found in a tiny domed nest, but also of its bearing markings resembling those of the bird in whose nest it is seen. I do not think this a likely explanation, or that a satisfactory one has yet been found.

When the young cuckoo is still sightless and apparently helpless, he uses the hollow in his back, which it would almost seem is specially provided for the ruthless purpose, to oust his foster-parents' legitimate offspring. After manœuvring the unwanted birds or eggs into this hollow, he then rears himself laboriously against the side of the nest, and tips them out. After the first four days the cuckoo seems to lose this convenient hollow in his back, when he becomes occupied solely with an insatiable desire for food.

I have seen the legitimate family lying dead under a nest while the young cuckoo is being continually fed by the seemingly unnatural father and mother. I find this puzzling, as the apparent heartlessness is so unlike the natural habit of birds with their young. I venture a theory that the parents may regard this huge fledgling as a sort of king-bird that they have produced and that it may be pride which makes them devote all their energies to keeping him alive at the expense of the rest of their brood.

Yet another of the strange things that we cannot understand about the cuckoo is that those birds who have submitted to the wanton destruction of their own brood will again return to the same site the following year and

[1] Two cuckoos have been found in the nest of a pied wagtail in Warwickshire. In the ornithological world this was an important event as it had never happened before, at any rate within the memory of bird-watchers, neither had it ever been recorded. The nest was in a crevice at the foot of a very old lock-gate. Attempts were made to raise the gate so as to get easier access to the nest but it was too stiff and rusty to be moved. The discovery was made by a workman who told Eric A. Constable, leading Birmingham ornithologist, who had the bird under observation.

once more submit without protest or any apparent distress to the ejection of their own offspring in order that yet another cuckoo may be reared.

I have always thought there must be some strange mesmeric power about cuckoos because their egg is brooded and the young bird fed not only by the foster-parents but also by other birds in the neighbourhood. I have seen him perched on the top of a fence uttering his everlasting cry for food and a host of small birds, often of quite differing species, bringing their donations and endeavouring to satisfy his voracity. Kay Robinson tells us that he has seen a young cuckoo fed, first by a cock housesparrow, then by pied wagtails, and then by a spotted flycatcher. He seems to be a sort of beloved rascal whom none of the small birds can resist. It is remarkable that none of the chosen foster-parents ever appear alarmed or even surprised by the arrival of this large bird; indeed they would seem to have a certain pride in his welfare and so he is continually fed through the whole summer without any personal effort of his own: they are so busy feeding the alien that they never have a second brood of their own so far as I have seen. Time and energy being more than occupied, the natural instinct for procreation necessarily fades.

There are, however, isolated instances when the cuckoo does not come off best; I have been fortunate enough to see one of these myself. Watching a linnet's nest in which a cuckoo had placed her egg, I found that the cuckoo hatched out one day in advance of the linnets. Owing to five days' stormy and exceptionally wet weather with very cold winds, the hen linnet brooded even more closely than usual. The cuckoo, according to his habit, worked himself under the nestlings in order to eject them but, owing to the elements, he met with an unusual fate. Watching until the hen linnet left her nest for a short space for food, I looked inside to find that the cuckoo, who evidently had not been able to lift the whole of the linnet family, was suffocated, while the linnets were still alive. With mixed feelings of repugnance and satisfaction I removed the cuckoo, leaving the nestlings to their mother, who reared them safely.

The young cuckoo must of necessity be constantly well-nourished as it is essential for him to develop quickly in order to be fit for his migration. Even so it will take place later than that of his unknown parents. He knows nothing of his own species and therefore cannot profit from the sort of communication which doubtless is given in many ways by other birds to

their young. How is this adventurous migration embarked on and successfully effected ? By instinct, magnetic currents, winds? We just don't know.
But we do know that the bird must fly over jungles, desert, and sea, travelling by night and feeding by day, without guide or experience of any kind;
he leaves for Africa or Asia a month or so after the last adult cuckoo has
left us. This is yet another part of the mystery of this strange bird and remains as confounding to us to-day as it was to the ancients. The earliest
mention of a cuckoo that I can find is about 1490 B.C. when it was described by Moses as 'an abomination'. It is noticeable that birds seem
always to have been worthy of interest to man, but according to the period
and outlook of a particular generation, how varied this interest has been!

The American cuckoo has none of the habits which are so reprehensible
in the bird we know so well. Instead it is their cow-bird who is the intruder
and parasite.

WHEATEAR

The wheatear sometimes finds his most desirable residence in a burrow,
often utilizing one for his main roof, sides, and floor. The nest itself is
actually composed of coarse grasses and moss, lined with finer grasses,
feathers, and bits of wool, but it would seem very little trouble is taken
with construction; the birds do occasionally build in the cavity of a stone
wall.

The wheatear is pioneer of the annual migration back to our shores.
Dates collected over a period of many years give him this honour, but by
one day only over the chiff-chaff; the most venturesome have been known
to undertake the perilous journey and reach England by the end of February. The cock arrives first, presumably because he is the stronger flier,
and he is followed about ten days later by the hen. When she is sitting the
male always tries to lure away any intruder, misleading the curious human
by means of his short flights and making a circular return to the nest only
when danger is past.

At all times the birds very quickly take fright, when they will run lightly
over the grass, taking a number of rapid low flights from one spot to another. The flash of their conspicuous white rumps makes them easily re-
cognizable. They never fly high save during migration, but flit restlessly
over the ground, particularly favouring fields left fallow, where they readi-

ly obtain the food they desire; grubs, snails, and insects are consumed, the latter being taken on the wing.

These birds were once very common on the Sussex Downs but they suffered disastrously from being trapped by shepherds and sold for food. The very fact that they so easily take alarm made them all the more ready to run into any trap; a single shepherd has been known to capture eighty-four dozen in a day. The passion for eating wheatears dates from some centuries back, increasing with the growth of coastal towns. The shepherds who were engaged in taking the birds made a substantial increase in their incomes, sometimes as much as fifty pounds a season, catching the birds principally from July to September. In 1880 the farmers began to prohibit the shepherds from catching wheatears, not from any consideration for the bird but because they found that the men became so occupied in catching them that they failed to attend to their work of shepherding.

In the course of one season a certain district in Sussex sent twenty-four thousand wheatears to market; twenty-eight thousand and eighty were caught on the Downs above Eastbourne alone in one year. These birds were mostly lured to their deaths by the making of artificial holes or tunnels, in which were placed horsehair snares. When the birds entered to search for the downland snails and similar food they were only too easily caught.

The many hundreds of these artificially made holes spoilt the grasslands, and this damage in addition to the waste of shepherds' time moved the farmers to stop the wholesale snaring of wheatears. But then the poulterers engaged the services of the ordinary bird-catchers, most of whom came from Brighton slums. Fortunately in 1897 the wheatear was scheduled under the East Sussex Bird Protection Order. Even so to-day there is a sad dearth of these little birds, and as I walk over the Downs I miss their once familiar *weet, weet, weet* and their song, with its notes resembling those of the skylark, which they utter from April to June.

COAL TIT

This bird sometimes uses a mouse-hole or the old nest of another bird, re-upholstering it to his taste, lining it with moss, hair, and down. I found a coal tit's nest for the first time in my garden this year, in a mouse-hole in the rockery, underneath a rock-rose. I should never have seen it had not my Pekinese puppy shown a determined interest, continually nosing and then springing backward. While I was watching him a coal tit flew out and then it was I found the nest. I had to place some wire-netting as a barrage and explain to the disgruntled pup that there was a difference in the human mind between mouse and bird, and though to hunt mouse was allowed, chastisement followed any interference with bird. I was rather surprised that both the cock and the hen were far from shy; they did not appear to resent my presence and came to feed at the bird-table on my verandah with other tits. This may have been because I had fed them all the winter and had become a customary, even a welcome sight; but however hungry, they were clannish always, leaving when birds of other species came to feed. A writer, whose name unfortunately I do not remember, gave an amusing description of the coal tit as 'a bald old gentleman with a skull-cap, rather too small for him, tipped on his nose'. The baldness I do not agree with, though the bird does have light plumage at the back of his head just below his black cap. A common country name for him is *coal head*, and there can be little doubt the bird was originally called a coal tit because of his black head: for this reason I prefer the spelling coal to cole.

TURNSTONE

This is not normally a British nesting bird but I once heard from a watcher, whose veracity is beyond question, that he had found a nest in a puffin's burrow in the Shetlands, so I have placed the bird in this company of easy take, easy make. I feel that the turnstone's choice of locality must have been accidental, for the birds' breeding haunts are in the far northern countries, where they seek shelter for their eggs in a puffin's burrow or perhaps under stones. It is strange that the colder the country the more exposed is the site they choose for laying their eggs; when it would seem the burrow is likely to be of real service it is neglected. This bird has always been one of my favourite waders, perhaps because of his variable notes, sometimes trilling, sometimes liquid, and I like his protesting twitters when the tide comes in and disturbs his snoozes (for he is fond of catnaps). I am also vastly entertained by the manner in which the pair will carefully and methodically turn over stones in search of food.

PEREGRINE FALCON

This bird, king of falcons, is a superb flier and his acrobatics in the air when in gay mood are amazing to watch. In common with the sparrow-hawk and kestrel, peregrines must come into the category of intruders, for they are not above taking advantage of other birds' nests, usually that of the rook or crow, using it as a foundation, though they have their own ideas and generally reshape it to serve their requirements. They also lay their eggs on the ledges of cliffs and I have known them to nest in very unexpected places. A pair I watched with interest at Salisbury had chosen the cathedral spire for their home and were evidently well content.

KESTREL

The kestrel does not hunt in bushes but hovers in the open; indeed he is frequently called the 'windhover'. He fascinates me into watching him with grudging admiration: when he sights his prey he appears to remain rigid in the air for an unconscionable time, though actually his wings vibrate so quickly it is impossible to detect the motion. He appears to anchor, as it were, then turn head to windward—dart forward—anchor again—then dive. And there is something for his dinner.

Whenever I watch the kestrel I remember Julian Grenfell's lines:

> The kestrel hovering by day,
> And the little owls that call by night,
> Bid him be swift and keen as they,
> As keen of ear, as swift of sight.

Though hawks are fierce they are sometimes outwitted, or perhaps I should say bested, by an excessive courage engendered by affection. A personal instance of this was afforded to me. A young flycatcher, owing to some accident, was unable to fly; it had only one eye and a twisted beak—in fact, it was thoroughly crippled. The kestrel-hawk spied it and swooped on the helpless little creature, but the flycatcher's parents darted at the hawk, pecking at the fierce bird's head until he finally made off—valour rewarded.

Whenever I watch these birds I always feel what a cruel thing is this urge for food—one cannot save the life of one creature without starving another. Kestrels are the least harmful of all hawks, at least from the human point of view, feeding chiefly on mice and rodents, and farmers are beginning to look upon them as their friends.

A neighbour of mine rescued an injured kestrel and now, though the bird's wings are fully restored, he still prefers to remain with his human companion. Though usually living in the country, my friend often brings the bird with him when he comes up to see me at my London flat, the kestrel travelling unfettered on his shoulder and seeming to be perfectly content amid the London traffic, indeed, anywhere and everywhere, provided he is with the man he trusts so completely.

Though I can never have the same liking for birds of prey as for other birds, I remember that hawks were held sacred by the Egyptians; the god Ra is often depicted hieroglyphically by a hawk. To me the strangest thing recorded of kestrels is that they were taught to hawk for bats in France at the court of Louis XIII.

Kestrels are often intruders, taking advantage of another's building, but also they favour for nesting sites the crannies in old ruins, towers, lofty trees, or precipitous cliffs. I have observed pairs nesting in the Lake District and at Dovedale in Derbyshire; unlike the sparrow-hawk both sexes incubate the eggs, though most of the work of nest-building—a simple construction of moss and sticks—is undertaken by the industrious female.

It is remarkable that a hawk, one of the wildest of feathered creatures, should so often favour towns. I did not know until I was informed by Ludwig Koch that the German name for kestrel is *turmfalk* (tower-hawk).

London has been many times chosen by these birds. The first record I know of is an interesting one: in 1871 they nested on the top of Nelson's Column. Then there seems to have been a long lapse, anyway as far as authentic records are concerned, though the birds were frequently seen on observation flights. From 1924 onwards, however, pairs chose a variety of sites for their homes. Among these were the Imperial Institute, the Power Station at Greenwich, St Paul's School, the Palace of Westminster, and Dean's Yard. Later, nests were located at St Giles' Cripplegate, the County Hall, the Victoria Tower, Westminster, the roof of Broad Street Station, and Christchurch, Southwark. The last record that I have is from 1952, when a pair of kestrels chose the Savoy Hotel, electing to bring up their family behind the leg of a cherub in a group of statuary a hundred and twenty feet above the pavement.

N

LONG-EARED OWL

These birds always strike me as very weird in appearance, especially when they raise their ear-tufts like horns and follow me with their eyes without moving their bodies. They certainly look very fearsome when bristling their feathers and depressing their ear-tufts—something like an angry cat—and they have the faculty of seeming to push their faces forward, giving them a peculiar look of menace.

It is very rare to see long-eared owls during the day, for they tuck their bodies up in such a way as to form a camouflage which makes them seem to be part of the tree chosen for day-time perching. At such times, though they appear to be asleep, it is evident that one eye and one ear are on the alert, for the slightest sound will arouse them.

They give voice in quite a different way from other owls; to hear their sighing sounds in the pine woods is uncanny—ghosts might well be abroad. The female in particular has a soft moaning call which is very eerie; when hunting, these owls mew like cats, and the chicks if hungry, will hiss.

In spite of their favouring conifers, and although my Sussex garden is bordered with fir trees to the west, I have never yet been honoured by a visit from them. I have therefore had to rely on observations made in Ireland, where I knew a pair who nested in the same place year after year and their children after them.

Long-eared owls will certainly make use of a ready-made open nest in which to lay their eggs. The buildings of the pigeon, crow, heron—even the squirrel's dray—seem to serve them very well, though I have never actually known them to turn out the owners. They are satisfied to take what others have abandoned. I am afraid these owls cannot be given an altogether good character; indeed they are often mobbed and for excellent reasons: they never respect other birds' territory and not only make use of their nests but kill the owners and their young for food.

17

AT WATER SITE

I. DAMP BEDS

Great-crested grebe; little grebe or dabchick; divers; moorhen;
water-rail; coot

FEW things equal the sight and sound of wild fowl or of a drift circling before alighting on the water, when the whole surface of a quiet pool will suddenly become alive with splashings, paddlings, spraying; then, as suddenly, there is silence and the water is still again. There is to me a never-failing thrill in the voicing of dabchicks, as there is in the wild cries of the peewit, curlew, plover, and sandpiper, the drumming of snipe, the booming of bittern, or honking of wild geese as they pass overhead in V-formation; but on the other hand, I cannot appreciate the enjoyment which sportsmen assure me they experience in shooting wild fowl. I have never forgotten as a young girl crouching for hours beside my uncle who was out after wild duck: cold and stiff I listened silently to the sounds of the night. In the light of the moon I caught sight of wings, then came a fluttering, and a thud. I know a sportsman will assert that he cares more for the time and place, the fact that he is pitting his skill, endurance, and energy against wild life; this may be true but to me the sight of dead birds cannot bring an iota of the pleasure that is mine in the sight and sound of living wings or of vigilant bright eyes brooding over a nest.

I have never myself seen water-fowl actually sleeping; one eye always seems well awake, scent, sight, and hearing being particularly sensitive to danger; but they must sleep sometimes and I imagine it is probably in the period before dawn or after sunset. In the evening little groups may often be seen going forth to feed, but they always return with the dawn and in the day they preen and rest. They take a considerable time with their toilet, rubbing their beaks over the oil-glands at the base of the tail and distributing the oil over the plumage as we might brilliantine our hair. It always entertains me to watch how water rolls off the feathers of these birds; should any lodge in the middle of the back, they will turn their heads and sup it up.

GREBES

Although grebes are closely related to divers they have many differences physically and in their habits. Grebes appear to have no tail, though I believe vestiges can be discerned. The breastbone of the grebe is short and wide; that of the diver is long and narrow. The grebes have a varied diet; the divers are almost invariably carnivorous. Unlike the divers and many other birds, the grebes swallow no stones to aid their digestion, but habitually consume their own breast feathers: this may serve to protect the intestines from injury as they also constantly give these feathers to their young.

I have always been interested in the heart-shaped patch of vermilion skin on the head of the young great-crested grebe and suppose this may have been bestowed by nature to help the parents when feeding the chicks and may make it easier for them to recognize and collect their young when straying amongst the reeds.

Grebes will visit the sea only when driven by frost; divers come to freshwater haunts only to breed; and, after the manner of aquatic birds, their toes are fully webbed, while with the grebes this is not the case, each bird having feet adapted to its natural habitat.

GREAT-CRESTED GREBE

The great-crested grebe is a very handsome bird with richly coloured frills and lappets. His head is set in an Eliazbethan ruff which he can spread at will and which is made even more conspicuous by his white eye-stripes and cheeks. The ruthless demands of milliners for his lovely white, satin-like feathers very nearly exterminated him, but since the end of the last century he has been strictly protected during the close season.

No watcher can fail to be struck by the affection and protective instinct shown by the male to his mate. Her safety comes first with him even before that of his prospective family, for if she is being molested he will immediately leave the nest and eggs to attack whatever may threaten her.

I have often watched them both together enjoying relaxation from family cares; they will dive, and as they rise from the water again, their breasts touching, they offer each other titbits.

The nest may appear to the casual observer to be nothing but a lump of water-weed. It is usually built among weeds and sedges on the margin of inland waters or lakes. It is composed of sticks, ivy, water-lily leaves, and aquatic plants procured by diving, all anchored to the favoured position by rush stems. Usually a sheltered spot is chosen, but sometimes nests are found in the middle of a stream held by what appears to be very questionable security; yet though apparently the nest is so perilously placed it continues to hold together, withstanding both weather and water. The birds invariably see that the cup is above water-level.

Both male and female brood, and when either leaves the nest the eggs are covered, sometimes with material taken from the edge. This may be for the purpose of camouflage or to retain the heat of the eggs, perhaps both.

I have often watched their chicks being fed with insects; when they are first born these are put directly into the bill but at a later period the insects are placed temptingly before the young birds on the surface of the water which is very soon regarded by them as their natural habitat. When tired by their early attempts at swimming, they will mount on the back of one of their parents, who raises both legs horizontally to the surface of the water, enabling the young chicks to clamber up more easily and to rest comfortably between the wing-feathers. Sometimes the male will swim up and give food to them when they are being carried by the female. I noticed they were taught to dive by the parents' offering them food, then taking it away and diving with it, thus enticing the chicks to follow. This practice induces a continuous dulcet piping from the young birds, sounding rather like the jingle of distant bells, but probably denoting remonstrance. At night they scramble back home and snuggle under their mother's breast so that they keep quite dry.

The nest demands continual care, otherwise it would soon become saturated, and every day one may see the mother bird occupied in giving it the required attention. I have seen the most stalwart of the brood help in the collecting of the material needed. By the time the nest actually subsides the young are able to sleep on the water with their parents.

To me the flight of grebes is most memorable when, in the fading light, they fly in a straight line like a streak of silver against the darkening sky.

LITTLE GREBE OR DABCHICK

Dabchicks are great favourites of mine and these squat little divers must surely induce at least a smile on the face of any watcher. If danger threatens they dive immediately; in the twinkling of an eye they disappear, leaving hardly a ripple on the water and coming to the surface some distance away.

Julian Huxley thinks birds deal with jealousy, which it is quite obvious they experience, in an amusing and satisfactory way. It seems that when the female does not respond to the male's demonstrations of affection he will go off in search of another. He is not unfaithful but wishes to have relaxation. When he finds a responsive hen, he begins a certain amount of display; then his rightful mate, who has kept one eye open, is immediately roused to action. She dives, and rising under her temporary rival gives her a sharp peck which doubtless acts as a salutary warning. She then wisely approaches her roving lord with no air of injury but with every sign of affection, and conjugal relations are resumed.

Young dabchicks' chubby little bodies of plushy down are very entertaining to watch. When very small they cannot do anything but crawl and use their wings as forelegs; later they scramble on to their mother's back for a ride while she swims about contentedly, which no doubt serves as both a treat and adventure. If their security should be threatened they snuggle under her wing-feathers while she conveys them to a place of safety; when they are not in hiding they keep up a continual bell-like piping which is also given by the chicks of the crested grebe.

Dabchicks are among the birds who do not tolerate greed in their offspring. Almost invariably they will give food to a less importunate bird first and not to the one who squeaks loudest, the feeblest being often allowed to remain with the parents until they hatch another family. Father dabchick fishes very strenuously while mother shows her brood the world, no doubt pointing out its many dangers and delights.

Dabchicks choose inland waters or slow-flowing rivers and streams for their nest. It is built under the shadow of overhanging branches, moored to reed-stems, and composed of leaves, dead weeds, and sticks. Whenever there is any threat of danger, whichever parent is brooding will remain quite still, probably feeling there is safety in this immobility. But alas! I have known these tactics to be in vain and have seen the bird shot on the nest, protecting eggs and young to the last. Occasionally I have seen these birds employ another method to mislead an enemy; with lightning movements they will collect beakfuls of weeds and cover their eggs, then leave the nest until the danger is over.

London parks give the resident and visitor interested in water-fowl plenty of opportunity to observe them, and the dabchicks play no small part in affording entertainment; their note is easily distinguishable from the many other cries and calls, suggesting, in a quieter degree, the whinny or neigh of a horse. Their food being insects, crustaceans, and small fish, they do not benefit by the liberal dole of bread bestowed by the public. Never being quite at home out of water these smallest of the grebes cannot seek their living ashore and have to migrate in winter to avoid being frozen out; in other respects this merry, plucky little diver prospers well enough and adapts himself to circumstances.

I have mentioned only the two grebes I know best and who are resident with us. The black-necked, the red-necked, and the Slavonian grebe are more uncommon visitors, though regular transit migrants. The black-necked is most like the dabchick and has the same small, squat appearance, with no horns or tufts on the crown. In the breeding season he has golden plumes on the side of his head over the ears, but in winter these head-adornments are lost. The red-necked are next in size to the great-crested; they lose their crest-tufts and the red on the neck in winter. The Slavonian has a short frill and golden horns or ear-tufts which he also loses in winter. The pied-bill grebe I have seen in the United States where he is more often called the *hole-diver*. I was very interested to find that the nest was not anchored but rose and fell in the water. When the chicks were hatched they climbed on the mother's back and were brooded under her wings. If disturbed she clamped down her wings upon them, carrying them off to the shelter of the undergrowth or brush.

DIVERS

Two members of this family nest in Britain, the black-throated and the red-throated. They favour desolate and remote places for breeding, particularly the northern islands, and it is here that I have seen their nests, which are little more than a depression made with negligible building material. The site is usually within a foot or two of a loch; the red-throated chooses a smaller loch and fishes in salt water, while the black-throated prefers a deeper and larger loch and fishes in fresh water.

Both these birds are wonderfully faithful, sharing the incubation of their two eggs and later feeding and caring for the chicks, which they very often carry on their backs. It is obvious that they choose the position of their nests so that when the sitting bird is disturbed she can slip down into the water and dive, sometimes only reappearing two hundred yards distant; my intrusion has often caused this manœuvre to take place.

They have a wonderful mastery of the water; even the young can dive almost directly they are hatched; also they are expert swimmers under water, their streamlined shape probably making this easier. They swim low, neck awash, turning from side to side, and when alarmed dip their bills repeatedly in the water; their legs are set far back which makes walking on land very difficult.

The plumage of both divers is at once remarkable and distinctive. I find the black-throated more outstanding; the head looks like soft grey rubber, eyes wine-red, wings black, covered with white lines, streaks, dots, squares, and oblongs, and the breast white with lines of black curving from the throat—a lovely bird indeed.

The red-throated diver is a more northerly bird and smaller; on the front of his neck he has a large orange-coloured patch and he voices a peculiar hoarse moan, but when flying he barks repeatedly. Alas! I have often seen him coming into Pagham Harbour, Sussex, suffering from the effects of oil-discharge. In this age of scientific discovery surely some method of dealing with the matter could be found, for it causes indescribable torture to all sea birds.

MOORHEN

Moorhens, also called *mere-hens* or *pond-hens*, have always been favourite birds of mine. The name moorhen does not seem suitable for a bird that is rarely seen on the moor but the word 'moor' is believed to be derived from the Anglo-Saxon *mor* meaning a bog or morass and this is probably the reason they were so named; they undoubtedly favour damp beds.

I should say they pair for life but it is difficult to be sure; they certainly always remain together. I have heard them described as shy, modest, retiring, although I have not found this invariably to be true. There is something unusual in their appearance with their shiny dark plumage, almost black, white jagged line on the flanks and under the tail, crimson bill with yellow tip, green legs, and exceedingly long toes. I find these compact, rather spruce, little birds most intriguing and have enjoyed special opportunities of watching them at close quarters, for year after year moorhens have built among the iris surrounding my pond and it seems not unlikely that the knowledge of a desirable nesting place has been somehow or other handed down from one generation to another. They never seem quite satisfied with their building for they are indefatigable in their efforts at improvement, the continual alteration and reconstruction going on even through the incubation period and after the chicks appear. The nest is compact and about the size of a soup-plate, composed of reeds, sedge, and other water-plants. Sometimes more than one is built, and that not chosen for the actual incubating is often used later by the young ones for shelter. Or again, I have seen the chicks hatched in one nest, and after about three days the cock building a second, obviously for the nursery. In the actual brooding-nest that I was watching on my pond the higher leaves of the sedge were ingeniously bent over so as to conceal it from above, and the cock brought fresh rushes and dry grass every morning; the hen was thus able to sweeten the nest without seeking the necessary material herself.

This year I was surprised to find that two cocks acted as guardians, one evidently the mate, the other probably a male who had lost his partner and for some reason or other was permitted to render his willing service. Moorhens have two broods and I saw that the young ones of the first assisted with the feeding of the second; I presume this practice is usual with moorhens, for Viscount Grey writes:

> apparently it was against the rules for the young ones to receive food from a parent at first hand, for when a parent did put food directly into the beak of a July bird, one of the May birds at once ran up, took the bread out of the beak of the infant bird and then replaced it.

I find it of absorbing interest to note the parents giving instructions to the young birds as to when they may be active and voice or when they must remain still; they will almost invariably obey orders upon the instant. I have seen them become absolutely frozen. There is something baffling about the pre-natal obedience of the young, which in some way exists in the chicks when still in the eggshell, for as they are chipping their way out of the egg they will stop immediately mother gives a warning cry, which she never fails to do when occasion warrants; even at night it may be heard and there can be no doubt she has sensed danger. The vigilance she exercises in the care of her young must never cease or that ruthless enemy of all moorhens, the water-rail, will certainly seize one of her precious chicks whom she will protect at the risk of her own life, as will most of the feathered tribe.

Moorhens, like many other birds, wisely build their nests to match their surroundings. At Barnwell in Northamptonshire is a house with a moat, and floating on the water used to be a log which drifted as the wind blew, sometimes lying still. The birds decided this was a good place to build and chose a lining of grass which blended with the bank against which the log was lying. A breeze then blew up which induced the log to drift until it rested against an earth bank; the moorhens evidently decided the lining must be changed to harmonize with these new surroundings and superimposed dead leaves on the grass lining; then the wind again drifted the log to another resting-place which necessitated a third lining; yet once more the log was moved by the wind, but the moorhens were not deterred. Whether the hen would ever have been able to settle and lay is problematical, but the owner of the house took pity and made the log fast to the bank, thus enabling the birds to raise their family. This determined preference for a certain site is strange, for there was an islet in the moat which offered eligible nesting spots such as moorhens usually desire.

To illustrate that there is no hard and fast rule about the site birds choose for their nest, I may mention that I once saw moorhens build in a weeping willow in St James's Park at a height of at least twenty feet from the ground. I was not the only observer who was amazed at the birds' approach, which was invariably to flutter up four or five feet and then continue by climbing up the sloping branches to the nest. There can be no doubt that birds have strong likes and dislikes about the particular spot they choose for home, not so very different from the human who will sometimes prefer the slum to the garden suburb, the mean street to the spacious avenue.

Though moorhens usually select a site perilously near the water, they always seem to know, almost by instinct, when floods threaten their home, even as other water-fowl, and they add material to the nest until the eggs are safe from rising water. I have often wondered whether this action is purely instinctive, or dictated by a peculiar sense of premonition (which we lack) enabling birds to forecast weather conditions.

Moorhens have a remarkable trick for self-protection, for when flight does not serve their purpose, they submerge, beak uppermost, seeming to freeze completely; the body, inert, looking lifeless, its plumage blending with the colour of the water, is almost invisible. They seem able to remain under water for some minutes and can be fished out looking like debris. How they are able to achieve this condition, for how long and why, actually shamming death, is something known only to the bird.

It was only recently that I became aware that moorhens eat apples. I was amazed to see them climb up the branches of an adjacent apple tree, or sometimes fly straight into it, and eat quite a large apple in a few minutes. The pair I was watching had incubated two broods, about fifteen young in all, and between them they were responsible for taking quite a large toll from my tree which, of course, I was very willing they should have.

I find these little water-birds entertaining and interesting. They have a most amusing, somewhat mincing gait, almost seeming to walk on tip-toe, and when seen at close quarters their feet appear too large for their bodies, giving the effect of wearing boots. Provided they are undisturbed they will walk slowly, raising their tails at every step, displaying the white under the tail coverts. If alarmed they lower their heads, run rapidly, and then show no white. When swimming they proceed slowly with a bobbing motion of head and neck, the head moving constantly and rhythmically. I very much hope they will always remain faithful to my small sanctuary.

WATER-RAIL

These birds, so feared by the moorhen, build their nests just above water level, and though they are relentless enemies, few will not admit they are good parents. They are more often heard than seen; their clear, eerie cry has been described as a mixture of groan and squeal; in the eastern counties this is called *sharming*.

They are very secretive birds and excessively nervous, which makes them difficult to approach. When alarmed they will conceal themselves among rushes or sedges, being loth to take wing. They are best seen during severe weather, as then herbage is scantier and lack of food often compels them to leave their safer harbourage.

I find their lavender-grey cheeks, necks, and breasts most attractive, while their chestnut backs and wings, spotted and streaked with black, long, lightish-brown legs and feet, and long red bills all harmonize well with the habitat they favour.

It seems to me little short of a miracle that the water-rail, who apparently can hardly fly over a moderate hedge, yet on migration reaches the shores of Africa. The urge of necessity can do much, but this flight is one of the bewildering mysteries I constantly find with birds; perhaps that is why they are invariably intriguing.

COOT

One of the many vivid memories of my old pond with its water-fowl is of the family of nine little coots scattered among the reeds, voicing their continual *qu-eeps*. They very soon visited an adjacent sheet of water which is more open, as coots appear to favour reeds and herbage only during the nesting period and the early days of their chicks.

They usually begin to construct their nest in mid-March; at first the building seems to be undertaken in a rather disinterested, casual manner but as time goes on the birds become more enthusiastic. The nest is well concealed in the bordering vegetation of the pond or lake chosen for the site, which is one that invariably supplies the food they need—the shoots of reeds and water-plants, grain, worms, and small freshwater fish. Occasionally they are destructive to eggs of other water-fowl, and are even said to be responsible for killing ducklings, though they never eat them.

Both male and female will jealously guard the nest and take their turn brooding the eggs. When the chicks first appear, and during the very early period of their lives, they are apparently much more helpless than those of the moorhen. At that time their parents are assiduous in their care, but later they appear to find this constant attention something of a nuisance, or perhaps they feel they have done enough for them and realize that their piping babies have actually become perfectly able to take care of themselves.

The plumage of the adult coot is sooty black with feathers crowded solidly together, white frontal shield and bill, diminutive tail, ruby eyes, dark green legs and feet, with rounded lobes along the side of the toes. Why these should have developed I have never yet been able to discover.

The head of the young bird is in striking contrast to that of its parents, with small vermilion nipple-like projections, similar to those that cover the red wattle of the pheasant. Distributed among these are yellow hair-like feathers which, within a few weeks, disappear and the young birds become even as their parents. There is to me something cosy about the coot: it is a tidy and compact bird, reminding me of a well-cared-for domestic hen.

Their personality does not conform with this description, for they are often called aggressive, snappish, even bad-tempered. It would certainly seem that they are easily irritated; this I think is partly because they are excessively jealous of their chosen territory. I think most would agree that the sound of the coot's voice is always somewhat explosive.

When alarmed they splash the water vigorously, smacking it repeatedly with one or both of their green, lobed feet. Some say this practice is not only one of defence but also employed by them in the courting season.

Coots are difficult to observe at close quarters as they quickly take fright and wing. They obviously cannot rise at once, as they skim the water for some distance before becoming air-borne, when their flight is strong and rapid. Save in the breeding season they are usually seen in flocks, and for this reason, unfortunately for them, they become an easy prey to the wild fowler.

I always think of coots as being as it were the unconscious sentinels among water-fowl and certainly of value to them. The mallard in particular often becomes occupied with pleasuring, and this laxity might well be disastrous to his family if it were not for the vigilance of the coot.

2. DOWN BEDS

Swan; mute swan; whooper; Bewick's swan; swan legends and beliefs; eider duck; shelduck; goldeneye; pintail; teal; mallard or wild duck; domestic duck; wild goose; barnacle goose; white-fronted goose; greylag goose; legends of wild geese; domestic goose

SWAN

There are many water-birds who do not favour damp beds but rather provide a down mattress, often procured from their own breasts, for the comfort of their young. First among such builders I think of swans; the territorial instinct of these birds is very great and they will if necessary fight fiercely to protect their domain. Their dignity, elegance, and beauty are proverbial, and they demonstrate an affection and devotion for their chosen mate and family which is singularly touching.

When three years old, the cob chooses a wife and is ever faithful; he starts courting her in autumn with attentions and caresses until mating in the spring. During the brooding he does long sentry-duty to guard her and this desire for close proximity and evidence of watchful care continues throughout the life of the pair.

The nest is usually one yard across and two feet high; it is the cob who collects the material and the pen who arranges it, presumably to suit her own individual taste.

Until the pen is actually brooding the birds go through delightful cere-monial movements together, and when gliding over the water still keep as close as possible.

At first the cygnets are carried on the back of the pen between her wings. To effect this she will usually stretch one leg behind, the webbed foot being on the surface, while the cygnet climbs on to the foot and then on to the back, the wings being slightly raised to keep it from falling off. Sometimes as many as three or four will be carried at one time in this position. Later, when able to swim, they are conveyed from one spot to another, usually led by the mother with father as rearguard—a lovely spectacle which no doubt appealed to Shakespeare:

> So doth the swan her downy cygnets save,
> Keeping them prisoners underneath her wings.[1]

Swans are usually wonderful parents, but that they sometimes have a favourite among their cygnets is evident; another one may be discredited and treated almost with ferocity. When I was last in Kendal, Westmor-land, I saw an instance of this with a pair who, for some reason known only to themselves, decided to exile one of their family of six. This unfortunate was driven away with determination from the family circle; an attempt was made to protect him by erecting a barricade against the onslaught of his adamant parents, but it was broken down and the young bird again expelled. Though the barrier was then reinforced the parents persisted in this unaccountable decision. I always wondered whether, if the bird

---

[1] I *Henry VI*, v. iii.

lived and grew to maturity, memory would make him harbour any resentment. Perhaps he would wisely withdraw to another stretch of water and found a colony of his own, but I never heard what actually happened to him, neither has there been, as far as I know, any explanation of his parents' behaviour.

There can be no doubt that swans are habitually valiant in defence of their young; in the nesting season the male is particularly dangerous and will attack with bill and wings to protect his pen and cygnets. A well-directed blow from his strong wings may break a man's leg or arm and I have seen an angry bird buckle an iron pail.

I have heard it asserted more than once that swans have little intelligence but I do not see how anyone can make such a statement unless they are very casual observers.

Lady Dunsany told me that at Shoreham village in Kent there is quite a remarkable sight when every day a swan waddles up the little street to the door of the *Rising Sun*. If this is not open he sometimes manages to turn the handle; if he does not succeed he knocks continually and always receives an answer. Whether opening time or not he is admitted, and stretching his long neck over the bar receives the desired nourishment. It seems that, when a cygnet, he was orphaned by a fox and the villagers took pity on him; their hand-feeding was quite satisfactory and in due course he was taken back to the river Durant, but he obviously remembered those good times and those that dispensed them. So far he has marvellously escaped the fox and the menace of the road, for every day when he crosses it cars and buses pull up to allow him safe passage.

Another evidence of their obvious intelligence must be known to many. At Wells in Somerset, swans and their descendants have lived on the moat of the bishop's palace for over one hundred years, always ringing a bell near the drawbridge for their meals. At the beginning of the last war there was only one remaining pair of swans and unfortunately the female lost her mate. The bishop, hearing of a lonely male swan on the canal at Bath, drove over and brought him back in a crate to join the bereaved pen on the palace moat. Happily these two grieving birds consoled each other: the Wells swan quickly taught her new mate to ring the bell and their three cygnets soon learnt to adopt this practice as effectively as their forebears had done.

There are many stories of swans in connection with the saints, notably the touching belief held to be true of St Hugh. But I have already written of saints and birds and bird legends in my book *The Wonder of Wings*.

Swans have always attracted both ornithologists and the ordinary watcher; they enrich our collection of legend and our vision of to-day; they need neither poet, scholar, nor folklore to lend them romance, for no man can see the long skeins pass northward, far and high above the mud flats and crawling tides of some great estuary, without feeling his heart beat faster; nor hear their wild bugles unmoved.

There can be no more thrilling sight than swans in flight formation; they fly at deceptive speed for they appear to be moving leisurely, but the flight is powerful and because of their size and weight they seem little affected by adverse winds. Before swans start on their great flight their heads move up and down almost as if testing air currents, they taxi for some distance before rising, and when actually air-borne they fly in a straight line with strong, even strokes. The whirr of these powerful wings can be heard from the distance of a mile and their wild strange cry is never to be forgotten; once heard the hearer will always long for the sound again. I have seen many of these birds arriving from their long migratory journey back to our shores. As they are then obviously very weary they appear to appoint a relay of sentinels who stand guard while their companions sleep.

Frost may be calamitous for this great water-bird. When I was in Windermere during a very severe winter, a greater part of the lake was frozen over and one morning I found to my distress ten whoopers frozen firmly into the ice, just south of where the ferry-boat crosses. When the high tarns are frozen and there is no open water they sometimes descend to Windermere. For more than two days these swans remained fixed to the ice and it was fortunate for them that a short thaw, lasting but a few hours, set in and freed them. First one, then another, broke loose, but not until all were freed did they take off and the wonderful swan-music float across the bay as they rose in V-formation heading for, I hope, kindlier waters.

I have noticed that swans sometimes spend long periods floating close inshore with their heads tucked under their shoulder feathers; very often this may mean they are weary with the flight, but I am amazed that they should remain motionless so long that ice could form quickly enough to

Great Crested Grebe on nest

Sanctuary

hold them prisoner. I would have thought this was the last catastrophe to befall a visitor from the Arctic regions.

MUTE SWAN

Mute swans are migratory; they favour for habitat Siberia and some parts of Russia, and are often seen in large flocks on the shores of the Caspian Sea. They live in a state of semi-domesticity on our lakes and rivers and, their existence being more placid, they usually attain length of days unknown among their wilder relations. They are easily distinguished from their cousins by a beak of vivid orange-brown, the upper mandible of which has the familiar knob or 'berry' upon its base.

The nest of the mute swan is usually a huge structure of water-weeds and rushes. Unfortunately the pen will allow herself to be pushed off the nest with nothing more than a protesting little hiss. Mute swans are relatively silent and are supposed to utter their cry only at the approach of death. Socrates said that 'good men might well imitate swans, who, perceiving by a secret instinct what gain there is in death, die singing with joy.'

An author who is unknown wrote a delightful verse concerned with this belief:

> The silver swan who living had no note,
> When death approached unlocked her silent throat;
> Leaning her breast against the reedy shore,
> Thus sung her first and last, and sung no more:
> 'Farewell, all joys; O death, come, close mine eyes;
> More geese than swans now live, more fools than wise.'[1]

The Thames swans add to the beauty and interest of our great river and are regarded as good weather-forecasters, for they invariably raise their nests before a storm and there is no doubt that they appear to have a foreknowledge of floods. I am fond of taking a walk to the Round Pond in Kensington Gardens, but I am careful to make it either early or late in the day so that I may watch these lovely birds undisturbed by the mechanical toy boats. I have noticed that they invariably sleep and rest on the water with their left leg over the back: there must be a reason for this that I have never heard explained.

[1] Set to music by Orlando Gibbons 1583–1625.

O

We cannot be certain who first brought this graceful and beautiful bird into England. Some say Julius Caesar was responsible; others assert that Richard Cœur-de-Lion, returning from one of his Crusades, brought the first pair into this country from Cyprus. It is certain that at an early period, even prior to 1186, the bird was regarded as royal property and was under the protection of authorized swan-herds. In the sixteenth century Ticehurst estimates that in the Fenland alone the population of swans totalled 'somewhere in the region of 24,000', belonging to eight hundred registered owners. It is on record that in the time of Elizabeth I there were nine hundred registered swan-marks. Today perhaps the best-known and largest swannery is at Abbotsbury in Dorset where up to a thousand pairs may be seen.

WHOOPER

The whooper is by far the largest bird that visits Britain, weighing from eighteen to over twenty pounds; his expanse of wing is eight feet and his length five feet. While the mute swan holds his neck in an arch, the wild swan, the whooper, holds his erect, and on his bill is a tongue of yellow which extends from the eye to the nostrils, leaving the tip black; the cygnets are the softest brown-grey with flesh-coloured bills.

I have known the bird to breed only in the Orkneys, and the same nest is often used year after year, becoming in the course of time a large erection of earth and weeds with a centre depression for the sitting bird, soft with down and feathers from the breasts of the birds themselves.

It is perhaps remarkable, and gives the human something to consider, that when these wild birds come to our shores and stay for a time with the mute swans, fights are rare: tolerance seems to prevail between visitor and resident, live and let live appears to be the rule in their relationship towards each other.

Alas, that these beautiful birds should ever be destroyed for commercial purposes! I often wonder whether women who wear feathered garments and decorations realize the torture inflicted to obtain them. Beauty, suffering, death: how one wishes these need never be associated!

Those who have ever seen whoopers in flight can never forget the inspiring spectacle or the thrill of their deep-ringing bugle-calls. One evening in Westmorland will always be associated in my mind with these great white birds: the hills were wrapped in snow, glistening with a million jewels. The sunset had been one of the most beautiful I had ever seen; at first rich in glory, then the splendid colours melting and becoming gentle and soft. As I watched I heard what might well have been the baying of a pack of hounds; I soon realized that the strange sound was made by swans circling round the head of the lake trumpeting all the time, then in V-formation setting off towards Rydal. I watched them silhouetted against the marvellous sky, the white string flying across the purple of Loughrigg; and even when they disappeared round the hill I could still hear their music for some minutes. Next day I went to Rydal to look for them but found they had landed on Grasmere; I counted forty-two standing on the ice; some were asleep on one leg, their heads tucked under a wing, others lying down. Two that were evidently appointed sentinels remained alert and continually uttered soft sounds, but when they thought I was getting too near the note became high-pitched, all the heads went up, and the whole white company began talking, obviously discussing the situation. They then moved a few yards farther away, at each step sliding a little, and though their tails steadied them to a certain extent they evidently found it very difficult walking on the ice. When at last they sensed there was no imminent danger, being plainly very exhausted they allowed themselves to relax and sleep. They had probably flown hundreds of miles and come to rest in a place which they felt offered sanctuary, but they were deceived. The serenity which seemed to exist in the still night, the great white hills, and frozen lake was suddenly shattered by a man with a gun, and one of the lovely great birds was shot—sanctuary was violated. I could not get near the savage (for so he seemed to me) before another bird was shot. At last succeeding in scrambling to his side, with strength given by furious indignation, I knocked the gun out of his hand. That I escaped a charge of assault was perhaps proof that the man was either ashamed or even experienced a change of heart.

BEWICK'S SWAN

When I was younger I saw many things without their actually registering in my mind but with the years registration certainly becomes deeper and clearer. So it was that Bewick's swans came to me only in middle age but early enough to store their memory gratefully.

My acquaintance with them began in the Hebrides on a bitterly cold day in winter. The world at the time was to me a bleak place and I sought solitude as a friend, congenial and companionable. On this memorable day I suddenly heard loud strange cries like the honking of wild geese in flight; the sound suited well the time and place, and the mood with which I was obsessed.

Then it was that one of those rare chance meetings occurred that often illuminate my haphazard wanderings. I saw the figure of a man gazing upwards with the intensity I had learned to associate with bird-watchers.

'Geese?' I asked.

'No, Bewick's swans,' he replied.

'I did not think them big enough for swans.'

'They are ten inches smaller than either the whooper or the mute, but their windpipe is of great length and is responsible for their loud trumpet-note which is so arresting.'

'I do not know them at all,' I said, 'but I have always understood they do not nest in this country.'

'That's true,' he replied, 'but when I was in North Russia last year I saw a nest. I was astonished that it was so large, even though I had been told that the birds used it for many years. In the centre of an apparent mass of weeds, turf, and earth, there was a hollow in which were three eggs. Unfortunately I never could find out how long the birds brooded them.'

After we had watched the last of the swans disappear and their honking had faded into the distance, we still ambled along together for a time and my companion took some little trouble to show me where I could watch these swans to the best advantage while in the Hebrides. When I found them I was again impressed by the fact that they were so much smaller than the swans I knew and I noticed that their black and orange bills had no 'berries'; but it was not for size or any special difference in form or plumage that I remember them but rather that they dispelled a dangerously black mood for me and were responsible for a pleasurable chance meeting.

I have always thought ornithologists and all the vast brotherhood of bird-watchers, in company with gardeners, ever ready to share the knowledge that they have acquired and some of the pleasure they have gained thereby. There is a sort of freemasonry with them, they are at once known to each other and recognized as part of the same family. No introduction is necessary but the mutual interest and enjoyment reaped from all those things which are learned outside four walls.

SWAN LEGENDS AND BELIEFS

The oath on the swan is no doubt the survival of swan worship. When in 1304 Edward I was knighted, he swore an oath on two swans decorated by golden nets. Hence probably comes the expression 'I swan' which survives, meaning 'I expect', and the same expression exists in the German: '*Es schwanet mir*'.

In all folklore and legend the swan is prominent. According to the common legend Zeus visited Leda in the form of a swan and from one of her eggs Helen of Troy was born. Greek legend says that the soul of Apollo, the god of music, passed into a swan, which is probably the origin of the swan-song; the swan was the favourite of foam-born Aphrodite. According to Pythagorean fable the souls of all good poets pass into swans: perhaps that is why Ben Jonson calls Shakespeare the 'Swan of Avon', even as Virgil was styled the 'Swan of Mantua', and Homer the 'Swan of Meander'. In Donegal wild swans coming off the sea are thought to be spirits of maidens who were in this life pre-eminently pure, and therefore they are never shot.

It is curious that mediaeval writers who found no difficulty in believing in centaurs and mermaids should have regarded the idea of a black swan as an extravagant impossibility: yet the black swan is common in Australia.

'From troubles of this world I turn to ducks.'

EIDER DUCK

The eider duck's nest may be found on rocks, shingle, a sandhill among herbage, or sometimes in the shelter of a boulder. I discovered to my joy an eider's nest on a cliff edge on the Northumberland coast. I believe this is rather an unusual sight; it was composed of grass and seaweed, made soft and lovely by the grey down which the bird plucks from her own breast. This down is also used for covering the eggs if the sitting bird has to leave for any purpose and it is usually stolen in great quantities for eiderdown quilts. The eider is a devoted mother, sitting on her eggs for weeks without moving for either food or water; the young birds do not remain long in the nest, the parents taking them almost immediately to the sea, and it is a lovely sight to watch the fluffy little chicks paddling along over the stones and rocks to the water.

When I was in the Farne Islands I found many nests round the ruins of St Cuthbert's chapel and no doubt the saint found relaxation and amusement in watching them. The local fishermen still call them St Cuthbert's ducks and they tell me that the birds easily become tame and will even take food from the hand.

Though the general effect of the eider is black and white, on looking closer one sees that the breast is pale rose and that on each side of the neck is a patch of sea-green, while the bill and legs are a dull green. The cry of these birds when in flight is harsh, very different from the soft coo which is voiced when on the water they love.

SHELDUCK

During the courtship of the shelduck the male bows his neck constantly, the female sways hers from side to side with a little clap of her beak each time; her conversation is chiefly purring, while he indulges in piping.

The nest is usually in sandy places near an estuary and is composed of grass and down, again from their own breasts; unfortunately this down is little inferior to that of the eider duck and therefore has become a commercial commodity. Their desirable residence is often found several feet down a burrow, and sometimes they are called *burrow ducks* because they will hollow out a hole to their liking. I have found these birds nesting inland under a gorse bush quite a distance from the coast, and they were extremely clever in their attempts to divert me from the nest; this ingenuity is probably the reason for the bird being called *sly goose* in the Orkneys: the French also use the descriptive term, *tadorne*.

At the first possible moment the young are led to the nearest water. I have actually seen the parents carrying them to the sea on their backs; their urge to do this is so strong that they will even cross a busy main street. There have been many attempts to make these ducks domestic, but they prefer the wild places. If their eggs are taken and hatched under a domestic hen, the ducklings will always, when old enough, make every effort to get to the sea and will even cover miles of land to gain it: I believe it is a fact that nothing will stop this migration save death.

The shelduck is the largest of our wild duck, some think the handsomest; the bird certainly has a very striking appearance. Both sexes possess a chestnut-coloured band across the breast and over part of the back, a dark-green head, scarlet bill, and pink feet. 'Sheld' actually means particoloured and the word is still used with this meaning in the eastern counties where these birds are often seen.

Their flight rather suggests that of the wild goose, and in the air they seem to be wholly pied, black and white, their distinctive decoration of ruddy chestnut across the breast not then being seen.

PINTAIL

The pintails with their distinctive dark tails, long and pointed, may be seen in London sporting themselves on the Serpentine, though the birds' usual haunt is the sea, or fresh water near the coast; perhaps that is why they are called by some *sea-pheasants*. I have seen their nests only in Scotland, though I believe they may be found on the east coast. They are usually in a hollow on the ground in a dry, sheltered situation, dead grasses and heather being used and the interior lined with down from the female's breast, she alone brooding her eggs.

It is unfortunate for the pintail that he is regarded by the human as good food. I have been told by a sportsman that he had bagged thirty-seven birds at one shoot. His jubilant pride cast a shadow upon me which time has lengthened and deepened, for I realize more and more that man will still continue to rejoice in the slaughter he is able to effect.

TEAL

Though teals haunt drier ground than most ducks they must always be within reach of water. The birds usually nest under the shelter of a bush or among bracken, generally in more or less open ground. Teals take the material they require for the nest from anything they find near by—for example dry grass and bracken—lining the interior with down.

The drake does not share the three weeks' brooding of the eggs, and this is the case with most water-fowl as tne male's time is mainly occupied in seeking the necessary food.

One cannot but be touched by the affection of the female for her brood; I was told that when a family of teals were being driven the mother followed, keeping close, and when they had been forced into a shed she still remained, in spite of dogs and men, faithful to her trust even unto death.

MALLARD OR WILD DUCK

The mallard or wild duck has always interested me; perhaps that is why I so much like Masefield's lines in his *Good Friday*. His observation and understanding are very evident:

> The wild duck, stringing through the sky,
> The south away.
> Their green necks glitter as they fly,
> The lake is gray.
> So still, so lone, the fowler never heeds.
> The wind goes rustle, rustle through the reeds.
>   .   .   .
> There they find peace to have their own wild souls.
> In that still lake,
> Only the moonlight or the wind controls
> The way they take.
> Through the gray reeds, the cocking moorhen's lair,
> Rippling the pool, or over leagues of air.

There are few who do not feel a thrill at the sight of mallard rising into the sun, all their iridescent feathers gleaming, with 'wings like garden-shears clipping the misty air'.

The wild duck has well been called cosmopolitan in his taste, for he is found almost everywhere save in the Arctic Circle or the Equatorial regions. Perhaps this is because he can eat most things and can feed by night as well as by day. I like best to see him plunging his bill into some oozy marsh and, with the minute teeth which line his mandible, sifting and filtering that food which is nutritious while discarding the valueless.

Mallards find their desirable residence in many different places but all within call of water—the marsh, lakeside, or reed-bed. I have seen a surprising and original taste in locality on the part of a pair of mallards who chose the roof garden at Canada House, which overlooks Trafalgar Square. There the female laid her eggs in a flower-box, sitting on them for hours each day and covering them carefully with leaves and straw when she flew away. She evidently found the position to her liking for she nested there two years in succession, hatching five out of eight eggs. When her family was ready she led her procession of ducklings across the Horse Guards Parade to St James's Park.

The nest is always constructed of grass and any other material to hand and lined with down which the hen plucks from her own breast until it is almost bare. This down often rises above her head as she broods and if it is necessary for her to leave the nest for any reason the down is always spread over the eggs to keep them warm until her return.

Wordsworth was much impressed by the beauty of a wild duck's nest he found on the largest island of Rydal Water:

> The Imperial Consort of the Fairy-king
> Owns not a sylvan bower; or gorgeous cell
> With emerald floored, and with purpureal shell
> Ceilinged and roofed; that is so fair a thing
> As this low structure, for the tasks of Spring,
> Prepared by one who loves the buoyant swell
> Of the brisk waves, yet here consents to dwell;
> And spreads in steadfast peace her brooding wing.
> Words cannot paint the o'ershadowing yew-tree bough,
> Of golden leaves inlaid with silver down.

The mallard is certainly a wonderful mother and lays from twelve to nineteen eggs. Not only does she build her nest and strip herself practically bare to line it but she has also to feed her ducklings, for her husband is a lazy fellow who takes no part in rearing his family. If it were not for the care she exerts to keep them warm during the periods when she has to search for food they could not survive, for the drake in company with other attractive males is then enjoying himself at ease on some neighbouring sheet of water, with little apparent heed or thought for his mate and family. I have seen many of these drakes all together, occupied with their own particular interests, obviously relieved at regaining their bachelor, carefree existence.

The chicks can swim almost immediately they are hatched, but they cannot fly for about nine weeks and the mother bird is always vigilant during this vulnerable period. Faithful, and fearless of personal danger, she falls an easy victim in the duck-shooting season, refusing to leave her young and guarding them with her life. I have always understood that no true sportsman will care to shoot a sitting bird, so surely the season for this sport should be later than it is.

The drake loses his wonderful plumage at the close of the breeding season, when he is thoroughly humiliated. In July you can hardly tell the duck from the drake but the very fact that his feathers become dull may be nature's way of protecting him during the moult because, bereft of his flight-feathers, he would be an easy prey.

In China mallards are kept in large numbers, housed at night in boats on the rivers, thousands being hatched by artificial means. The eggs are placed in tiers of boxes filled with sand and subjected to the necessary degree of heat upon a floor of bricks; the ducklings are fed at first with boiled crawfish, or crab, cut in very small pieces. When the young birds are a fortnight old they are able to shift for themselves. They are then placed under the guidance of an old foster-mother who leads them at stated times to feed, to and from the boat in which they are kept and which is moved about by the owner to places likely to afford a plentiful supply of food.

It is curious to see how well a flock of three or four hundred ducks is trained to obey; some thousands of birds, belonging to different boats, will feed at the same spot but on a given signal will follow their leader to each of their respective boats without a stranger bird being found among them.

DOMESTIC DUCK

Birds have individuality and there are always exceptional builders among every type. I have known more than one ordinary farmyard duck to build on the side of a busy road. Some think they are foolish birds, not showing much sense to make their homes in built-up areas but this taste is shared by many living creatures. Their wisdom is constantly shown in other ways, for they usually rear their ducklings safely, always carefully covering their eggs with dry leaves and bits of rubbish whenever they leave the nest so that it is difficult to locate: I have often watched a duck looking carefully all round to see if she is being watched during this process.

It is said 'all ducks take to water' but I had a pet duck who would leave dry land only when her friend, a cocker-spaniel, went for a swim and she rode on his back. This comradeship, founded on evident trust, went further, for she ate her food out of the same plate as the dog and even slept on the same chair. Eventually, however, this admiring friendship led to her following and even exceeding his example in chasing all dogs and children who ventured near. So it was reluctantly decided that it was wiser to send her away to a friend who lived twelve miles distant in a more isolated district and possessed neither child nor dog. But the duck refused to settle down and evidently felt that life without her four-footed companion was not worth while. She actually found her way back, a long trail for a duck on webbed feet. This valiant effort so impressed my disgruntled neighbours that they relented and her sentence of exile was therefore commuted to one of severe reprimand and imprisonment for any further offence that might be committed.

WILD GOOSE

There is so much to be said about wild geese that they require more than a section to themselves. Indeed, several books might be written on these birds about whom Peter Scott is constantly providing interesting material.

I never see a skein of wild geese in flight without experiencing a thrill. I have watched them flying not only over the desolate marshes but also in Sussex, making for the sea in perfect V-formation. The last skein I saw from my cottage verandah was in the middle of October at three o'clock in the afternoon. The wheeling of the skein seems to have a composite directing force. I have seen the leading bird flash his wings before taking to the air, as a signal to the others to join up in formation, and one cannot but imagine that by some means unknown to us he regulates the remarkable movement of those who follow, for they maintain a perfect unity. It has been noted that each bird in the limb of the V is slightly to the outside of the one in front so as to be free of the disturbance of air caused by the powerful wings of his neighbour.

To the bird-watcher few things can surpass the wonder of the sight and sound of wild geese in flight, perhaps best seen silhouetted against the silver light of the moon: first a faint honking in the distance, then louder until the high-pitched whistle of many hundreds of wings grows nearer. Then as they circle overhead, the honking ceases and they drop noiselessly from the air to feed. Hungry geese will congregate in thousands on a rocky shore close to that spot where their instinct tells them there are shoals of mackerel and pilchards. I have seen numbers of solan geese in the Hebrides diving from high cliffs into the sea at least two hundred feet below, tracking their invisible and unsuspecting prey far below the surface of the water. They are so well padded with soft down that the high dive does not harm their heavy bodies. When seen for the first time this diving operation must thrill even the most phlegmatic; the swift diagonal descent, the folded wings, and the seizure of the prey is a breath-taking spectacle. The Scottish fishermen watch birds even as the birds watch the sea and they follow them with nets gathering in a rich harvest.

The countryman thinks that when wild geese fly high or out to sea it is an indication of fine weather but if low and towards the hills the reverse may be expected; when the birds gaggle in the air it is thought that cold and wintry conditions will prevail.

Geese are particularly cautious and never unmindful of danger at any time; it has been said it is easier to stalk deer than geese, and anyone who has tried to catch a goose will realize the truth of the expression 'wild-goose chase'. Fowlers say that they are both wise and wary and have a sense of smell. It appears that when feeding or sleeping at least one of their number keeps watch so that none of the gaggle may be taken unawares. In spite of this wariness on their part certain geese are becoming a rarer sight. Almost invariably they are shot, the pink-footed being among those unfortunates.

GREYLAG GOOSE

I believe the greylag goose nests only in Britain (Scotland and the Hebrides); he is the ancestor of the farmyard goose and makes much the same sounds. The nest is formed with a mixture of heather twigs, moss, and grass, lined with down and feathers from the breasts of the birds themselves, and is usually found among reeds in marshland or in heather.

DOMESTIC GOOSE

It is generally believed that the domestic goose is a descendant of the greylag whose feathers winged the arrows of our bowmen ancestors.

When I worked on a farm during the last war, one of my duties was looking after geese and I realized then their intelligence, sense of gratitude, scrupulous cleanliness, and the manner in which they co-operated in the care of their young. I was never tired of watching the goslings being escorted for their first outing which seemed to me an interesting and delightful picture; a triangle was formed with a gander at the head, the geese flanking the whole cavalcade, all the goslings of the various families walking for safety in the middle. Woe betide anyone who came too near!

I have many memories of those geese. Alas! space does not permit me to record them, but I remember one very small weakly gosling who had to be reared in an incubator, eventually being catalogued as of little worth and being taken home by one of the carters, where she became not only a pet of the family but of the whole village. The care with which she was surrounded probably made up for the lost comfort of the mother's downy breast; in any case she survived and grew to be a fine goose. Yet I found to my bewilderment and dismay that in spite of being beloved, particularly perhaps by the children, she was to become the Christmas dinner of the family who had adopted her. Her subsequent history was however a happy one, for I was fortunately able to effect a rescue, placing her with a vegetarian family. In these new quarters her very special friend was a donkey. Whenever possible the ill-assorted pair were never out of each other's company and evidently mutually understood the language of 'bray' and 'honk'. In the bitterest weather I watched this goose frequently rapping loudly on the kitchen door; when admitted she would stand in a dignified manner on the hearthrug.

One of the last Sussex blacksmiths that I knew was companioned upon all occasions by a goose who followed him everywhere, even to the 'local', where the bird was always given his own tipple—a drink of milk. When the blacksmith died Billy Gander followed the coffin and refused to move from the grave in spite of every effort to coax him away. On the third day he also died and was given honourable burial by the village. I erected a small headstone on which was carved:

BILLY GANDER

Migrated

LEGENDS OF WILD GEESE

Geese are particularly solicitous for any one of their fellows who may be injured and there are many incidents recorded of their grief when one of their company is missing.

Of the many legends one I like is concerned with wild geese and St Werburga. Her father, King Wulfhura, gave her a farm which the wild geese favoured but unfortunately they destroyed much corn in the fields. She told her steward to drive them into the house: they all obeyed, waddling most gloomily with down-bent heads. They were kept there as a punishment till the following day when the saint came to see them. She inquired if they were all assembled, at which there was a great cackling of obvious dissatisfaction, the steward having stolen one for his dinner. The saint told the birds to hold their peace while she addressed them with much rebuke and admonishment as to their wrong-doing. This done, she told them they might depart, provided their offence was not repeated; to her astonishment, not one of the geese would budge but all continued to cackle louder than ever with undoubted discontent. Then the clear eyes of the saint turned to the steward who confessed his theft. She bade him bring the bones of the missing bird and, as she stretched her hands over them, the skin, flesh, and feathers reappeared and the bird with eager hope and joyful cackle was again soon on the wing; then all the others, uttering their thankfulness, departed. I have often wished I had hands with the miraculous power of St Werburga's.

3. AT SPLASH POINT

DIPPER OR WATER-OUSEL

No wanderer or mountain-climber in our Fell country can fail to have seen and heard the water-ousel, the dapper little bird with black and white plumage which seems designed to harmonize with the spray of waterfalls and bubbles of the stream.

He is well described by Rex Warner:

> Urbane, rotund, secretive, dashing dipper,
> O daintier and gentler than the alderman
> We know in life, bowing not to highness
> But to wealth of running water in shine or
> Shower, the gliding race shaken into a shiver
> Of foam beneath your feet.
> Dapper you go, stout, bowing at the edge of cascades.

To many this bird is known as the dipper; undoubtedly he owes the name to his frequent habit of bobbing up and down on a stone and constantly dipping in the water. I find him a most intriguing and entertaining water-bird, one that I can watch for hours. For those who are jaded and disillusioned, whose bodies require rest and a renewal of strength, and for those who would have beauty and interest, I would suggest they leave the complications that gather within four walls and seek the habitat of the dipper beside some friendly stream or voluble waterfall. Then watch the bird who seems to possess so completely the aptitude for living every moment of his hour in which he assuredly rejoices. His attitude to life is contagious.

There are few who will not be refreshed by his entertaining companionship, the multitudinous variety of his movements and exploits, his confidence and intimacy with water. Few, however lugubrious, will not smile as they see him taking his pleasure and exercise, wading like a heron, swimming on the surface like a duck, diving like a kingfisher, hovering like a hawk, and swooping like a gannet. He must be dull indeed if he is not intrigued as he watches the water-ousel walking with ease under water on the bed of a stream, clinging to the stones with his claws, seeking the larvae which are his food and using his wings even as when in the air. The bird delights in the spray of a waterfall, standing on some favourite stone, jerking his body about, dipping up and down with his continuous bob and curtsy. He obviously rejoices in his diving practices and it is astonishing to note that his family will dive even before they can swim. He not only indulges in this sport from a jutting rock but even from a block of ice, and I have seen him disappear undismayed into turbulent waters: added to this, as Mary Webb said, he has 'such a flight as archangels might envy'.

It is not only entertainment but admiration I experience when watching him occupied with his more serious work of building his domed nest, which is often on a ledge under a waterfall. When feeding his family he will fly in and out a cascade of water without even a shake of his feathers; that the nest remains dry is astounding. It is usually difficult to find, seeming almost a part of the dripping, mossy rock; one I saw was about eight inches deep and twelve in diameter with an entrance at the side, the whole structure interwoven with delicate green moss, yet in spite of this water-site the nest remains cosy and warm.

Water-ousels are among the earliest nest-builders, returning to a parti-

cular chosen spot year after year, in fact I am inclined to believe as long as
they live.

Every beck in the Fell country knows the sweet trilling notes of this
bird who seems inspired by the water he loves; he gives his bright cascade
of song all the year round and I have heard him even in mid-winter. But
if he senses a watcher he will quickly dive and, when he reappears, will
find a temporary place of concealment until the intruder is accepted as a
harmless addition to his world.

Mary Webb's poem on the water-ousel is so lovely and true a description that little else is needed:

> There on the wrinkled stream where willows lean,
> A water ousel came, with such a flight
> As archangels might envy. Soft and bright,
> Upon a water-kissing bough she lit
> And washed and preened her silver breast, though it
> Was dazzling fair before. Then twittering
> She sang, and made obeisance to the Spring . . .
> Maybe she dreamed a nest, so safe, so dear,
> Where the keen spray leaps whitely to the weir;
> And smooth warm eggs that hold a mystery;
> And stirrings of life, and twitterings that she
> Is passionately glad to hear; and a breast
> As silver white as hers, which without rest
> Or langour, borne by spread wings swift and strong,
> Shall fly upon her service all day long.

4. BERTHED ALONGSIDE

Bearded tit; wagtails; greenshank; red-necked phalarope;
osprey

BEARDED TIT

A whole family of these rather quaint little birds once visited my garden
in Sussex but only for a short space of time, when I watched them bathing
in a puddle, twittering all the while. Afterwards the hen snuggled under
the spread wing of her mate, the two birds cuddling close to one another;
she dried first one side and then reversed her position to dry the other.
When they saw me they gave their peculiar scolding cry, which has been
well described as the sound made by 'drawing a finger lightly across the

Bearded Tit. Male at nest with young

Pied Wagtail at nest amongst tomato plants in a greenhouse

strings of a violin'. The call-note again suggests plucking one string with the finger, thus producing a pizzicato note. Some authorities say this species has no song, but I think they have, and I would say it has a soft, silvery quality, though it is not well known, as the bird itself is rare. The visit of these birds was a very unusual occurrence and caused much excitement at the time. I have never seen them anywhere since in Sussex; they favour the eastern counties, finding their pleasure and means to live among the hedges and reeds; probably this is the reason they are sometimes called *reedlings*.

I find their acrobatics most entertaining; these can be seen very clearly against the background of the green reeds. The nest I saw was on a platform of decaying vegetation fringing the water; it was deeply cup-shaped, composed of flat, dead portions of reed-leaves; the lining was thick and principally of fine grass and reed-flowers.

The female lacks the unique ornament of the cock bird's black Victorian moustache, which is part of his attraction; whether this is just one of nature's decorations given him to attract his mate or for some other specific purpose I have never been able to discover. The mouths of the nestlings are very remarkable, the roof being brilliant red outlined by yellow, and there are a number of glistening white nipple-like protuberances resembling teeth. These of course disappear at a later date.

After the young ones are hatched the family still keep together and usually sleep in a tight row. Bearded tits were very nearly wiped out by the severe winter of 1947, and if it were not for vigorous protective methods, the bird would have been exterminated by the pernicious egg-collector. Now drainage further limits its numbers and with the exception of that one isolated visit, when the family landed in my garden, I have never seen the birds, other than in the Norfolk Broads.

WATER OR PIED WAGTAIL

Among the delightful and interesting family of wagtails, I have chosen the three perhaps most familiar to bird-watchers. The white and blue-headed are both uncommon birds of passage; the water or pied wagtail is very well known to me for these birds particularly favour a pile of wood near the pool in my garden where they have built a nest for several years in succession. I found most of the work was done in the early hours of the

P

morning; on the whole the nest was rather carelessly built but scrupulously clean, consisting of roots, moss, and fibres of grasses, lined with feathers and wool. They had two broods, but I never saw the cock help with the incubating, though both parents showed great courage in defence of their young and fed them with ceaseless energy all day. I noticed the cock collected many flies and insects in his search for food, taking these to the nest one only at a time. When the fledglings were able to leave the nest they were carefully guided into the adjacent marshy fields. I was once fortunate enough to find that a cuckoo had deposited her egg in a nest my wagtails were building, before even the lining was complete. I was able to take it out and so circumvent the cuckoo's design, for my birds went on with their building unaware of what might have been.

Though the pied wagtail's nest is usually at the edge of water, I have a friend who had a pair build and lay their eggs in the disused nest of a thrush, but this, I think, is something quite unusual, though they do sometimes favour old pollard-willows or ivy. I always allow this parasite growth to flourish over any stumps of trees and my fences as it gives shelter to many birds.

Although these birds favour the water-site they apparently do not mind dry land, as I frequently see them on my lawn. There is a plantation on the Downs not far from my cottage where pied wagtails nest and I often stop to watch them performing their acrobatics, cleaving a way through the air and singing a low sweet song which they invariably repeat many times. I find them very amusing birds to watch; they always appear gay, a quality worthy of appreciation in a complaining, grumbling world. They bob their heads and flash their tails in a characteristic, quick little run—movements reminiscent of a mechanical toy, for when their heads go down, their tails go up. They will run two or three yards, then stop, apparently considering, dash off again, soaring a foot or two into the air to catch their food; dart forward again, and again stop dead, finally digging their beaks into the grass with their jaunty tails high in the air.

Many people know the water-wagtail as *Polly Dishwasher*; in France the bird is called *lavandière* no doubt because the country washerwomen shake out their clothes in much the same way as the bird flicks his tail.

They do not appear to resent the company of man; rather the opposite,

I once saw pied wagtails roosting together in a tree in O'Connell Street, Dublin. These lodgings, apparently, became more and more popular with the birds, for I have been told some thousands came to roost on the trees in this busy street. Again, amid a crowded market I have seen a water-wagtail flicking his tail while customers and stallholders alike stood watching the daring little bird.

They are among the birds who peck at my cottage windows and I have never yet been able to learn any satisfactory explanation of this habit, which I find is shared by many birds. It has been suggested that it is because they see their reflection, but they often observe this practice in the day-time when no reflection is visible, so it remains one of the many things about birds to which we have as yet no answer.

Though the bird is obviously sociable and will often feed with a flock, he chooses but one mate, pairing for life. His devotion to her is very moving. I once saw a bird that I think had been shot. She was lying, evidently dying, beyond any possible help of mine. Her mate was flying round her, his distress only too evident; he voiced a few uncertain notes and touched her with his beak, no doubt hoping this would rouse her. The sight affected me very much. I watched them for a few minutes, only too conscious of my impotence; when the bird died I left, but I looked round once and saw the cock was still by the side of his dead mate and I always wondered how long it would be before he accepted the inevitable.

Bosworth Smith gives a most touching example of a wagtail's grief at the death of his mate who was killed by a catapult; he records that the living bird seemed beside himself with grief and kept running up to the body with loud and plaintive calls. He caressed it, trying to coax a movement, then drew the body after him with his bill for a yard or two, even trying to rise with it in the air. All efforts proving vain, he flew off in uncertain, wavering flight as far as the eye could follow, as though trying to blot out the pitiful fact of receiving no response, but soon hurried back in straighter and quicker flight in the hope that there might now be some sign of life. This abandonment of grief Bosworth Smith watched from the window of his house throughout the afternoon till darkness came. Next morning the body was no longer there and the survivor was seen no more.

There is no doubt that wagtails are very useful to the feathered tribe generally in warning them of the approach of a hawk. I have seen them gather collectively and mob this dreaded bird of prey, even driving him off.

This bird is also of service to cattle. I have no doubt cows welcome him, for he catches a multitude of the flies which torment them. I have seen him in his anxiety to catch these, apparently stand on his tail in the air, at times hovering and swooping like a hawk.

To be beautiful, entertaining, and useful is not given to many but the wagtail may claim to be all three.

GREY WAGTAIL

The grey wagtail is by no means altogether grey; though he has a grey back and cap, he has white stripes above and below the eyes, white on the long tail feathers, and a sulphur-yellow breast which touches the ground when he runs.

In courtship the male spreads his lovely tail when he rises to show the beauty of the white under-feathers, then he slowly descends with wings spread and tail expanded; whenever I watch him I feel something of the thrill which he intends to communicate to his prospective mate.

He comes to this country in the autumn and returns north in the spring. I have seen him quite often in the Fell country, also in Wales, and I believe he is frequently found in the eastern counties though I have not seen him there myself. He prefers hilly and rocky districts for nesting, indeed he is called the *rocky wagtail* by some country people, but he will never build far from water as he likes to jog about in the shallow bend of a stream. I have seen a brood hatched only just above the water, on a stone; I have also found his nest in a hole in a wall, and a fellow-watcher told me he had seen a nest beside running water at a height of one thousand, seven hundred feet.

At first the young birds have but stumpy little tails, a mere suggestion of the future when they will be blessed with the delicate, graceful body, beautifully moulded bill, and handsome tail. It is a lovely sight to watch the mother bird feeding her young. These are very adventurous and anxious to fly before they are able, sometimes giving a little flight over a stretch of water, then sinking exhausted at the other side; the mother then administers food as a restorative, probably following on with a mixture of encouragement and admonition.

YELLOW WAGTAIL

I have seen yellow wagtails in Norfolk, nesting among the ling. They are perhaps the daintiest and loveliest of all the five species. They come to us exclusively in the summer and prefer the stream and water-meadow, though sometimes favouring the open Downs. When the plumage of these birds catches the light either in brilliant sunshine or in the setting sun the effect is wonderful.

I have included only the three wagtails I think most generally known; the white and blue-headed are both uncommon birds of passage.

GREENSHANK

There is one thing I have in common with the greenshank and that is a love of peat, though for different reasons. I like peat for a fire with its delicious, pungent fragrance; he favours it for a nesting site and there lines his nest with leaves and lichen, though some members of this family prefer a stone on which to build. Although he haunts moorlands he feeds near the neighbourhood of water which is essential for his life.

As far as I know greenshanks are the only birds who appear to lay a trail of bits and pieces in the direction of their nest, apparently using them as landmarks; why they do this none can say, for birds certainly know their own individual nests among thousands. Yet here is one who seems to require guidance.

The olive-green legs of the greenshank distinguish him from the redshank, also the upward curve of the bill, and the white rump is much more in evidence, though the cry and nests are very similar. Both these birds usually lay four eggs, but I did find a redshank's nest in a marsh near Carlisle which appeared unusually large, with four eggs marked alike and two quite different, which suggested to me that two hens had laid in the same nest. This does sometimes happen with the redshank, though I have never heard of it happening with the greenshank.

RED-NECKED PHALAROPE

The finding of any nest gives me a thrill, but one so rare as that of the red-necked phalarope was indeed a unique experience. The Outer Hebrides gave me this discovery. The nest was a deep cup, composed of dead grasses and concealed in a tussock on marshy ground, near water. The phalarope is the only cock bird in the British Isles who entirely incubates and rears the young without assistance from the hen. She, after laying her last egg, continues to assert her supremacy, insisting that her mate alone shall brood; it might therefore seem that she takes no interest in her eggs, but I believe, though indolent and not desiring the arduous duties of incubation, she is yet determined the clutch shall be brooded, and for this reason drives her mate back to the nest the moment he has acquired the necessary food. He then apparently assumes all the natural paternal duties with a better grace than that with which he accepted the initial wooing. Then he was reluctant and unwilling but, once wooed and won by the female, he not only guards the eggs but shields them carefully with grass when hunger forces him to leave them. In the meantime, his light-o'-love may be seen enjoying her carefree days, frequently accompanied by more than one lover.

OSPREY

I remember seeing ospreys and even being taken to a nest when I first went to the Lake District as a very young girl. I believe they also nested quite freely in Scotland. They are now lost to us save for a very occasional migrant, and we have to thank fishermen, collectors, and ill-informed gamekeepers for this depredation.

They are guarded in Sweden almost as jealously as the fishing-rights, and there it was I again had the opportunity of watching them and seeing their remarkable nest; sometimes it weighs quite half a ton and smaller birds often build their home in its fabric. Both male and female share in the brooding, and I was much entertained to note that when they changed over they were always meticulous in first cleaning their feet; if by any chance they forgot to do this they immediately remedied the omission before taking their place on the nest.

See Appendix, page 233.

18

SOME STRANGE HOMES

AMONG the records of nests built in apparently unlikely places, I have chosen only those I feel to be of exceptional interest and that I have been fortunate enough to see for myself or of which the authenticity is assured.

It is surprising that many birds should build, brood their eggs, and actually bring up a family in railway bridges with trains constantly roaring past; there is no doubt that birds get accustomed to noise when they find this does not bring disastrous results. It is also remarkable that building should take place in railway stations; pigeons evidently favour several of the London termini. They certainly appear to find at Brighton station a desirable site, and this spring while waiting for a train at West Worthing I counted six nests. At West Sutton I watched a hen blackbird brooding her eggs in a nest built on a girder under the glass roof of the station. She was attending to the sanitation of the nest, finally flying off with the excrements as my train came in; this was the second time in one month I had seen a blackbird nesting there. Probably she was the same hen, who, having reared her first brood safely, decided the site was desirable. When I was working on a farm in the north I was taken to see a pied wagtail's nest in the wheel of a railway wagon standing in a siding at Windermere station.

A pair of starlings chose for themselves a peculiar nesting site in the station at Crewe Bridge near Ferryhill, Durham. They had built in a small hole in the large metal ball at the top of the column carrying the water-cistern apparatus and hose from which locomotives obtain water. Although the column was swung round fully thirty times a day in order to reach the boilers, the starlings were apparently unperturbed, flying in and out feeding their young.

The most remarkable instance of devotion to a nest that I know is that of a pair of thrushes, who, having chosen to build their nest in a horse-box at Holyhead, were faced with the fact that the van was hitched on to a train bound for East Grinstead. The thrushes followed their home along some of the busiest rail routes to its destination three hundred miles distant. The energy and persistence this journey entailed can be appreciated when it is considered that it must have taken approximately ten hours and the birds' wing-beats are a hundred and sixty to the minute; in addition there was the continual and ceaseless roar of railway traffic. At East Grinstead good fortune rewarded the birds, as one of the railway staff, discovering the nest and seeing the thrushes, communicated with the stationmaster and found him sufficiently interested to order that they should be left unmolested. He further prevailed upon the District Officer to provide an alternative horse-box if one should be required. Such a remarkable achievement as that of the thrushes certainly deserved the consideration it happily obtained.

Many an observer of bird life and even an ornithologist was interested in this very remarkable instance of the tenacity with which birds cling to their nests. The pair of thrushes concerned were the principals in an achievement that must be unique and remains for us among the many wonders of bird life. Ludwig Koch's opinion was that if the nest itself were not disturbed the birds might follow it anywhere; thrushes can fly at fifty to sixty miles per hour.

It is strange that there are fewer casualties among feathered creatures from rail than from road traffic. The casualty list is rare with rooks, who delight in feasting on the grain that falls from the trucks, but they seem to sense the approach of a train, hopping on to the nearest rail or fence that borders the line and returning as soon as the train has passed. Those that do suffer are often game birds in search of grain which trickles out of vans and wagons; they fly away only at the very last minute. I am always delighted when I see the railway banks uncultivated, abounding with flowers and weeds, because I know the finches, linnets, tree-pipits, yellow buntings, and yellow wagtails will rejoice; both they and their young will be fed and comparatively safe from human menace.

I saw that a pair of pigeons had built this spring in a lamp on Victoria Embankment; it was not in use—inside there was no bulb, and on the south side no pane of glass. It was necessary for me to pass that way frequently and I was very interested to see the hen brooding her eggs, unmoved by the thousands of city workers passing beneath. There is no doubt pigeons in our cities become fearless, perhaps unfortunately, and accept man not as a potential enemy but as part of their surroundings.

A swallow's nest which I had been watching, built in a barn on the Sussex Downs near my cottage, was destroyed by boys. I could not help being affected by the thought of the birds' loss, the destruction of their work and home, and I wondered if I should see anything of them again. However, when I visited the barn I saw several swallows were flying to and fro with the necessary material for a rapid rebuilding of the nest that had been destroyed. This was already half way to completion, in exactly the same place, and I thought it a most remarkable and moving exhibition of co-operative service.

I have known several instances of swallows choosing unusual sites for their nests. In the old church at Lowdham, Nottinghamshire, I once saw one at the side of the altar; and I remembered the psalm: 'the swallow hath found a nest for herself, where she may lay her young, even thine altars, O Lord of Hosts.'[1] At a farm adjacent to my cottage a pair built in the cycle-shed on a long-handled clipping tool. While the hen was brooding the cock always roosted on the tool near the nest. Two broods were hatched and the young frequently returned to the shed and slept in a row on the same tool, the perch they had doubtless seen their father use.

Another unusual nesting site was recorded at Corton, Lowestoft, when an amazed naturalist discovered young birds in a nest which had been built on a recess in the outer edge of one of the sails of a 'smock' windmill, still in action, the revolutions averaging thirty a minute; the young birds would certainly be adventurous travellers before they left such a nest. The mother bird when entering or leaving the mill had to make use of a hole through which the shaft projected; to do this it was necessary for her to touch the wheels which hung close to the walls. When the creaking and shaking of a windmill are taken into account, one can hardly fail to be struck by the courageous spirit of the bird that chose such an apparently dangerous spot in which to build her nest and rear her young.

A remarkable nest was built by nuthatches who, with an unusual taste for a site, decided to burrow in a hayrick near East Grinstead. Building occupied about two months, and the nest was lined with mud which had

[1] Psalm lxxxiv. 3.

to be conveyed from a pond a hundred and fifty yards distant and was mixed with the inner scaly bark of a near-by fir; the birds made an entrance five to six feet from the ground. When the nest had served the birds, it was preserved and found to weigh eleven pounds, measuring thirteen inches from top to bottom and eight inches at its widest, the walls being four inches thick. The amount of mud that a bird of less than six inches long can carry is not great, and the labour undertaken must have been prodigious.

Tits often appear to favour letter-boxes. A blue tit elected to build in a wooden letter-box attached to one of the gateposts on Lord Leconfield's estate in Sussex; this box is on the main road from Worthing to Petworth. The tit had lined the bottom of the box with a thick mattress of moss and in the front right-hand corner had made her nest, laid her eggs, brooded, and raised a family two years in succession. All this in spite of the fact that the daily newspaper, in addition to letters, was pushed into the box and that it was opened each day for collection. Any 'doubting Thomas' can write to Mr Pring at Palfrey Farm near Petworth and he will verify this statement. I should never have believed it possible had I not seen both nest and bird myself, because those who have a tit-box know if they but raise the lid once and look inside the little bird usually deserts.

In a post office letter-box on a telegraph pole at Stanley, near Chippenham, a pair of tom tits made a nest, laid ten eggs, hatched them, and reared the young in spite of the fact that the box was cleared twice a day. The postman reported that he often found letters across the hen's back; once she was even pinned in by a package, but when this was removed she continued undaunted to brood her eggs.

At Pot Hill Common off the Horsham and Worthing road, I was once amused and delighted at reading the notice 'BIRD NESTING, WAIT FOR POST-MAN!', regardless of the fact that the postman might not be coming until the next morning!

Tits choose many curious places to build, curious at least to the human. Upon lifting an inverted flowerpot which had been standing on a grass plot all the winter near a path in my Sussex cottage garden, I found a nest composed of horse and cow hair. The hole across the pot was one inch in diameter, this being the only means of ingress and egress. When I lifted the pot on one side I found there were seven young blue tits. How the nest had been built and the young birds fed was beyond my comprehension.

Another nest I found on the Douglas Nurseries, Durrington, near Worthing. This had been fashioned half way down a disused eight-foot waterpipe (well beyond the reach of any cat's paw); I have always been puzzled as to how the birds fed their chicks and how they eventually made their exit. It *was* achieved, for later I saw nine of these tiny creatures like blue and yellow butterflies being fed with insects on a near-by bush. I was told by Mr Douglas that the parents had actually been seen hauling up five of them by the beak.

Robins certainly lead in choosing unusual nesting sites. Is it possible these birds, having always shown a certain fearlessness and indeed liking for man, often favour his possessions for their building? There are many records of robins building in old coats, boots, kettles or pots, even in machines.

A robin was discovered to have built a nest in a semi-automatic machine in the Kleen-e-ze Brush Company's factory in Bristol. The discovery of the nest caused considerable astonishment and pleasure; it was decided that the birds must not be disturbed, and the machine was put out of use. The hen had already shown her appreciation of the surroundings by using the firm's material—bristle, hair-fibre—in the making of her nest. A large notice was put up over the machine to prevent any inadvertent interference. During the period of sitting on the six eggs which she laid, the hen was frequently observed being fed by the cock. She usually sat for as long as four hours, then vacated the nest for about half an hour, returning to brood again; all the eggs hatched. The hen disposed of the eggshells by cracking them up and consuming the pieces, and the cock, who was in attendance at the time, helped her in the process. Both adults and young appeared to be quite oblivious of the coming and going of the workers and the noise of the machinery. The best maternity home in the land could not have shown more concern over the welfare of its inmates than did the employees of that factory.

A robin who favoured modern transport laid three eggs in a nest built under the dashboard of a car, and went motoring with the host, Mr F. Hogan. If the run was long the hen got tired of the continual movement entailed and, probably feeling somewhat bewildered, would leave her nest and hop on to the back seat of the car until it was brought to a standstill, when she would immediately return to the nest. This process naturally intrigued Mr Hogan and, though he does not say so, doubtless caused him to be particularly careful. But whatever induced the tolerance shown to the uninvited guest, it is certain she was enabled to achieve her purpose of raising a family.

Mr F. E. Cordy, a timber merchant of Lingwood, Norfolk, travelled for some days with a robin sitting on a nest built on a cross-bar near the winding-chain of his tractor. He was so impressed by this fearless hen that when the eggs were laid he decided to put the tractor out of commission until they were hatched and the birds had flown.

The most adventurous bird I ever heard of was the robin who built her nest in an aeroplane at Denham aerodrome. The robin appears to have made up her mind about the site she fancied and nothing deterred her, for half a dozen times the aerodrome staff pulled the nest to pieces, feeling that this was the kindest thing to do, but the robin hen's persistence and courage were so determined that at last they let her remain. Both nest and eggs went on many short flights, for the plane was in constant service, and though the mother bird hopped off the nest when the machine 'took off', she remained near by until its return when she immediately went back to brood. The engine, being just in front of the nest, kept the eggs warm and Wing-Commander Bickerton tells me that when the wings were fixed in place the nest was entirely encased and in no danger. After the eggs were hatched out this particular plane was not used until the birds had flown.

I do not feel we can leave robins without reference to the fact that throughout the centuries they seem to have particularly favoured country churches. At the Parish Church at Hampton-in-Arden for two years in succession robins fixed their nests to the church Bible. The vicar would not have the birds disturbed and accordingly brought another Bible into the church from which he read the lessons. It was noted that the bird in constructing the nest used pieces of the rope-ends from the belfry. In the village it was thought that robins building on the Bible foreboded ill to the vicar, who died in the second year of their nesting. Nevertheless whether robins build in church Bibles or not we must all die sooner or later.

Many clerics and their congregations regard a robin in a church as fortunate; their company is welcomed and their well-being fostered. In the lectern of Ringfield Church, Suffolk, I saw another robin's nest. The rector sent me the following record of the bird's interesting building:

It began as you saw during Holy Week and the nest was left unfinished for nearly three weeks. The Church doors were left open day and night. Early in May it was found that the nest was completed and by the evening of May 3rd four eggs had been laid and later there were six. The mother bird continued to brood through all services, while the male bird flew in and out. The only sound made by the birds was that very curious one described by W. H. Hudson as 'a prolonged note rather like that of some insects and of the bat which is inaudible to many people'. Within the quiet walls of the little Church it was a clear, beautiful sound, especially towards evening. The hatching out began and with it many fresh interesting incidents. The birds chose to fly, not through a near window but the whole length of the nave to reach the out-of-doors, and the great toilsome scramble to feed six hungry beaks began. The female bird was the braver in overcoming the natural dislike of a human being watching. Whit Sunday was a day of much interest to all who came to Church, especially the children. Both parent-birds hopped with beaks full of green caterpillars on to every possible alighting point, not daring for many minutes to approach the nest. Then, a sudden dart towards the hole in the lectern, a quick gobbling down, the light tremulous twitter of the fledgeless ones and a dash over the heads of the pews and out through the porch for more. This continued for one more week, the birds growing rapidly every day and their shrill piping cries for food ever more incessant. On the eve of Trinity Sunday the first of the six tumbled out of the nest. By the next mid-day the nest was empty and only one fledgling was left perched, defiant and demanding, on the base of the font. It seemed altogether appropriate that the robins should first see the glory of a perfect June day on Trinity Sunday. A linen cover is being embroidered with local wild flowers at its border and a robin for centre-piece.

I could not help feeling that the robin's song of ecstasy and thanksgiving may well have been as acceptable to the Creator as the often tuneless and mechanical voicing of our *Te Deum*.

It is noticeable that thrushes seem to favour building in cars and lorries. On a site at Great Missenden, Buckinghamshire, where motor vehicles were parked preparatory to an auction, thirty nests were discovered. In a lorry marked *Lot* 1605 a thrush had built her nest and laid four eggs;

she hatched out her family only a few hours before the lorry was sold. Even then this thrush's luck still held for an understanding official carefully lifted the nest and nestlings to a nearby sheltering hedgerow, where the anxious mother followed, giving the incident a happy ending by continuing to feed, bring up, and launch on the world four valuable songsters.

Blackbirds are certainly catholic in their taste for both site and nesting materials. Sir Eric Studd of Limpsfield Common planted a number of new plants in his herbaceous border with light, metallic name-labels. These disappeared and it was discovered they had been collected by a blackbird who was building in a forsythia at the back of the border. The labels had been used to make a solid foundation for the nest.

In July 1957 a blackbird nested on a ledge inside the garden court of the Bank of England; the spikes on the ledge inserted to deter pigeons from roosting provided a good anchorage for the nest. The birds were seen collecting the nesting material on a blitzed area off Moorgate, a quarter of a mile away. They then had to carry this over seven storeys and down to the ledge situated at third-floor level; this applied later to the conveyance of food.

When the fledglings left the nest, they were virtually prisoners within the high walls for several days, until strong enough to fly away.

Most men will respect a brooding hen. Recently a professional golfer sacrificed his chance of the championship because he would not play his ball which was resting against a lark's nest.

A hen partridge was found nesting on a gamekeeper's grave at Hatfield Peveril, Essex. It almost seemed that she might have remembered that in the nesting season a gamekeeper is always a careful guardian!

A nest which I found very amusing in the making, and showing the determination of the hen bird, was built by a pair of starlings in my garden. I watched the couple obviously consulting as to a site for their nest and the hen deciding on a bird-box in which I had hoped tits would build. The pair had been viewing the box for several days before the hen definitely made up her mind, then with difficulty both the birds pushed themselves in turn through the very small hole, just large enough for tits to get in and out; for starlings it meant time, infinite patience, and some discomfort. They performed the feat by first pushing in one wing and leg, then drawing the other slowly after; then flew some distance for the necessary building material. I noticed that after three or four journeys the cock grew tired of the difficult process of entering the new home. Then he evidently resolved on a plan that might assure his mate that he was working and at the same time discourage her building. Directly her back was turned he put his beak into the hole, took out the piece of straw the hen had just brought and sat on the roof of the bird-house with it in his beak until she returned, as if to impress upon her that this straw was his own gathering. Then directly she went off again in search of more material he dropped it in the hedge near by; he repeated this performance, taking out every piece that she brought. After a time it evidently struck her as very surprising that the nest proceeded so slowly, considering how many journeys she had made and that her mate was apparently equally busy. Suspicion seemed gradually to dawn upon her, for later in the day I saw them both on the bird-table quarrelling. However, their rival efforts continued, the cock determined on demolition, the hen still bent on building. Unfortunately just at that time I had to leave my cottage for a few weeks and I wondered what I should find on my return, whether the cock's manœuvres or the hen's determination had succeeded. I was delighted to see that the hen had gained her desired purpose. This could not have been an easy victory but her reward was evident, for the beaks of young starlings protruded from the little round hole. I was amused to find that the unwilling cock had now become a willing and anxious family man.

I was thrilled by the discovery of a nightingale's nest close beside a bus-stop at the entrance to a little lane which leads to the Downs at High Salvington, Sussex. A roadman was swapping the long grasses as I passed and I noticed what I first imagined to be a piece of brown paper.

It was evident, I thought, that the man did not regard it as part of his job to remove litter, so hoping he would be suitably shamed I went to pick it up. Then I found the offending litter was a small heap of dead oak-leaves. The roadman then called to me, 'Bide still—nightingale's nest it be and 'er's asettin' on eggs.'

It would seem that even a roadman is stirred by a nightingale for he continued sheepishly: 'If I'd a-knawed I wouldn't never a' swapped they near-by nettles.'

I suggested that we should collect some grass and cover the nest carefully again, which we did. For the next ten days I spent my time guarding it from man and beast, particularly the prowling cat, and all the time the plucky little bird continued to brood. During this period both work and sleep suffered; I was up at dawn and I think the last to go to bed on the Hill. I pretty nearly lived on my camp-stool, making numerous bad sketches of Honeysuckle Lane as an excuse for my constant presence. When off duty I was always careful to leave an efficient and understanding substitute; at the end of the vigil I think I was as worn out with anxiety and strain as the mother bird herself but well rewarded by the ecstatic cascade of song which constantly poured forth from the throat of a passionate and faithful lover. Also by the fact that five more potential little music-makers were safely launched on a usually indifferent and ungrateful world.

I once found a linnet's nest in a broccoli. I have never heard of such a site for a linnet before. That a vegetable should house a nest of this lovely little singing-bird I found remarkable.

One of the most puzzling nests I have known was that of a redstart. I was shown this nest inside an inverted large flower-pot. How the nest was built and the birds subsequently fed remained something of a miracle. One presumes the parents must have entered by the drain hole at the top; there is no question that the young were hatched. The discovery of the nest led to the young birds' liberation, otherwise it is hard to understand how they could have been freed. I have heard many theories to explain this incident but none that I find entirely satisfactory.

Hawks do not always have it their own way for, evidently scared by a cat, a pair abandoned their nest twenty feet up a tree at Tydd St Giles, Cambridgeshire. A Mr George Pentelow became interested in this nest as he thought he saw something very strange looking over the side. He found that a tortoiseshell cat had taken over the nest and there were three kittens in it.

I hope this small collection of 'Strange Homes' may at least demonstrate a little of the adventurous and intrepid spirit of birds and that they have individual taste.

I realize ever more certainly how little I know, how much is still a mystery; my amazement at the diversity, industry, capacity, and wisdom of the feathered creatures only increases with continued observation. I have experienced constant wonder and delight in watching them, in their beauty, the great variety of their plumage, form, and movement, the joy of their song, their haunting cries and call notes, the miraculous feat of migration which puzzles the wisest of men; all these things afford me endless interest. I am astonished by their ceaseless industry, the ingenuity of their building, the means whereby they live with so many odds against them. I find inspiration in their never-failing endurance of personal injury and all forms of disaster and the fact that they will sacrifice life itself for safety of their young; surely, 'greater love hath no man than this'.

Q

APPENDIX

The Observer of June 14th, 1959, reported: 'Relays of watchers are keeping a day-and-night guard on a brood of young ospreys, hatched out a week ago in a Highland pine forest. They are the first known to bird-watchers in Britain for over fifty years.'

Egg collectors and skin collectors are active and, alas! usually successful. This in spite of the fact that if a thief is caught within six months of the deed the penalty is £75 and a month's imprisonment. On this occasion, however, the Royal Society for the Protection of Birds was leaving nothing to chance, and a sum of £2,000 was spent to equip and mount a guard on the clutch for three months.

This determined effort was financed by bird-lovers from all over Britain and the protection was organized on military lines, a field telephone giving immediate contact with the police in case of need.

The Manchester Guardian of August 22nd, 1959, reported the complete success of the above operation and that the young birds 'are flying and can take care of themselves'.

INDEX[1]

[1] Where *Plate* is indicated it will be found from the alphabetical List of Illustrations.